The Key to Prosperity

The Key to Prosperity

CONQUERING POVERTY THINKING

Dr. Orison Swett Marden

Published 2020 by Gildan Media LLC
aka G&D Media
www.GandDmedia.com

THE KEY TO PROSPERITY. Copyright © JMW Group Inc. All rights exclusively licensed by JMW Group Inc., jmwgroup@jmwgroup.net.

No part of this book may be used, reproduced or transmitted in any manner whatsoever, by any means (electronic, photocopying, recording, or otherwise), without the prior written permission of the author, except in the case of brief quotations embodied in critical articles and reviews. No liability is assumed with respect to the use of the information contained within. Although every precaution has been taken, the author and publisher assume no liability for errors or omissions. Neither is any liability assumed for damages resulting from the use of the information contained herein.

Front cover design by David Rheinhardt of Pyrographx

Interior design by Meghan Day Healey of Story Horse, LLC

Library of Congress Cataloging-in-Publication Data is available upon request

ISBN: 978-1-7225-0332-1

10 9 8 7 6 5 4 3 2 1

Contents

PART I
The Poverty Habit
11

One POVERTY A MENTAL DISABILITY 13

Two ENTANGLING ALLIANCES 25

Three HAD MONEY BUT LOST IT 31

Four RESIGNED TO POVERTY 39

Five ECONOMY THAT COSTS TOO MUCH 51

PART II
Your Thoughts and Your Prosperity
57

Six HOW WE LIMIT OUR SUPPLY 59

Seven THE LAW OF ATTRACTION: DRIVING PROSPERITY TOWARD ONESELF OR DRIVING IT AWAY 64

Eight ESTABLISHING THE CREATIVE CONSCIOUSNESS 74

Nine WHERE PROSPERITY BEGINS 81

Ten MAKING YOURSELF A PROSPERITY MAGNET 86

Eleven HOW TO MAKE YOUR DREAMS COME TRUE 97

Twelve WHAT DISCOURAGEMENT DOES TO YOU AND HOW TO CURE IT 104

Thirteen HOW TO MAKE YOUR SUBCONSCIOUS MIND WORK FOR YOU 113

Fourteen HOW TO MAKE YOURSELF LUCKY 120

Fifteen THE ATTITUDE OF EXPECTANCY 128

Sixteen THE LAW OF OPULENCE 135

Seventeen HOW TO ATTRACT PROSPERITY 142

Eighteen HEART-TO-HEART TALKS
WITH YOURSELF 152

Nineteen SUCCESS AND HAPPINESS ARE FOR YOU 169

PART III
The Prosperity Habit
177

Twenty GETTING AWAY FROM POVERTY 179

Twenty One ONE UNWAVERING AIM 185

Twenty Two CONQUERING THE ULTIMATE
PROSPERITY OBSTACLE 194

Twenty Three USES OF OBSTACLES, OR ATTAINING
PROSPERITY UNDER DIFFICULTIES 202

CONTENTS

Twenty Four THRIFT AND CHARACTER 218

Twenty Five FINANCING YOURSELF 231

Twenty Six SELF-FAITH AND PROSPERITY 236

Twenty Seven "TIME IS MONEY" ... AND MUCH MORE 251

Twenty Eight MAKING YOUR DREAMS COME TRUE 256

Twenty Nine LOOK LIKE A SUCCESS 271

Thirty SELF-HELP & PERSEVERANCE 277

Thirty One THE SECRET KEY TO PROSPERITY 290

Thirty Two MAKING ROOM IN YOUR LIFE FOR PROSPERITY 294

Thirty Three THE MASTER KEY: TO BE GREAT, CONCENTRATE 301

Thirty Four SEIZE YOUR OPPORTUNITY 308

Thirty Five HOW TO INCREASE YOUR ABILITY 314

Thirty Six BRING OUT THE PERSON YOU CAN BE 320

Thirty Seven WHY DON'T YOU BEGIN? 324

PART IV
Another Look at Prosperity
329

Thirty Eight RICH WITHOUT MONEY 331

Thirty Nine RICHES WITHOUT WINGS 336

Forty THE GREATEST PROSPERITY 341

PART V
Appendices
345

Appendix A A LESSON IN PROSPERITY THINKING 347

Appendix B THOUGHTS ON PROSPERITY 349

Appendix C PROSPERITY AFFIRMATIONS 369

PART I
The Poverty Habit

One

POVERTY A MENTAL DISABILITY

Poverty itself is not so bad as the poverty thought. It is the conviction that we are poor and must remain so that is fatal. It is the attitude of mind that is destructive—the facing toward poverty and feeling so reconciled to it that one does not turn about face and struggle to get away from it with a determination which knows no retreat.

So long as you carry around a poverty atmosphere and radiate the poverty thought, you will be limited.

You will be but a poor person while you think poverty—just as, relatedly, you will be a failure while you think failure thoughts.

If you are afraid of poverty, if you dread it, if you have a horror of coming to want in old age, it is more likely to come to you, because this constant fear saps your courage, shakes your self-confidence, and makes you less able to cope with hard conditions.

The mind is a magnet, and a magnet must be true to itself: it must attract things like itself. If your mind is saturated with the fear thought, the poverty thought, then no matter how hard you work, you will attract poverty.

You walk in the direction in which you face. If you persist in facing toward poverty, you cannot expect to reach abundance. When every step you take is on the road to failure, you cannot expect to reach the success goal.

Holding the poverty thought keeps us in touch with poverty-stricken, poverty-producing conditions—the constant thinking of poverty, talking poverty, living poverty, makes us mentally poor. This is the worst kind of poverty.

I have never known a person to be successful who was always talking about business being bad. The habit of looking down, talking down, is fatal to advancement. Those who are always thinking of their hard luck and failure to get on, can by no possibility go in the opposite direction, where the goal of prosperity lies.

If you would attract good fortune you must get rid of doubt. As long as that stands between you and your ambition, it will be a bar that will cut you off. You must have faith. No one can make a fortune while convinced that he or she can't. The "I can't" philosophy has wrecked more careers than almost anything else. Confidence is the magic key that unlocks the door of supply.

When we lose the confidence that we can rise, improve ourselves, then every other success quality gradually leaves us, and life becomes a grind. We lose ambition and energy and become less and less capable of conquering poverty.

A young man of remarkable ability, who has an established position in the business world, recently told me that for a long time he had been very poor, and remained so until he made up his mind that he was not intended to be poor, that poverty was really a mental disease of which he intended to rid himself. He formed a habit of daily affirming abundance and plenty, of asserting his faith in himself and in his ability to become a man of means and importance in the world. He persistently drove the poverty thought out of his mind. He would have nothing to do with it.

He would not allow himself to think of possible failure. He turned his face toward the success goal—turned his back forever on poverty and failure.

He says that he used to pinch in every possible way in order to save in little ways. He would eat the cheapest kind of food, and as sparingly as possible. He would rarely get on a bus or streetcar, even if he had to walk for miles.

Under the new impulse he completely changed his habits. He resolved that he would go to good restaurants, get a comfortable room in a good location, and would try in every way to meet cultured people, and to form acquaintance's with those above him who could help him.

The more liberal he has been, the better he has been to himself in everything which could help him along, which would tend to a higher culture and a better education, the more things have come his way. He found that it was his pinched, stingy thoughts that shut off his supply.

Although he is now living well, he says that the amount he spends is a mere bagatelle compared with the larger things that come to him from his enlarged thought, his changed attitude of mind.

Nine-tenths of the people in the so-called industrialized, advanced countries who complain of being poor and failures are headed in the wrong direction, headed away from the condition or thing they long for. What they need is to be turned around so that they will face their goal, instead of turning their backs on it by their destructive thinking and going in the other direction. The Carnegies, Rockefellers, Vanderbilts, think prosperity, and they get it. They don't anticipate poverty, they don't anticipate failure, they know they are going to be prosperous and successful because they have eliminated all doubt of *not being so* from their minds.

Doubt is the factor which kills success, just as the fear of failure kills prosperity. Everything is mental first, whether failure or success. Everything passes through our consciousness before it is a reality.

That is why stingy, narrow minds do not attract money. If they get money they usually get it by parsimonious saving—like Ebenezer Scrooge—rather than by obeying the law of opulence. It takes a broad, liberal mind to attract money. The narrow, stingy mind shuts out the flow of abundance.

It is the hopeful, buoyant, cheerful attitude of mind that wins. Optimism is a prosperity builder; pessimism a prosperity killer.

Optimism is the great producer. It is hope, life. It contains everything which enters into the mental attitude which produces and enjoys prosperity.

No matter if you have lost your property, your health—your reputation even—there is always hope if you keep a firm faith in yourself and look up.

As long as you radiate doubt and discouragement, you will be a failure.

If those of you who believe that your opportunity has gone by forever, that you can never get on your feet again, only knew the power of reversal of your thoughts, you could easily get a new start.

But before you can live in a new world, you must believe in it.

I know a family whose members completely reversed their condition by reversing their mental attitude. They had been living in a discouraging atmosphere so long that they were convinced that success was for others, but not for them. They believed so thoroughly that they were fated to be poor that their home and entire environment were pictures of dilapidation and failure. Everything was in a run-down condition. There was almost no paint on the house, no carpets on the floors, and scarcely a picture on me wall—nothing to make the home comfortable and cheerful, All the members, of the family looked like failures. The home was gloomy, cold, and cheerless. Everything about it was depressing.

One day the mother read something that suggested that poverty was largely a mental disease, and she began at once to reverse her thinking habit—to gradually replace all discouraging, despondency, failure thoughts with their opposites.

She assumed a sunny, cheerful attitude, and looked and acted as if life were worth living.

Soon her husband and children caught the contagion of her cheerfulness, and in a short time optimism took the place of pessimism.

The husband changed his habits. Instead of going to his work unshaven and unkempt, with slovenly dress and slipshod manner, be became neat and tidy. He braced up, brushed up, cleaned up, and looked up. And the children followed his example.

The result of all this was that it brought about what many people would call "good luck." The change in the mental attitude, the outlook toward success and happiness instead of failure, reacted upon the father's mind, gave him new hope and new courage, and so increased his efficiency that he was soon promoted, as were also his sons. After two or three years of the creative, inspiring atmosphere of hope and courage, the entire family was transformed—as was the house! It was repaired—renovated within and without.

We must play the part of our ambition. If you are trying to be prosperous, you must play the part. If you are trying to demonstrate opulence, you must play it—not weakly, but vigorously, grandly. You must *feel* opulent. You must *think* opulence. You must *appear* opulent. Your bearing must be filled with confidence. You must give the impression of your own assurance, that you are large enough to play your part and to play it superbly.

Suppose the greatest actor or actress living were to have a play written for him or her in which the leading part was to represent a character in the process of making a fortune—a great, vigorous, progressive character, who conquered by his or her very presence. Suppose this actor, in playing the part, were to dress like an unprosperous character and walk on the stage in a stooping, slouchy, slipshod manner, as though he or she had no ambition, no energy or life—no real faith that he or she could ever make money or be a success, shuffling around the stage with an apologetic, shrinking, skulking manner, as much as to say, "Now, I do not believe that I can ever do this thing that I have attempted; it is too big for me. Other people have done it, but I never thought that I should ever be rich or prosperous. Somehow good things do not seem to be meant for me. I am just an ordinary person. I haven't had much experience and I haven't much confidence in myself, and it seems presumptuous for me to think I am ever going to be rich or have much influence in the world."

What kind of an impression would he make upon the audience? Would that actor or actress give confidence, radiate power or forcefulness, make people think that that kind of character could create a fortune, could manipulate conditions which would produce money? Would not everybody say that that character was a failure? Would they not laugh at the idea of that character conquering anything?

If you talk poverty, think poverty, live poverty, assume the air of a pauper, dress like a failure, how long do you think it would take you to arrive at the goal of prosperity?

Our mental attitude toward the thing we are struggling for has everything to do with our gaining it. If you want to become prosperous, you must believe that you were made for prosperity and happiness.

Erase all the shadows, all the doubts and fears, and the suggestions of poverty and failure from your mind. When you have become master of your thought, when you have once learned to dominate your mind, you will find that things will begin to come your way. Discouragement, fear, doubt, lack of self-confidence, are the germs which have killed the prosperity and happiness of tens of thousands of people.

If it were possible for all the poor to turn their backs on their dark and discouraging environment and face the light and cheer, and if they should resolve that they are done with poverty and a slipshod existence, this very resolution would, in a short time, revolutionize civilization.

Every human being from childhood on should be taught to *expect* prosperity, to believe that the good things of the world were intended for him or her.

Wealth is created mentally first; it is thought out before it becomes a reality. Those who decide to become physicians, talk medicine, read medicine, study medicine, and think medicine until they become saturated with it. They do not decide to become a physician and then put themselves in a legal atmosphere—read law, talk law, think law.

In a like manner, if you want success and abundance, you must think, walk, and talk success—you must think, walk, and talk abundance.

Stoutly deny the power of adversity or poverty to keep you down. Constantly assert your superiority to your environment. Believe that you are to dominate your surroundings, that you are the master and not the slave of circumstances.

Resolve with all the vigor you can muster that since there are plenty of good things in the world for everybody, you are going to have your share, without injuring anybody else or keeping others back. It was intended that you should have a competence, an abundance. Prosperity is your birthright, and you should resolve to reach your divine destiny.

Poverty is an abnormal condition. It does not fit any human being's constitution. It contradicts the promise and the prophecy of the divine in a person. There is not a single indication in our wonderful mechanism that we were created for a life of poverty. There is something larger and grander for us in the divine plan than perpetual slavery to the bread-winning problem.

No one can do their best work—bring out the best thing in themselves—while they feel want tugging at their heels, while they are hampered, restricted, and forever at the mercy of pinching circumstances.

The very poor, those struggling to keep the wolf at bay, cannot be independent. They cannot always afford to live in decent locations—and surely not in healthful houses. They cannot order their lives. Often they cannot even afford to express their opinions or have individual views.

Praise it who will, poverty in its extreme form is narrowing, belittling, contracting, ambition-killing—an unmitigated curse. There is little hope in it, little prospect in it, little joy in it. It too often develops the worst in people, and kills love between those who would otherwise live happily together.

It is difficult for the average human being to be a real man or real woman in extreme poverty. When worried, embarrassed, entangled with debts, forced to make a dime perform the proper work of a dollar, it is almost impossible to preserve that dignity and self-respect which enable a person to hold up his or her head and look the world squarely in the face. Some rare and beautiful souls have done this. Amidst dire poverty, they have given us examples of noble living that the world will never forget. But how many has poverty's lash driven to the lowest depths?

Poverty is more often a curse than a blessing, and those who praise its virtues would be the last to accept its hard conditions.

I wish I could fill every youth with an utter dread and horror of it; make them feel its constraint, its bitterness, its strangling effect—the way it can make one feel less of oneself.

There is no disgrace in unpreventable poverty. We respect and honor people who are poor because of ill-health or misfortune which they cannot prevent.

What we denounce is preventable poverty—that poverty which is due to the lack of effort, to wrong thinking, or to any preventable cause.

The trouble is that many of poverty's victims today have no confidence that they can get away from poverty. They hear so much about the poor person's lack of opportunities, that the great money combinations will compel nearly everybody in the future to work for somebody else; they hear so much talk of the grasping and the greed of the rich, that they gradually lose confidence in their ability to cope with conditions and become disheartened.

I do not overlook the heartless, grinding, grasping practices of many of the rich, or the unfair and cruel conditions brought about by unscrupulous political and financial schemers, but I wish to show the poor person that, notwithstanding all these things, multitudes of poor people *do* rise above their iron environment—and that there is hope.

The mere fact that so many continue to rise, year after year, out of just such conditions as you may think are fatal to your advancement—if you are currently struggling financially—ought to convince you that you also can conquer your environment.

Poverty begins in the mind. The majority of poor people in out cities remain poor because, tragically, they are mental paupers to begin with. They don't believe they are ever going to be prosperous. Fate and conditions are against them, they believe—they were born poor and they expect to always be poor: this is their unvarying trend of thought, their fixed conviction. Go among the poor in the slums and you will find them always talking about poverty, bewailing their hard luck, the cruelty and injustice of society. They will tell you how they are ground down by the upper classes, kept down by their greedy employers, or by an unjust order of things which they can't change They think of themselves as victims instead of victors, as conquered instead of conquerors.

The worst thing about poverty, then, is the poverty thought—the conviction that we are poor and must remain so.

Holding the poverty thought keeps us in poverty-stricken and poverty-producing conditions.

When you make up your mind that you are done with poverty forever; that you will have nothing more to do with it; that you are going to erase every trace of it from your dress, your personal appearance, your manner, your talk, your actions, your home; that you have set your face persistently toward better things and that nothing on earth can turn you from your resolution, you will be amazed to find what a reinforcing power will come to you, what an increase of confidence, reassurance, and self-respect.

The very act of resolving that you will have nothing more to do with poverty; that you will make the best possible out of what you do have; that you will put up the best possible appearance; that you will clean up, brush up, talk up, look up, instead of down—hold your head up and look the world in the face instead of cringing, whining, complaining—will create a new spirit within you which will lead you to the light. Hope will take the place of despair, and you will feel the thrill of a new power, of a new force coursing through your veins.

If you feel that you are down and out and everything about you looks bleak and discouraging, just try the experiment of turning squarely about and facing the other way—toward the sun of hope and expectancy—leaving all shadows behind you.

Cut off all currents of poverty thoughts, of doubt thoughts. Tear down from the walls of your mind all gloomy, depressing pictures, and hang up bright, hopeful, cheerful ones.

Remind yourself that thousands of people before you and around you in this country have *thought* themselves away from a life of poverty by getting a glimpse of this great principle: that we tend to realize in the life what we persistently hold in the thought and vigorously struggle toward.

Two

ENTANGLING ALLIANCES

"Beware of entangling alliances!" said George Washington to the young nation. There are thousands of victims of entanglements of all kinds in this country today who, if they could only gain the ears of the young just starting out in life, would repeat to them Washington's words of warning.

Is there a sadder picture than that of promising individuals of great ability, conscious of power which they have no opportunity to use to advantage, mocked by an ambition which they cannot satisfy, because they are hopelessly in debt or so bound by other self-forged chains that they cannot extricate himself? Instead of being a king or queen and dominating their environment, they are a slave to their entanglements—dogged for years by creditors.

Keep yourself free. Keep clear from complications of all kinds that may possibly compromise your manhood, your womanhood. An entanglement, whatever its nature, is imprisonment, no less terrible because it is voluntary. If your brain is intact, your mind unburdened, your hands and all your faculties free, you can do great things even with small money capital, or, perhaps, even without any. But when you are ground under the heel of debt and are not at liberty to act of your own accord, are pushed hither and thither by those to whom you are under obligations or with whom you have formed entangling alliances, you cannot accomplish much. You are a servant, not a free person.

There are hundreds today in middle life or older, working in ordinary positions who are as able as or abler than those who employ them. Good, honest men and women are everywhere struggling with superhuman efforts under loads which almost crush them, and are barely getting a living, who could do wonders if they were only free. But every avenue of opportunity seems closed to them because they are not in a position to seize whatever chance may offer—are not free to work it out. Everything they do is done at great disadvantage. They have to employ personal work and sheer force to accomplish what a little planning would do if they had not lost their money in some foolish investment, or were not so tied up by mortgages and debts that they are practically business prisoners. They cannot go where they would, but where they must. They are pushed instead of pushing; forced instead of forcing. They do not choose; iron circumstances compel them.

I know one of these victims who earns five hundred dollars a month, but for years half of his salary has gone for what business people call "paying for a dead horse." When quite a young man he made a foolish investment, in which he not only lost every dollar he laid up, but also gave notes for a large amount, which fall due every three months. He cannot get free from these notes without going into bankruptcy, which he is too honorable to do, and so his whole life has been handicapped. He is now fifty years old, with several sons and daughters, whom he has not been able to educate as he was ambitious to do. The comfort and happiness of his family as well as his own peace of mind have been ruined by this debt which will not die down. He has lived all these years in constant fear that he might be sick, or that something might happen to him, and that his wife and children might suffer in consequence.

The result of all this is not only a disappointed ambition, but the loss of the man's hopeful disposition, his buoyancy, and natural optimism, and he has become sour and pessimistic. His monotonous life of compulsory service, of slavery to a foolish transaction, entered into without investigation way back in his young manhood, has crushed all the spirit out of him. He has practically given up the thought of ever doing anything more than make a bare living for himself and his family. Existence has become a mere joyless drudgery because in a weak moment he mortgaged his whole future.

Struggling just for something to eat and something to wear, while forced to give up most of one's earnings for past errors, is not life. It is not freedom. It is slavery. It is slow strangulation.

The mania for getting rich—the mad, false idea that we must have money—has played worse havoc among ambitious people than war or pestilence. A member of the Chicago Board of Trade says that the men and women of this country contribute a hundred million dollars a year to the sharpers who promise to make them rich quick. They work the same old scheme of a confidential letter and shrewd baiting, until the victim parts with his money. Thousands are plodding along in poverty and deprivation, chagrined and humiliated because they have not been able to get up in the world or to realize their ambitions, for the reason that they succumbed to the scheme of some smooth promoter, who hypnotized them into the belief that they could make a great deal very quickly out of a very little.

The great fever of trying to make one dollar earn five dollars is growing more and more contagious. We see even women secretly going into brokers' offices, investing everything they have in all sorts of schemes, drawing their deposits out of the banks, sometimes pawning their jewelry—even their engagement rings—and borrowing, hoping to make a lot of money before their husbands or families find it out and then to surprise them with the results; but in most cases what they invest is hopelessly lost.

Thousands of young Americans are so tied up by financial or other entanglements, even before they get fairly started in their life-work, that they can only transmute a tithe of their real ability or their splendid energies into that which will count in their lives. A large part of it is lost on the way up, as the energy of the coal is nearly all lost before it reaches the electric bulb.

Don't tie yourself or your money up. Don't risk all your savings in any scheme, no matter how much it may promise. Don't invest your hard-earned money in anything without first making a thorough and searching investigation. Do not be misled by those who tell you that it is "now or never," and that, if you wait, you are liable to lose the best thing that ever came to you. Make up your mind that if you lose your money you will not lose your head, and that you will not invest in anything until you thoroughly understand all about it. There are plenty of good things waiting. If you miss one, there are hundreds of others. People will tell you that the opportunity will go by and you will lose a great chance to make money if you do not act promptly. But take your time, and investigate. Make it a cast-iron rule never to invest in any enterprise until you have gone to the very bottom of it, and, if it is not so sound that level-headed men will put money in it, do not touch it. The habit of investigating before you embark in any business will be a happiness-protector, a fortune-protector, and an ambition-protector as well.

Many looking in earnest to "get ahead," often get involved with questionable characters, and, before they are aware of it, they compromise themselves financially—finding themselves in an unfortunate, embarrassing position.

There is something humiliating in being poor. The very consciousness that we have *nothing to show for our endeavor* besides a little character and the little we have done, is anything but encouraging. We feel that we have not amounted to much, and we know the world looks upon us in the same way, if we have not managed to accumulate something.

What is the use of having a giant's intellect if you bind your faculties in such a way that you must do a pygmy's work, the work of mediocrity? Average ability accompanied by persistent determination and the freedom to pursue it is better than genius so tied up that it cannot act.

Value freedom and an unobstructed passage in your upward climb. Do not tie yourself up—financially, socially, morally, or in any other way. Keep yourself clear of crippling obligations of all kinds, so that you can act with freedom and with untrammeled faculties. Keep your manhood, your womanhood, and your independence—so that you can always look the world squarely in the face. Do not put yourself in a position where you must apologize or cringe or bow your head or crawl before anybody.

Keep your freedom at all costs.

Three

HAD MONEY BUT LOST IT

A prominent New York lawyer of wide experience says that in his opinion, ninety-nine out of every hundred of those who make money or inherit it, lose it sooner or later.

How many thousands of good, honest men and women there are in this country who have worked very hard and made all sorts of sacrifices of comfort and luxury in order to lay up something for the future, and yet have reached middle life or later without having anything to show for it—many of them, indeed, finding themselves without a home or any probability of getting one, without property or a cent of money laid by for sickness, for the inevitable emergency, or for their declining years!

It seems incredible that strong, sturdy, self-made people, who have had to fight their way up from poverty, and who feel the backache in every dollar they have earned, should let their savings slip through their fingers in the most foolish investments, with scarcely any investigation, often sending their money thousands of miles away to people they have never seen, and about whom they know practically nothing—except through an advertisement which has attracted their attention, or through the wiles of some smooth, unprincipled promoter.

Great numbers of vast fortunes in this country have been and are being built up on the very ignorance of the masses in regard to business methods. The schemers bank on it that it is easy to swindle people who do not know how to protect their property. They thrive on the ignorance of their fellows. They know that a shrewd advertisement, a cunningly worded circular, a hypnotic appeal will bring the hard earnings of these unsuspecting people out of hiding places into their own coffers.

For the sake of your home, for the protection of your hard earnings, for your peace of mind, your self-respect, your self-confidence, whatever else you do, do not neglect a good, solid financial training—and get it as early in life as possible. It will save you from many a fall, from a thousand embarrassments, and perhaps from the humiliation of being compelled to face your spouse and children and confess that you have been a failure. It may spare you the mortification of having to move from a good home to a poor one, of seeing your property slip out of your hands, and of having to acknowledge your weakness and your lack of foresight and thoughtfulness, or it may prevent your being made the dupe of con artists.

Many who once had businesses of their own are working as clerks, floorwalkers, or superintendents of departments in other people's stores, just because they risked and lost everything in some venture. As they now have families depending on them, they do not dare to take the risks which they took when younger, so they struggle along in mediocre positions, still mocked with ambitions which they have no chance to gratify.

How many inventors, discoverers, artists, writers, and the like have fought the fight of desperation amidst poverty and deprivation for years and years, have succeeded in giving the world that which helps to emancipate it from a life of drudgery and ameliorate the hard conditions of civilization, yet have then allowed others to snatch their victories away from them and leave them penniless, just because they did not know how to protect themselves!

Thousands of people who were once in easy circumstances are living in poverty and wretchedness today because they failed to put an understanding or an agreement in writing, or to do business in a business way. Families have been turned, penniless, out of house and home, because they trusted to a relative or a friend to "do what was right" by them, without drawing up a hard and fast, practical business arrangement.

Commit transactions to writing. It costs but little in time or money. It does not matter how honest people are, they may forget—and it is so easy for misunderstandings to arise, that it is never safe to leave anything of importance to a mere oral statement. When all interested parties are agreed, formulate the agreement in exact terms. This will often save lawsuits, bitterness, and alienations. How many friendships have been broken because understandings were not put in writing! Thousands of cases are in the courts today for this reason, and a large part of lawyers' incomes is derived from them.

Many people have the idea that others, especially friends or relatives, will think their honesty or confidence or trustworthiness questioned if they are asked to put their proposition, or agreement, or understanding in writing. It is not a question of honest, confidence, or trust. It is a question of, business, and business should be done in a business way—so that in case of death, or some other unforeseen event, every possibility of complication or misunderstanding will be eliminated.

Many a cultured woman has been thrown suddenly on her own resources by the failure or the death of her husband—and has found herself wholly incapable of administering his affairs or of earning a living. Many women, their husbands having died suddenly, are left with large business responsibilities, which they are utterly unfit to assume. They are at the mercy of designing lawyers or dishonest business men, who well know that these women are mere babies in their hands when it comes to important transactions.

We find young men and women graduating from college, full of theories and of all sorts of knowledge or smatterings of knowledge, but without the ability to protect themselves from human thieves who are trying to get from them something for nothing. No one should be allowed to graduate, especially from any of the higher institutions, without being well grounded in practical financial methods. Parents who send their children out in life, without seeing that they are well versed in ordinary financial and investment principles, do them an incalculable injustice.

I have heard a young woman boast that she did not know anything about money matters, and had no desire to. She said that it was distasteful to her to discuss economy. And there are many women who think it is not necessary for them to know anything about money from the purely business point of view, as they consider that that phase of life belongs wholly to their fathers or brothers or husbands.

I once met a lady who had lost her property through a lack of business knowledge. She told me that she knew nothing whatever about business. She had never known finances or investing. Her husband died and left her with a large property, and it was her custom to sign any paper or document that her lawyer or agents presented to her, usually without reading. The people who had charge of her property knew that she knew nothing about business and took advantage of her ignorance. They got her property away from her, and she did not have enough left even to conduct a legal fight to get it back.

Another woman presented a check for payment to the teller of her bank. He passed it back to her with the request that she be kind enough to endorse it. The lady wrote on the back of the check, "I have done business with this bank for many years, and I believe it to be all right. Mrs. James B. Brown."

I know of a lady whose husband made a deposit for her in a bank and gave her a cheek book so that she could pay her bills without calling on him for money. One day she received a notice from the bank that her account was overdrawn. She went to the bank and told the teller that there must be a mistake about it, because she still had a lot of checks left in her book. She knew so little about business methods that she thought she could keep drawing any amount until the checks were all gone.

These stories sound ridiculous and almost incredible, yet the very girl or woman who laughs at it may make even more absurd blunders. Many an accomplished woman, when given a pen and asked to sign an important document drawn up by an attorney or business man, will sign it without reading it or even asking to be informed of its contents, only to learn afterwards by disastrous results that she has signed away her property and turned herself out of her home.

Only a short time ago I read of a lady who had won a suit involving about $20,000. New evidence, however, was brought forward, which caused the court immediately to reverse its decision. It was proved that the lady had sworn falsely. She was perfectly innocent of any such intention, but she had sworn that she had never signed her name to a certain document. The document was produced, and, to her utter astonishment, she saw her signature affixed to it. She acknowledged at once that the signature was hers, although she had just sworn that she had never signed the paper in question. It appeared that, during her husband's lifetime, whenever papers were to be signed, he told her where to write her name, and she did as she was told, without having the slightest idea of the contents of the papers.

Many people have come to grief by giving full power of attorney to their lawyer or business agent. Very few understand the significance of a full power of attorney, which authorizes the person so empowered to deal with your property in all respects as if it were that person's own, or as if he or she had for the time being assumed your personality. A person with power of attorney may sign your name to any instrument, may bind you to anything he she pleases, may draw money from your bank, may impersonate you in all business transactions. In short, as far as business arrangements are concerned, a person with power of attorney stands practically and legally for yourself: This is a tremendous power to place in the hands of another, and people should be very careful to whom they assign it. It should never be conferred on any person but one whose honesty is above suspicion, and whose knowledge of the administration of the financial affairs of others has been tried and proved.

"Oh, I signed a paper, giving full power of attorney to my lawyer before I went abroad I trusted everything to him, and when I came back practically everything was gone. My business affairs were so complicated that I have not had the money to fight the man I trusted." This, in brief, was the story of one man's wrecked finances, as he told it to me.

If everyone had a thorough financial training, tens of thousands of promoters and schemers who have thriven on the people's ignorance, would be out of an occupation.

This ignorance of practical business principles is amazingly very common among professionals. I know clergymen, journalists, authors, doctors, teachers—people in every profession—who are constantly subjected to serious embarrassment by their incapacity in business matters. Some of them do not know how to interpret the simplest business forms.

It is infinitely harder to save money and to invest it wisely than to make it. If even the most practical business people, those who have had a long training in scientific business methods, find it a difficult thing to hold on to money after they make it, what is likely to happen to the rest of us who have had practically no training in business methods?

Nothing will stand you in better stead, in the hard, cold practical everyday world, than a good, sound education in the uses and abuses of money. Your success in any trade, occupation, or profession will depend as much on your general knowledge of the dollar as on your technical training.

No matter what your vocation may be, in other words, you must be a businessperson first, or you will always be placed at a great disadvantage in the practical affairs of life. You cannot entirely ignore the money side of existence any more than you can the food side.

The foundation of a successful life is the ability to know how to manage the money side of it effectively.

Four

RESIGNED TO POVERTY

One of the worst things about being very poor is the danger of becoming reconciled to penury, expecting it, holding the conviction that we shall always be poor, that there is no help for it.

The habit of thinking we must remain poor because we are so is a paralyzing habit.

Whatever we have accustomed ourselves to for any length of time tends to become a fixed mode of life. Multitudes of people have become so accustomed to their poverty environment, so used to taking it for granted that they are going to remain poor, that they do not take the necessary steps to get away from poverty. They do not know that the first step toward prosperity is far easier than they think. Indeed, it is a mental one. It is how they *do* think. So they go on affirming their poverty, getting more and more deeply imbedded in the poverty condition by their poverty thoughts and convictions.

As long as you hold the poorhouse thought you are heading toward the poorhouse.

No matter how hard you may work, if you constantly hold the poverty ideal, the poorhouse thought in your mind, you are driving away the very thing you are pursuing. If you sow failure thoughts, poverty thoughts, you can no more reap success, prosperity harvests, than a farmer can get a wheat crop from sowing thistles.

Some one has said that no one ever went to the poorhouse who did not attract the poorhouse by a poorhouse mental attitude. Observation and long study of the question have convinced me that, as a rule, people who make miserable failures of their lives expected to do so. They had such a horror of the poorhouse, they lived in such terror of coming to want, that they shut off the very source of their supply. They had so warped their minds that they could see nothing ahead but poverty. They wasted the precious energy which might have been utilized in happiness and prosperity building, by expecting, dreading and preparing for the dire things that might come upon them—and, according to the law, they got what they dreaded and feared.

Thinking war, talking war, anticipating it, getting ready for it—in other words, preparedness for war, the perpetual war suggestion—has been responsible for the outbreak of virtually all wars. If all the nations involved had talked peace, thought peace, expected it, prepared for it, there would have been peace, not war.

Similarly, so long as you talk poverty, think poverty, expect it, get ready for it, you will have poverty. Preparedness for poverty, expecting it, attracts it—confirms poverty conditions.

We are constantly drawing to ourselves that which we expect. If you are sending out a perpetual poverty thought current, a doubt current, a discouragement current, no matter how hard you may be working in the opposite direction, you will never get away from the current you set in motion. The sort of thought current you generate will flow back to you.

Everywhere we see people trying hard to get on, struggling early and late to better their condition, and yet never expecting, or even hoping to be prosperous. They do not believe they are going to get what they are working for, and so they do not.

A typical example of those who keep themselves in the poverty current is a woman I know who is constantly affirming her inability to better her condition. She answers her better-off friends who tell her that she ought to have this and that by saying, "Oh, it is all very well for you rich folks to talk this way, but these things are not for me. We have always been poor, and I suppose we always shall be. We can only lave the bare necessities of life and are fortunate if we get these. Of course I might indulge in a little treat for myself and the children now and then, but that would be extravagant, and I must save for a rainy day."

Now, I have no quarrel with people who save for a rainy day. It is prudent to be prepared for all emergencies. It is a splendid thing to save for spending, to prepare for enjoyment in our later years. But people who begin early to provide for the "rainy day," and who deny themselves every little pleasure and enjoyment for the sake of adding to this provision, fall into the habit of pinching the themselves, and usually continue to do so throughout life.

This woman limits her supply by her conviction that every cent she can spare must go to the rainy day fund, because she is always going to be poor. She assures herself and others that she is never going to have the things she would like to have, because of her poverty, and so she starves the lives of herself and her boy and girl in anticipating a day of possible want. She is a type of a multitude of men and women who settle down to their poverty, become reconciled to its limitations, and do not make a strenuous effort to get away from it. That is, they never dream of exercising their creative, positive thought, but continue to live—and to realize in their circumstances—the negative, destructive, poverty thought.

These are the people who are always saying they "cannot afford" things; they cannot afford to send the boy or girl to college this year; they cannot afford the necessary clothes or the needed vacation, because of the rainy day, which, like a specter, rises at every feast and on every occasion when they try to get some enjoyment or satisfaction out of the present. They are always postponing things till next year.

But this "next year" never comes, and the children never go to college, and they never take the needed vacation—the travel their own country or the long promised trip abroad. They keep forever postponing the enjoyment of the good things of life until they can "afford it," and that time never comes for people of this apprehensive habit of mind, because they always want to lay up a little more for the future.

I know a number of people well along in years who are still pinching themselves—not only on the comforts but even on the necessities of life—in anticipation of the possible rainy day, for which they are always planning. They make life one long continuous rainy day, and little realize that they more often than not are creating the need for which they are perpetually saving.

We sometimes read in newspapers striking illustrations of the results of this starved, rainy day habit of mind. A New York daily recently reported a typical instance: that of an aged woman who had died alone in the slums of the metropolis. She had been dead several days when her body was found. So wretched were her surroundings that it was at first supposed that she was penniless. On investigation, however, it was found that the woman had had in ready cash and in bank deposits, almost ten thousand dollars.

Pauperized by her diseased mind, this wretched creature, like many another poverty-stricken soul, died of starvation in the midst of plenty. Her mind was so obsessed with the poverty thought that she even denied herself the necessities of life. For years she had shut herself away from the great stream of life flowing all around her, so that she might hoard, and hoard, and hoard. She would allow no one to enter her rooms, and died alone and uncared for, leaving behind her the money which would have made her comfortable, happy, useful, and would have prolonged her life. She was as much a victim of poverty as if she didn't have a cent.

"But where is our supply coming from? How are we going to pay the rent, the mortgage off the home, the farm? Where is the money coming from? What will happen to us if we cannot get it? Where are the children's clothes coming from? How are we going to get the necessaries of life? What if I can't get a job that will enable us to really live?" These are the questions multitudes of people ask themselves—expressing thereby the epidemic acuteness of the suffering of poverty disease.

Nothing else gives human beings so much anxiety, nothing else is such a perpetual irritant, as this fear of what is coming in the future, this dread of poverty, of not being able to provide for the necessities and the comforts of those dear to us, the fear of not being able to maintain ourselves and to rear our children in comfort and respectability. It demagnetizes us, driving away the things we want and drawing to us those we dread.

"The thing I greatly feared has come upon me," said Job. And just as surely, those who have an abnormal fear of poverty attract the very condition they dread and are trying to get away from—because the mind relates with whatever it dwells on. Our doubts and hatreds and fears—the things we mentally relate with—we attract.

Whatever you allow your mind to dwell on you are unconsciously creating. If you think continually of misfortunes, of poverty; if you fear you are going to fail in your work, that you may come to want; if you are always thinking about the possibility of your business declining; if you fear you are losing your grip on your trade or profession, you are aggravating your trouble and making it worse and worse. There are multitudes of people who never expect even to be comfortable, to say nothing of having luxuries. They expect poverty, hard times, and do not understand that this very expectancy increases their magnetic power to attract what they do not want.

Not long ago a young man who was greatly depressed because he could not get on in the world, asked me what I thought the trouble was. He said he had always worked hard, but did not seem to make any headway. About all he could do was to earn a bare living. Everything appeared to go against him. Fate, he complained, seemed determined to keep him down, no matter, how hard he might struggle against it, and he was doomed to be poor, to be a nobody. He said he believed that hard luck, poverty and failure were family traits, for his father and grandfather, he said, were hard workers too, but they could never get on, never get away from poverty, and he didn't expect he ever would either.

Another, an older man, who sought my advice in a similar difficulty, lamented the fearful inequality of human conditions and railed against his luck and the injustice of fate. "I work early and late, Sundays and holidays," he said, "and haven't taken a vacation for years. I have been struggling and striving and pushing to make my way in the world since I was a boy, and here I am past fifty and have never succeeded in anything yet. Now there is something wrong somewhere in society when such persistence and such constant efforts do not enable one to get anywhere, or to rise to any position worth while."

I asked him about his early training and education. He acknowledged that he had not made much of a preparation for his life work, because, he said, his father also had been a tremendous worker, had always tried hard to better his condition, but like himself had never succeeded, and so he had come to the conclusion that success was not in the family, and that it was no use to spend years in preparing for a career, for there was no chance that very much would come to him anyway.

These two are types of people who are constantly heading toward poverty and failure in their minds, and then complaining when they have got what they invited. By the law of mental attraction they could not get anything but poverty and failure. Each had desired success and prosperity, but had always expected the opposite. Each had slaved and toiled in an aimless sort of way, belittling himself and his talents, with the inner belief that it was all he was good for anyway, and that if success by any chance ever came his way it would be a stroke of luck, and not because it was his due by inherent right or though his effort.

None of us can become prosperous as long as we hold in our mind the picture of limitation, of lack and want. We do not get things in this world which we do not believe we can get. We do not accomplish what we doubt we can do—even though we have the ability to do it.

I knew a boy in college who always felt certain he was going to fail in his examinations, and he did fail invariably. Vet it was due more to his fear, his terror, of failure than to a lack of ability or preparation in his studies He had formed a habit of expecting failure, of predicting misfortunes, of looking and preparing for them—and, so far as I know, they followed him through life.

In every community, in every occupation and profession, there are able, conscientious men and women who try very hard, so far as their actual labor is concerned, to get on in the world, but who don't expect to get on. It is pitiful to see them toiling day after day, but always facing in the wrong direction. They are working for success in their vocations, working for a competence for themselves and their families, but all the time expecting failure, anticipating poverty, living in an atmosphere of mental penury.

There is no law of philosophy by which you can possibly produce just the opposite of what you are holding in your mind, what you are concentrating on. If you are thinking down, if you are afraid, are worried, if you have fears and doubts, if you keep visualizing, thinking, talking hard times, panics, and financial crises, your life circumstances will shrink and shrivel accordingly. A thought current saturated with the fear of failure, with doubts and discouragement will neutralize your most strenuous efforts. If, on the other hand, you have confidence, expectation of better things, if you are convinced that conditions are going: to improve, you set in motion a thought current that will back your efforts with an irresistible force.

The early years of multitudes of children are saturated with the poverty suggestion. They breathe a poverty atmosphere. They hear poverty talk perpetually. They acquire a poverty vocabulary. Their fathers and mothers are always talking poverty, bemoaning their hard conditions, complaining that they were born poor, and must die poor. Children reared in such a mental environment acquire a poverty habit from which it is very difficult to get away.

There is a tremendous difference between the prospects as well as the mental attitude and the facial expression of a poor child who dreams of one day going to college, who pictures himself or herself there, who believes with a steadfast heart that this dream will be realized, and the prospects, the mental attitude and face of another child, who also longs for an education but has abandoned all hope of ever going to college, or of ever getting away from the grinding drudgery and monotony of the life which he or she hates.

We must change our thought before we can change our conditions. The thought always leads in any achievement. It would be as impossible for the great mass of poor people to improve their position materially while holding the persistent belief that they are always going to be poor, and that they never can do what others have done to get out of their rut, as it would be for the child who longs to go to college—but who has made up his or her mind that it is impossible—to get a higher education. If you think that all others are lucky and you are unlucky, if you talk about your hard fate and think that the rich are getting all the good things of the world and that you are getting only the dregs and never will get anything else, then you will, of course, never indeed get anything else.

This facing toward poverty and despair, the assumption of the inevitability of heading toward hopelessness and failure, is the worst thing about poverty. The conviction that one cannot get away from poverty, the firm belief that one can never rise into prosperity—these are the most distressing things about the very poor.

Not long ago a man told me that he had accepted that it was not intended for him to have any luxuries; that having always been a poor man, he always expected to be poor and never expected to have anything better than he now had. He said that he would be perfectly satisfied if he could just be assured that he would never have to go to the poorhouse, that he would have enough to provide the bare necessities for his little family.

Now, this is just the thing that kept this man poor, for he was a hard worker. He always expected to be poor. He did not expect anything better. He merely worked for the bare necessities of life, did not expect anything else, and so, of course, he only just managed to squeeze along, making but a bare subsistence. This attitude of the poor toward poverty tends to increase it, to aggravate their circumstances. So long as we hold the poverty thought, we are making ourselves a poverty magnet, and continually drawing to himself unfortunate conditions.

Extreme poverty is a scourge that draws its victims down from depths to lower depths; that makes life a bitter struggle for the bare crumbs that hold body and soul together. When these are not forthcoming it drives the despairing to crime in order to keep themselves from starving. Or, they are too proud to steal or beg, then to end their lives.

The Bible tells us "The destruction of the poor *is* their poverty." Every investigator of slum life in our big cities, every record of the lives of the unfortunate poor and the starving children in our midst, proves that this is an absolute truth.

If you are in the clutches of a poverty so dire that it robs you even of the desire to get away from it, you are cursed with self-thought poisoning. This is what mars and embitters so many lives, drives away happiness, health and prosperity.

Poverty is usually a disease. It is just as much a disease as is smallpox or tuberculosis. It is just as abnormal to the human being as any disease of the flesh.

So is poverty's cousin, failure.

Every year poverty claims, among its tens of thousands, innocent children who die of disease and neglect.

As the race becomes more intelligent and better educated we eliminate a multitude of conditions to which people formerly thought they were born, and that there was no escape from them. Many evils which have been conquered by science and education were at one time regarded as scourges sent by God to punish us for our sins, to chasten us. Diseases which struck terror to the hearts of human beings a hundred years ago, and from which they fled in horror, are not feared at all today. Intelligence and science have mastered the great plagues which in the Middle and Dark Ages carried off their terrified victims by the million. We have no fear of those plagues today, because we have obliterated their causes. We know now that the prevention of those frightful epidemics is merely a matter of sanitation, scientific hygiene, intelligent, healthful living. We know that they were scourges forged by ignorance and not "judgments" of God.

The poverty disease, the poverty curse, is not a decree of Providence. In industrial nations, in prosperous nations, it is largely the result of a mental habit. Every human being in these countries could be living in comfort if they knew the powers locked up in themselves. If the mental poverty antidotes were as generally known as are the medical poison antidotes, there would be, in these countries, no poor people.

If we are to progress as a race, as a civilization, we must, emphatically, drive this crushing poverty disease from our midst. Instead of lauding its blessings, as some do, it is our duty to get away from it—and to help others, in ours and every nation, to do so.

Five

ECONOMY THAT COSTS TOO MUCH

"Thair iz sertin kinds of ekonomy that don't pa," said Josh Billings, "and one of them iz that thair iz a grate menny pepul in the world who try to ekonomize by stratenin' pins."

Many become slaves to the habit of economizing, and, without realizing it, constantly strangle their business. They handicap their prospects and kill their greater opportunities by keeping their eyes fixed on petty economies.

I know a rich man who has become such a slave to the habit of economizing, formed when he was trying to get a start in the world, that he has not been able to break away from it, and he will very often lose a dollar's worth of valuable time trying to save a dime. He goes through his home and turns the gas lights so low that it is almost impossible to get around without stumbling over chairs. Several members of his family have received injuries from running against half-open doors, or stumbling over furniture in the dark; and once, while I was present, a member of the family spilt a bottle of ink upon a costly carpet in passing from one room to another in the darkness.

He carries the same spirit of foolish economy into his business. He tears off the unused half-sheets of letters, cuts out the backs of envelopes for scribbling paper, and is constantly spending time trying to save little things which are utterly out of proportion to the value to him of the time thus consumed. He makes his employees save strings from bundles as a matter of principle, even if it takes twice as much time as the string is worth, and practices all sorts of trifling economies equally foolish.

A Paris bank clerk, who was carrying a bag of gold through the streets, dropped a ten-franc piece, which rolled from the sidewalk. He set his bag down to look for the lost piece, and, while he was trying to extricate it from the gutter, some one stole his bag and ran away with it.

I have seen a lady spoil a pair of fine gloves trying to rescue a nickel which had fallen into the mud.

Comparatively few people have a healthy view of what real saving, or economy, means. They injure their health seriously by trying to save money—purchasing cheap food which produces low vitality. They think they are wisely economizing because they spend a pittance for their lunch, or do without altogether. Sadly, what they too often discover that they have indeed been cutting back on was their health.

Others delay some needed trivial surgical or dental operation for months or even years, simply because they dread the expense, thus not only suffering a great deal of unnecessary pain all that time, but also incapacitating themselves from giving the best thing in them to their vocations.

We little realize what a fearful amount of energy and precious vitality is wasted in most lives through false ideas of economy.

Some people will waste a dollar's worth of valuable time in visiting numerous stores looking for bargains and trying to save a few cents on some small purchase they wish to make. They will buy wearing apparel of inferior material because the price is low, although they know the articles will not wear well.

There is no greater delusion than that cheapness is economy. I have watched for some time a New York skyscraper erected years ago under contract. The owners dickered with a great many builders, finally letting the contract to the one who bid the lowest. The original estimate, made by a reliable builder, for a thoroughly substantial, first-class building, was cut down over a hundred thousand dollars by this cheap concern. The result is that, in their grasping greed to save, the owners overreached themselves, and the building has been a source of anxiety to them ever since its erection. Everything about it is cheap, shoddy, or rickety. There is scarcely a day that something is not out of order somewhere. The walls crack, the floors settle, the doors warp, and the windows stick. There is constant trouble with the cheap elevators, and with the steam and electric fittings, and the boilers and all the machinery are frequently out of order. In the winter the building is cold, the pipes leak because of cheap plumbing, and the furnishings are constantly being damaged. As a consequence the occupants get disgusted and move out. Although the building is in a locality where rents are high, it is impossible to keep reliable tenants very long, because they become so exasperated. It attracts a class of people just like itself—

cheap, shoddy, unreliable—and the loss in the rents and in constant repairs, in the rapid deterioration, to say nothing of the wear and tear on the nervous system of the owners, will be greater than the amount saved by the cheap contract.

Trying to cut the payroll down to the lowest possible dollar has ruined many a concern. Many a hotel has gone down because the proprietor tried to save a few thousand dollars a year by hiring cheap clerks, cooks, and waiters, and by buying cheap food. Just that little difference between the cheap and the best help and the cheap and the best food has made the fortune of many a shrewd hotel-keeper.

Of course, we realize that those who haven't the money cannot always do that which will contribute to their highest comfort and efficiency. But they can emphasize the right thing, instead of handicapping their prospects and killing their opportunities by keeping their eyes fixed on petty economies.

Do not take a little, narrow, pinched, cheese-paring view of life. Live between extravagance and meanness. It is false economy never to take a holiday, or never to spend money for an evening's amusement on for a useful book.

Economy, in its broadest sense, involves the highest kind of judgment and level-headedness and breadth of vision. It means the wisest expenditure of what we have. It is not stinginess or meanness. It is not saving a nickel at the expense of twenty-five cents' worth of time. Indeed, the wisest economy often means liberal spending, a large outlay, for it always has the larger end in view. Thousands of dollars may depend on the spending of hundreds.

Some people, however, never get out of the world of pennies into the world of dollars. They work so hard to save the cents that they lose the dollars: the richer experience and the better opportunity. Such petty economizers are too narrow in their views, too limited in their outlook, too stingy in their expenditures, to ever measure up to large things. They hold the penny so close to their eyes that it shuts out the dollar.

The great thing is to make it a life principle never to delay the remedy of anything which is retarding our progress, keeping us down.

Power should be the goal of a worthy ambition. Anything which will add to one's personal force, which will increase one's ability to grow, is worth its price, no matter how much it costs. Spend generously for anything which will raise your achievement qualities, which will make you a broader, abler man or woman.

"He that soweth sparingly, shall also reap sparingly."

PART II
Your Thoughts and Your Prosperity

Six

HOW WE LIMIT OUR SUPPLY

What would you think of a prince, the heir to a kingdom of limitless wealth and power, who lived in the condition of a pauper, who went about the world bemoaning his hard fate and telling people how poor he was, saying that he didn't believe his father was going to leave him anything, and that he might as well make up his mind to a life of poverty and limitations?

You would say, of course, that he must be insane, and that his hard conditions, his poverty and limitations, were not actual, but imaginary; that they existed only in his mind; that his father was ready to load him with good things, with all that his heart desired, if the prince would only open his mind to the truth and live in the condition befitting a prince, the son and heir of a great king.

If you are living in pinching poverty, in a narrow, cramped, limited environment in which there seems to be no hope, no outlook for better things; if you are not getting what you want, though working hard for it, then you are living and acting just as foolishly as the prince who, believing that he was poor, lived like a pauper in the midst of his father's limitless wealth. Your limitations are in your mind, just as the prince's were in his. You are the child of a Father who has created abundance, limitlessness, for all of His children, but your fearful, doubtful, poverty-stricken thought shuts you out from all this abundance and keeps you in poverty.

A Russian laborer named Mihok, living in Omaha, Nebraska, carried a "luck" stone in his pocket for twenty years, never guessing that it had any monetary value. Time and again friends, who thought that it might be more than an ordinary stone, suggested that he have it examined by a jeweler. He obstinately refused until, finally, they became so insistent that he sent the stone to a Chicago jeweler, who pronounced it a pigeon-blood ruby, the largest of its kind in the world. It weighed 24 karats and was worth $100,000.

There are millions like this poor day laborer, living in poverty, thinking that there is nothing for them but hard work and more poverty who, without knowing it, are carrying in the great within of themselves possibilities of wealth beyond their dreams. Their wrong thinking is robbing them of their divine inheritance; shutting off the abundant supply provided for them by the Omnipotent Source of all supply.

The majority of people are in the position of a man who went out to water his garden, but inadvertently stepped on the hose, shutting off the water supply. He was getting only a mere dribble of water when he should have been getting a liberal flow. He was pinching his supply, limiting it to a disheartening drizzle—and didn't know it.

That is literally what all who are living in poverty are doing. They are pinching their supply by stepping upon the hose through which plenty would come to them. They are stopping the flow of abundance that is their birthright, by their doubts, their fears, their unbelief; by visualizing poverty, thinking poverty, acting as if they never expected to have anything, to accomplish anything, or to be anything.

Everything in life, everything in this universe, is based upon principle—follows a divine law. And the law of prosperity and abundance that applies to the universe as well as to humanity is just as definite as the law of gravitation, just as unerring as the principles of mathematics. But whereas gravitation will operate whether you think about it or not, it is only by aligning your thinking in accordance with the universal principle of abundance that can you realize the abundant, prosperous life that is your birthright. In other words, according to your thought will your life be: be that a life of supply or a life of lack. Your mental attitude will be flung back to you, every time, in kind.

We are the creatures of our convictions. We cannot get beyond what we believe we are; what we believe we have. If we think that we are never going to be strong or well liked other people, or to be successful in our calling, we never will be. If we are convinced that we will always be poor, we will be. You can't get away from poverty when you don't expect to; when you don't believe that you are going to.

Many of the people who are living in poverty to-day never really expect anything else. Their fixed belief that they can never become prosperous keeps them in poverty; that is, it keeps their minds negative, and the mind cannot create positively, cannot produce positively, in this condition.

It is only the positive mind that can create prosperity; the negative mind is non-creative can only tear down, inhibit, prevent the inflow of things. A hard-working person who longs for prosperity but is headed in the other direction mentally, who doesn't believe he or she is going to be prosperous, is neutralizing his or her hard work—standing on the hose that connects with his or her supply.

For your work to produce prosperity, it is not so much what you do with your hands as what you do with your mind that counts. Everything that has been accomplished by the hand or brain of man had its birth in the mind. The universe itself is the creation of Divine Mind.

When you limit yourself inwardly in your thoughts, you are limiting yourself outwardly in a way that corresponds with your mental attitude, because you are obeying a law which is unchangeable. When you are forever saving pennies, you are forever watching out for little things and never doing big things. And you cannot *do* big things because you are never *thinking* big things. No matter how much natural ability you have, your limited, poverty thoughts are dwarfing you, cutting off the big flow of supply that is literally at your command.

We often think of others as extravagant when we compare what they pay for things with what we pay for things of the same kind, and we pride ourselves that we are economizing and saving what they are wasting. But, are we really? How does our lifestyle compare with theirs? Does the enjoyment we get out of life measure up to what they get? Do the few dollars we save deny us the opportunity for finer foods, better clothing, the little pleasure trips, the social enjoyments, the picnics and various diversions which make life pleasant, healthful that our neighbors enjoy, whose extravagance we condemn? Or does our pinching policy leaves us *poorer* in the end?

Prosperity flows only through channels that are wide open to receive it. It does not flow through channels pinched by the poverty thought, by discouragement, doubt, or fear, or by a strangling narrow-visioned policy. A generous expenditure is often the wisest economy, the only thing that brings a generous success. If the great manufacturers should lose their broad visions and wide outlooks, should begin to skimp on necessary output, should substitute inferior goods and service for the best, should change from a broad, generous policy to a narrow, stingy one, they would soon find their businesses dwindling away to nothing.

There is no changing the principle behind the law of supply: Ultimately it's your mental attitude that will determine your success or failure. If you tap the great fountainhead of supply with a gimlet, you cannot reasonably expect to get an abundant supply. That is impossible. Your mental attitude gauges the flow of your supply, and to truly be prosperous, it must gauge life in terms of abundance, not limitation.

Seven

THE LAW OF ATTRACTION: DRIVING PROSPERITY TOWARD ONESELF OR DRIVING IT AWAY

It was never intended that God's children should ever want for anything. We live in the very lap of abundance; there is plenty of everything all about us, the great cosmic universe is packed with all sorts of beautiful, marvelous things, glorious riches, ready for our use and enjoyment. Everything the human heart can crave, the great creative Intelligence offers us. We can draw from this vast ocean of intelligence everything we wish. All that it is necessary for us to do is to obey the law of attraction: Like attracts like.

To realize prosperity and abundance depends on our ability to make our minds magnets to attract the things we want, to attract our desires.

All inventions, all discoveries, all the marvelous facilities of civilization—our hospitals, our schools, our churches, our libraries, and other institutions, our homes, with their comforts and luxuries—have all come to us by first being attracted to us by our minds.

What keeps our own from us is our ignorance of the law that would bring it to us.

When you were a child, experimenting with a little steel magnet, didn't you often try to make it pick up a variety of objects, including wood, copper, rubber? And, of course, you found it would not pick these things up, because it did not have the makeup to attract these things, nor they to attract it. You found that it would pick up a needle but not a toothpick. Unknowingly, you were demonstrating the law that *like attracts like*.

Not a day passes that we do not see this law demonstrated in different ways in human life. Sometimes the demonstrations are very tragic. Only a short time ago, a little eight-year-old girl, the daughter of a Pennsylvania farmer, died from fright in a dentist's chair, where she had been placed to have a tooth extracted. Although the child knew nothing about the law, it worked just the same; and, like Job, the thing she feared had come to her.

We all use the law of attraction no matter whether we know it or not. We use it every instant of our lives. The mind at any given time is a magnet for something. It is a magnet for whatever thought, whatever convictions dominate the mind at the time. By concentrating upon something, in other words—decidedly or undecidedly—we become a specialist in that line, and the law of attraction brings it to us. It is by this means that we draw to ourselves either poverty or opulence, success or failure.

The glorious thing about it all is that we can determine what the mind shall attract, what sort of a magnet it shall become.

If you have a prosperity mental attitude, if you have a vigorous faith that you are going to get away from poverty, that you are going to demonstrate prosperity, abundance, and strive intelligently and persistently to realize your vision, prosperity will be yours. That's the law. And it's a law that we cannot disobey. We are always obeying it, and however we obey it, those are the result we will get, accordingly.

Multitudes of people who work hard and try hard in every way to get on would be shocked if they could see a mental picture of themselves headed toward the poorhouse in fact, as they actually are in thought. They do not know that, by an inexorable law, they must head toward their mental attitude, that when they continually think and talk poverty and suggest it by their slovenly dress, their personal appearance, and by their environment, when they predict that there is nothing for them but poverty, that they will always be poor, no matter how hard they may work. They do not know that their doubts and fears and poverty-stricken convictions are making prosperity impossible for them. They do not know that as long as they hold such thoughts they cannot possibly head toward, the goal of prosperity.

If we could only see a picture of the mental processes of whatever is held in the mind, pulling the things which correspond to our thought; if we could see more failure, more bad business, more debts, more losses starting towards us because we have contacted with these things in our thought, we would understand the law of our lives and quit forever thinking on those things that attract less instead of more, poverty instead of abundance, failure instead of prosperity.

How often we make our mind a magnet to attract all sorts of enemy thoughts—poverty thoughts, sick thoughts, fear thoughts, and worry thoughts, and then somehow we expect that a miracle will be performed, and that out of these negative causes we will be sure in some way to enjoy positive results. No miracle could perform such a change as this. Results correspond with causes.

We may be born into poverty, or, owing to circumstances suddenly find ourselves in poverty, but *before we can be conquered by poverty, we must, first of all, be poor mentally.* The poverty thought, the acceptance of a poverty-stricken environment as an inevitable condition from which you cannot get away, keeps you in the poverty current and draws more poverty to you. It is the operation of the same law which attracts good things, a better environment, to those who think abundance, prosperity, who are convinced that they are going to be well off, and work confidently, hopefully, toward that end.

Not the things we long for most, not the things we wish for, but that which we *have*, which we own, by virtue of their living in our thoughts and minds, dominating our mentality and attitude—that is what the law of attraction brings to us. It may be that this law has brought us the very things we hated and wanted to get rid of, but because we have dwelt upon them, and, because they have formed the basis of our mental model, the life processes built them into our lives.

What you have, what you are surrounded with, is a reproduction of your thought, your faith, your belief in your efforts. Our thoughts, our faith, our beliefs, our efforts, all materialize, and are objectified about us. Our words become flesh and live with us; our thoughts, our emotions, become flesh and live with us; they become our environment and surround us.

I don't mean that if you were born into poverty that somehow *you* created that, I mean that if you *remain* in poverty, that that's a result of your mental attitude.

Until recently many of us did not understand what Job meant when he said, "The thing which I greatly feared has come upon me." Now we know that he expressed a psychological law that is as inexorable as the laws of mathematics. We know that the things we fear most, the things we have a horror of and want to flee from, we are really drawing to us, pursuing by our very fear of them. We are attracting them to ourselves by our beliefs, and when we do this we are turning our backs upon the very things which we long for most.

The time will come when the law of attraction will be known as the greatest power in creation. It is the law upon which all of our characters, all of our lives are built—be they successes or failures. Mental attraction is the only power upon which we build anything successfully. It is an inevitable law, an inexorable principle.

It is our task to make sure that what we are building is what is the best for us.

The saying "Money attracts money" is only another way of stating the law. The prosperous classes think prosperity, believe in it, work for it, never for a moment doubt their right to have all the money and all the good things they need. And, of course they get them. They are living up to the very letter and spirit of the law of attraction.

Many people wonder that bad people, wicked people, vicious people are successful in business, at money making, in amassing a fortune, while the good person, the upright person, often doesn't seem to be able to make any headway. Good things do not seem to come to them. If they make an investment they almost always lose; they buy in the wrong market, or sell in the wrong market. They don't seem to have the knack of making money.

The truth is that a person's morals do not have anything specially to do with his or her money-making faculties, except that honesty is always and everywhere the best business policy. But money-making is ultimately a matter of obeying the law of accumulation, the law that *like attracts like.* A very bad person may obey the law of accumulation, the law of attraction, and accumulate a vast fortune. Like all other laws, the law of attraction is amoral—it is neither moral nor immoral.

Multitudes of people are attracting the wrong things because they do not know the law. They have never learned that the great secret of health, happiness, and success lies in holding the mental attitude which builds, which constructs—the mental attitude which draws to us the good things we desire. They have never learned the difference between building and tearing down thoughts; the difference between success and failure thoughts. In fact, they do not know that whatever comes to us in life, in our undertakings, great or small, is largely a question of the kind of thoughts we hold in the mind. We can attract the thing we desire, and we can attract the thing we hate and despise and long to get rid of. It is simply a matter of holding an image of a thing in the mind. That image will then be the model which the life processes will build into our environment and which we will objectify.

What we most frequently visualize, what we think most about, is constantly weaving itself into the fabric of our lives, becoming a part of ourselves, increasing the power of our mental magnet to attract those things to us. It doesn't matter whether they are things we fear and try to avoid or things that are good for us, that we long to get. Keeping them in mind increases our affinity for them and inevitably tends to bring them into our lives.

Hatred attracts more hatred, envy more envy, jealousy more jealousy, and malice more malice. Everything has power to attract its kind. What we sow we reap, just as the soil will return to us exactly what we put into it. Nothing has the power to reproduce anything but itself. There is no exception to this law.

To think about and worry about the things we do not want, or to fear that they will come to us, is but to invite them; because *every impression becomes an expression*—or tends to become so—unless the impression is neutralized by its opposite. If we think too much about our losses, too much about our possible failure, our thoughts will tend to bring to us the very thing we are trying to get away from.

On every hand we see this law of like attracting like exemplified in the lives of the poverty-stricken, who, through ignorance of the law, keep themselves in their unfortunate condition by saturating their minds with the poverty idea; thinking and acting and talking poverty; living in the belief in its permanency; fearing, dreading, and worrying about it. They do not realize, no one has ever told them, that as long as people mentally see the hunger wolf at the door and the poorhouse ahead of them; as long as they expect nothing but lack and poverty and hard conditions, they are headed toward these things; they are making it impossible for prosperity to come in their direction.

The way to attract prosperity and drive poverty out of the life is to work in harmony with the law instead of against it. To expect prosperity, to believe with all your heart that you are going to become prosperous, *that you are already so*—no matter how present conditions may seem to contradict such a belief—is the very first condition of the law of attaining what you desire. You cannot get it by doubting or fearing. Whatever we visualize and work for we will get.

It is a curious fact that many people seem to think that one must spend years as an apprentice to become an expert in any line of endeavor, but that in regard to prosperity it is largely a matter of chance, of fate, something which cannot be affected very much by anything they may be able to do.

They say, "Well, I was not built that way. I am not a natural money-maker, and never can be." Or they excuse themselves on the ground that their parents and those before them were never money-makers, and never did anything more than make a bare living.

In my youth, one of the hardest things in the Bible for me to understand was the statement, "For whosoever hath, to him shall be given, and he shall have more abundance. . . ." (Mat. 13:12) I couldn't reconcile this with the rest of the Bible teaching. It seemed positively unjust. But now I know that it illustrates a law. "For whosoever hath, to him shall be given" is true because by virtue of having, one has made one's mind a magnet to attract even more. On the other hand, as the biblical passage goes on to tell us, "but whosoever hath not, from him shall be taken away even that he hath"—because such a person is headed in the wrong direction mentally. He or she does not have because he or she is closing the avenues of supply by doubt and fear thoughts. Such people are in no mental condition to get more, to attract more, but only to lose more.

There is nothing at all peculiar about attaining prosperity. Its realization is purely a matter of concentration and of preparation; a matter of focusing all our powers upon the prosperity law in order to attract prosperity and to make ourselves expert in attaining it.

As in the attainment of any goal, however, the first principle is mental. Wealth is created mentally first; it is thought out before it becomes a reality.

There is only one way to get away from poverty, and that is to turn your back upon it. Begin right away by putting the poverty thought, the poverty fear, out of your mind. Assume as far as possible a prosperous appearance; think the way you want to go; expect to get what you are after, the thing you long for, and you will get it.

It is just as easy to attract what you want as to attract what you don't want. It is just a question of holding the right thought and making the right effort.

It is just as easy to attract what you want as to attract what you don't want. It is just a question of holding the right thought, and making the right effort. If you want to attract success, keep your mind saturated with the success idea.

Remember, too, that our conviction is much stronger than our willpower. No willpower can help you to do a thing when you are convinced that you can't. For instance, if you are convinced that a fatal disease which you believe you inherited is overcoming you, this thought is infinitely stronger than your will to prevent it.

Develop, then, an attitude of mind that will attract success. Think success and prosperity. Act prosperity. Live prosperity. Talk prosperity. Don't think that by holding the constructive, creative thought now and then, or just when you happen to feel like it, that it is going to counteract the influence of holding the destructive thought most of the time. Many who work for prosperity and opulence hold the want thought, the lack though, also, and that is the reason their prayer is not answered—the expectation of lack still predominates in their minds.

When you once get this law of attraction thoroughly fixed in your mind, you will be careful thereafter about attracting its enemies, contacting them through your mind—thinking about them, worrying about them, fearing and dreading them. You will hold the sort of thoughts that will attract the things you long for and are seeking, not the things you dread, and despise, and are trying to avoid.

It was intended that we should have an abundance of the good things of the universe. None of them are withheld from us except by our poverty-stricken mental attitude. There is no more a lack of all that the heart can wish for than there is lack of supply for the fish in the great ocean. The fish swims in the ocean of supply, as we swim in the great cosmic ocean of supply that is all around us. All we have to do is to open our minds, our faith, our confidence, and direct our intelligent effort to this reality.

Then, when the prosperity, abundance thought is fully in your bearing, you will begin attracting it.

Eight

ESTABLISHING THE CREATIVE CONSCIOUSNESS

The great trouble with those of us who are living in a world of unfulfilled desires and ambitions is that we do not hold the right consciousness. Dr. Perry Green rightly says that Job's lament—"For the thing which I greatly feared is come upon me" (Job 3:25)—should be changed to *"The thing which I was greatly conscious of is come upon me."* In other words, it is the thing we hold in our consciousness that comes out of the invisible world of realities and takes visible form in our lives according to its nature—poverty or prosperity; health or disease; happiness or misery.

The whole secret of individual growth and development is locked up in our consciousness, for this is the door of life itself. Every experience, whether of joy or sorrow, of health or disease, of success or failure, must come through our consciousness. There is no other way by which it can enter and become a part of the life. You cannot live in accordance with what you are not conscious of; you cannot do what you are not conscious of being able to do. In short, it is an immutable law that whatever you hold in mind, believe that you can do or get, is the thing that will manifest itself in your life. The thing that Job held in his consciousness was the thing that came upon him. Joan of Arc saved her country, because from childhood she held the consciousness that she had been born to do that very thing. This poor unlettered peasant girl knew nothing about the great law of mental attraction, but unconsciously she worked with it. But for her consciousness of victory she never could have accomplished her stupendous work.

It is the victorious consciousness that achieves victory in every age and in every field. After many years study of the lives and methods of successful men and women in every department of life, I have found that those who win out in a large way are great believers in themselves, in their power to succeed in the things they undertake. Great artists, scientists, inventors, explorers, generals, business men, and others, who have done the biggest things in their specialty, have always held the victorious consciousness. Success was the goal they constantly visualized, and they never wavered in their conviction that they would reach it.

We fail less because of lack of ability than because we do not hold the victorious, the success consciousness. We do not live in the expectancy of winning, in the belief that we will succeed in reaching the goal of our ambitions. We live rather in the expectation of "just getting by," of "just having enough."

Our consciousness is a part of our creative force; that is, it puts the mentality in a position to attract its affinity, that which is like itself. A penury consciousness cannot demonstrate a fortune; a failure consciousness cannot demonstrate success. It would be against the law. If you are steeped in poverty and failure, you have no one to blame but yourself for your circumstances, for you are working against the law. You are holding the poverty consciousness, living in the thought of failure. Perhaps you are wondering why you can't create something that will match your ambition, your longings. You feel, perhaps, that something, some invisible force, some cruel fate or destiny is holding you back. Something *is* holding you back, but it is not fate or destiny; it is your discouraged mental attitude, the unfortunate consciousness that you have been holding for years. While you were trying to build on the material plane, you were neutralizing all your efforts by constantly tearing down on the mental plane.

All of life and its achievements, its possibilities, depend upon our consciousness, and we can develop any sort of consciousness we wish. The great musician has developed a musical consciousness of which most of us are ignorant, because we are not conscious of this mode of activity. Our musical consciousness has not been developed. The mathematician, the astronomer, the writer, the physician, the artist, the specialist in whatsoever line, has developed a particular consciousness and realizes the fruits of that consciousness. Each manifests and enjoys a special power just in proportion as he or she has developed his or her specialty consciousness.

What sort of consciousness do you want to develop? What do you want to get, to do, to become? Make yourself very positive on this point, for the first step toward the development of a new consciousness is to get a thorough grip upon your purpose, your desire, your aim; to get a picture of it firmly fixed in your mind to make it dominant in your thoughts, in your acts, in your life. This is how the successful lawyer at the start develops a law consciousness; the successful physician, a medical consciousness; the successful business man, a business consciousness. It is of the utmost importance to get started right, because whatever the consciousness you develop, your mind will attract that which has an affinity for it, will draw to you the material for your building.

The next thing is to establish the conviction that you can achieve whatever you desire. This is a tremendous step in the way of accomplishment, for as I have written in a previous chapter, conviction is stronger than will power. You may will ever so hard to do a thing, but if you are convinced that you can't do it, the conviction of your inability will prevail over your will power. Your conviction is your strongest lever of accomplishment. This is what has enabled so many poor boys and girls to climb to high place and power in spite of all sorts of obstacles, and often contrary to the opinion and advice of those who knew them best. They were so thoroughly conscious of their ability to do the thing they wanted to do, and so convinced that they could do it, that nothing could hold them back from their own.

The beginning of every achievement must be in your consciousness. That is the starting point of your creative plan. In proportion to the intensity, the persistence, the vividness, the definiteness of your consciousness of the thing you want, you begin to create.

Consciousness of power reveals power; the consciousness of supremacy is equivalent to supremacy itself; the consciousness of self-confidence is what gives us the assurance that we are equal to the thing we undertake. What we are conscious of, we already possess. But we cannot come into possession of anything we are not conscious of. That is, it cannot be ours until we become conscious of it. If you are not conscious of the ability to succeed, you can't succeed. If you are not conscious of your own superiority, you cannot become superior. But if you hold in your consciousness the picture of masterfulness; if you hold in mind the thought of superiority, you are putting in operation a law of mastership, a law of superiority, and you begin to manifest these things in your life. We have unlimited power, boundless resources, in the great within of us, but until we awaken to a consciousness of this hidden power, those invisible resources, we cannot use them.

Some time ago a friend of mine saw a small, delicate woman leap over a six-bar gate when frightened by the sudden approach of a cow which she mistook for a bull. He said that this woman told him she could no more have done this under ordinary conditions than she could have lifted a corner of her house from its foundations. But she thought her life was in peril. Seeing the cow running toward her, and imagining that it was an angry bull, she had no time to allow her doubts and fears as to whether she could leap over the gate to control her. It was the only means of escape in sight, and she cleared the gate without difficulty. But when the imagined danger was past, she lost the consciousness of this strength within her and relapsed into her ordinary condition of weakness.

There are numerous instances on record where invalids and cripples, people who had been paralyzed for years, who did not feel that they could do anything whatever, have risen up from their beds when a fire or some terrible accident endangered their own lives or the lives of those dear to them, and then and there performed marvelous feats: carrying heavy furniture out of a burning house, rescuing children, and doing other things that would have seemed miraculous even for strong men. Again and again unusual emergencies give us a fleeting consciousness of our vast reserve powers and we perform prodigies that amaze ourselves, but we don't continue to make the demand on ourselves, and the consciousness that it is possible for us to do anything out of the ordinary slips from us and our measureless resources remain untouched.

There is no limitation of anything we need except in our own consciousness. That is the door, which, according to its character, shuts us off from, or admits us to, the great storehouse of infinite supply. The closed or partially opened door never lets us get in touch with this supply. It is only the fully opened door that allows us the resources to meet whatever demands life may make upon us.

It is those who spend their last dollar fearlessly, because they know the law of supply and are in touch with the flow of abundance who that get on and up in the world. Those who hoard their last dollar in fear in fear and trembling, afraid to let go of it even though they must go hungry, who always carry in their minds a vivid picture of the wolf at the door, never conquer poverty, because they never get the prosperity consciousness.

A wonderful uplift and courage comes to those who trust and look up, no matter how dark the outlook. Faith in the Power that orders all things well tells them that there is a silver lining to the dark cloud which temporarily shuts out the light, and they go serenely on—feeling confident that their plans will succeed, that their demands will be met. Theirs is the consciousness that assures them, no matter what happens.

If you keep this one thing in mind, that we are always creating, always manifesting in our lives the conditions we hold in our consciousness, you will not make the mistake millions are making today: manifesting the things they don't want instead of the things they want. When you realize that your enjoyment, your happiness, your satisfaction, your achievement, your power, your personality, all depend on the nature of your consciousness—the aim and direction in which it is unfolding—you will not be building up a consciousness of the very opposite of all that you are struggling to attain. On the contrary, you will hold constantly in mind the consciousness of your ambition, whatever it is, the consciousness of your heart's longings, your soul's desires. You will hold the opulent consciousness, and then you shall *really* begin to live.

Emerson says: "Every soul is not only the inlet but may become the outlet of all that is in God." When we hold to this truth consciousness, then life will mean something more to all of us than it now does to most of us—a mere struggle for existence.

Nine

WHERE PROSPERITY BEGINS

During his lecture tour in the United States, the great scientist, Sir Oliver Lodge, speaking on "The Reality of the Unseen," said: "Our senses are no criterion of existence. They were evolved for earthly reasons, not for purposes of philosophy, and if we refuse to go beyond the direct evidence of our senses, we shall narrow our outlook and the universe to a hopeless and almost imbecile extent."

It is the most difficult thing in the world to convince people of the reality of anything they cannot perceive through the senses. Yet the realest things we know anything about are invisible; have never been seen by mortal eyes.

And right here lies the great difficulty for most people in changing undesirable conditions; in getting away from poverty and the things that are holding them back. They can't see beyond the material things about them into the unseen world, packed with all creative energies, where the mind starts the creative processes. They do not realize that everything in the visible world that human beings have produced began as a mental vision; that the power of mind picturing, of visualizing the things we want to come into our lives, enables us to bring into visibility out of the invisible world whatever we will.

If you know how to use this marvelous power, you can begin now to visualize your future; to see yourself as you would like to be; to see yourself mentally, doing the things you would like to do; occupying the position you aspire to; and thus you will draw to yourself the means necessary to build, step by step, in the material world the future as you see it in your vision. By its aid we can bring ourselves out of a discordant environment into harmonious conditions, with the refinements and, if we will, the luxuries of life; or we may pervert it, and hold ourselves in degrading lack and poverty, limited, held back from self-development, the unfoldment of our possibilities, and all the joys of living.

The forces operating in the universe which transport us over the globe and bring its uttermost parts into instant communion—the power of the principles of chemistry, of gravitation, of electricity—we cannot see, hear, or touch. We can appreciate them only as we feel their effects. They are things we know little about, yet we know they are great realities.

Gravitation, which holds the heavenly bodies in their orbits—none of them varying in their revolutions in their orbits the fraction of a second in a thousand years—which keeps the world so marvelously balanced in space, revolving at terrific speed around the sun, is an invisible force. Because we can't see or taste, or smell, or handle it, shall we say it is not a reality? That it does not exist?

We can see and feel the effects of electricity, but who knows what this invisible force is? Electricity carries our messages under oceans and across continents. It has already done away with a large part of the drudgery of the world, and is destined to serve mankind in ways perhaps not yet dreamed of by even the wisest scientists and inventors. This mighty force which Edison used in thousands of his inventions, he confessed that he knew nothing about. He stood in awe of this mysterious power which came out of the cosmic intelligence in response to his efforts. He regards himself merely as a channel through which some of its secrets were passed along to humanity—to make life less toilsome, more comfortable, and more beautiful.

It is nonsense for skeptics and materialists to say that they take no stock in anything that they cannot test with their senses, when we know that the real power in the universe—indeed, the elements in the food we eat that nourish and keep us alive—are all invisible.

Who can see or explain the mystery of the unfolding bud, the expanding flower, the generating of the wonderful fragrance and marvelous beauty of the rose? Yet we know that there is reality back of them, which shapes them, brings them to their glorious maturity.

We think we live in a visible world, but in reality we live in a world controlled and guided by invisible forces. The corporal part of us is fed, warmed and clothed by material things, but we live, move, and have our being in the unseen.

If we could only realize and measure our lives and their infinite possibilities from the standpoint of the invisible power within us, instead of from the bounded, limited, visible world of our material circumstances; if we could realize the tremendous significance of the reality of the unseen within us; if we could only hold the thought that we are a part of the creative intelligence of the universe, in possession of an illimitable power implanted in every one of us, how much more we could accomplish, how much higher we could climb, how much happier we should be!

When Christ emphasized the fact that the kingdom of heaven is within us, he meant that this kingdom within is identical with the Divine Mind, that the kingdom within is the kingdom of power, where all our creative work is started. It is there we connect with the universal substance, the great creative energy.

Your prosperity, your health, your happiness, your success, the fruition of your ambitions, all are in the great formless creative energy within you, ready to come into form when your thought does its part in starting the creative processes. Limitless wealth, inexhaustible supply to meet your needs, inventions, great productions of art and literature, music and drama, marvels in every field of human endeavor, are in the great intelligence waiting within you, the contact of your thought in order to come into visible form on our earth.

All the great powers in the cosmos are constantly awaiting the thoughts and desires of each of us. There is no favoritism in the unseen realities. Just as the sun and the rain avail their potencies to the wise and the unwise farmer alike, so to we all—the thief, the criminal, the murderer, the failure, the just, the noble, the inventors, the great men and women in every field who are uplifting the race and making the world a better place to live in—have the same materials to work with.

In other words, there is an invisible power in each of our hands, and we, according to our thoughts, mold our lives, destinies, and fortunes. We cannot think without creating, for every thought is a seed planted in the invisible, universal substance, and it will produce something like itself. We can sow in the invisible substance constructive thoughts, beautiful thoughts, thoughts of love, of goodwill, of health, of prosperity, of happiness, of success in our chosen work, or we can sow destructive thoughts, ugly thoughts, thoughts of hatred and ill-will, of disease, of discord, of failure, of poverty, of all sorts of misery.

If there is the specter of the wolf at our door, it is because we have made it real, we have manifest it in our lives by allowing it to first exist in our minds—by visualizing it, thinking on it, fearing it, it has become real for us.

One thing, then, is certain: Whatever we sow in the invisible world, we shall reap in the visible. That is the law, and there is no escaping from it.

The invisible world about us is packed with infinite possibilities, awaiting our thought seed, our desire seed, our ambition seed, our aspiration seed, our prosperity and success seed—backed by our effort on the material plane—which will be made manifest in our lives in the form upon which we concentrate on them, nourish them.

No matter what your present circumstances and environment, therefore, if you hold fast to a firm belief in the reality of the unseen, where your supply is, and work in harmony with the law, you can, through the creative power of thought, acting on the invisible universal substance, fashion and draw out of the unseen, the realization of all your hopes and visions.

Ten

MAKING YOURSELF A PROSPERITY MAGNET

*E*very human being is a magnet, the attractive power of which may be developed in any desired direction. Each one can so direct this power that he can draw to himself whatever he wills; Before your life can be really effective you must make yourself a magnet for the things that will make it so. You must learn how to attract, how to draw to yourself all that will help you to succeed in your work, that will enable you to attain your ambitions.

If poverty is holding you down, you can conquer it by making yourself a prosperity magnet. We are living in the midst of a stream of inexhaustible supply. It is one's own fault if he does not take from this stream whatever he needs.

What we get in life we get by the law of attraction. Like attracts like. Whatever you may have managed to get together in this world you have attracted by your mentality. You may say that you have earned these things, that you have bought them with your salary, the fruit of your endeavor. True, but your thought preceded your endeavor. Your mental plan went before your achievement.

The mere changing of your mental attitude will very soon begin to change conditions. Your decision to face toward prosperity hereafter, to cultivate it, to make yourself a prosperity magnet will tend to draw to you the things that will satisfy your ambition.

The text "He that hath a bountiful eye shall be blessed" (Prov. 22:9) is the expression of a fundamental truth. The pictures you make in your mind's eye, the thoughts you harbor are day by day building your outward conditions They are real forces working ceaselessly in the unseen, and the more you think and visualize favorable conditions the more you increase your power to realize them. You make yourself a magnet for the thing you desire. This is a psychological law.

If you want to become a prosperity magnet you must not only think prosperity but you must also turn your back resolutely on poverty. Begin today. Don't wait for tomorrow or next day. If you don't look, prosperous assume a prosperous appearance. Dress as far as possible like a prosperous man or woman, walk like one, act like one, think in terms of prosperity. A mental healer could not cure a cancer by holding in mind a picture of the hideous disease, with all its horrible appearances and symptoms. The healer must eliminate all this from his or her mind. He or she must see his patient whole, clean, healthy—free from all disease.

The same thing is true if you want to be prosperous: you must hold the prosperous thought, the prosperous picture in your mind. You must refuse to see or recognize poverty. You must not acknowledge it in your manner. You must erase all marks of it, not only from your mental attitude, but just as far as possible from your appearance. Even if you are not able to wear fine clothes at first, or to live in a fine house, you can radiate the hope and expectancy of the glorious inheritance which is your birthright, and everything about you will reflect this light.

Prosperity begins in the mind. You must lay its foundations in your thoughts, surround yourself with a prosperity atmosphere. In other words, you will build into your environment, into your life, whatever dwells in your mind.

We hear of some people that "they are always lucky"; "everything seems to cone their way." Things come their way because there are invisible thoughts forces radiating from their minds toward the goal they have set for themselves. Things fall in line and come our way just in proportion to the force and velocity of the thought forces we project.

Thinking better things might be called the first aid for those who want to be prosperous. To picture yourself as prosperous, living in a comfortable home, wearing good clothes, surrounded with the refinements of life, in a position to do your best work in the service of mankind, this is to put yourself into the current that runs success-ward.

It is a strange thing that most of us believe the Creator will help us in everything but our financial troubles. We seem to think that it is in some way almost sacrilegious to call upon Him for money to meet our needs. We may ask for comfort, for solace in our afflictions, for the assuaging of our griefs and the healing of our diseases, but to implore God to help us to pay the rent, to pay off the mortgage on the home or the farm, does not seem quite right.

Yet we know perfectly well that every mouthful of food we eat, the material for the clothing we wear and for the houses we live in every breath we breathe must come from this Divine Source, of infinite supply. If the sun were to be blotted out, or to cease to send its magic rays to the earth, in a few days there would not be a single living thing on the globe. Not a human being, not an animal could exist without it. Not a tree, not a plant, not a flower, no fruits, no vegetables, no grass, nothing green, no vegetable life, would be possible. Without the sun's energizing power all, life would cease on this planet. It would be as cold, barren and lifeless as on the moon. In a like manner, everything we have comes from the creator, and without the supply which flows from His abundance we could not live a single instant. Why should we not, then, look to this great Source for our money supply?

The truth is we were all intended to live the life abundant. Never for a moment harbor the thought that anything can come to you but prosperity, for this is your birthright; and because it is, you should demand it.

Turn your back on poverty. Make up your mind that you will never again have anything to do with it, that you will not encourage it by dwelling on and visualizing poverty suggestions. Face toward prosperity. Think of and plan for prosperous conditions; struggle toward prosperity with all your might and you will draw it to you.

Suppose you are poor and live in a humble home, just have a talk with your spouse and children, and make up your minds that you will all focus on your objective—improved conditions—that you will face the other way, toward prosperity instead of poverty. Tidy up your little home and make it as neat and cheerful as possible. Do the same with your dress and general appearance. Keep yourself better groomed; look up brace up, brush up, struggle up. Surround yourself with an atmosphere of hopefulness and show everybody by the new light in your eyes the light of hope and expectancy of better things, that there is a change in you. Your neighbors will notice it. They will see a change in your home and your family. The change in the mental attitude of yourself and family, through facing toward the light instead of darkness, toward hope instead of despair, will make a tremendous change in your whole outlook on life.

In this way you are making yourself a prosperity magnet, you are radiating thought waves of hope, of ambition, of determination. Your new mental attitude is expressed in an erect carriage, in squared, thrown back shoulders, in a neat, clean appearance—even though the clothing be old and threadbare—in a winning, forceful, magnetic countenance. You are thus establishing the conditions of success. The positive prosperity thought flows out like a wireless current and connects itself with similar thought currents. Hold the prosperity conviction, work steadily toward your object; see opportunity and success in your vista, determine to be somebody, hold firmly to the resolve, and your mentality will direct the invisible magnet of your personality to lift you higher and higher, to attract toward you others who will help you in the direction in which you are moving.

If you want a better position, more salary, money to pay off debts, or to get what you need, whatever it may be, cling with all the power of your mind to the thing you are trying to get, and never for a moment doubt you will get it.

As long as you keep yourself saturated with the poverty conviction you cannot rise out of poverty. You must think yourself out of it.

Abundance will never flow through pinched, doubting, poverty thoughts, any more than clear, crystal water can flow freely through foul, grease-clogged pipes. A right view-point must be your mental plumber to keep the connection open and free. Things of a kind attract one another. The poverty thought attracts more poverty, the fear thought more fear, the worry thought more worry, the anxiety thought more anxiety. On the other hand, the faith thought, trust thought, and the confidence thought attract things like themselves.

Poverty is a mental disease, and you carry the antidote to its poison in your mind. The prosperity thought is the natural antidote for the poverty germ. It kills it. The poverty thought cannot exist in the mind at the same moment with the prosperity thought. One will drive out the other. It rests with you which one you will harbor and encourage.

The trouble with us is that we have been in the habit of looking for a material supply when our first supply must be mental. We keep the supply avenues open or we close them with our thoughts, our convictions. We materialize poverty by our doubting thoughts, by our fears of it. We are just beginning to find that we get out of this world what we think into it and work out of it, that our thought plan precedes its material realization just as the architect's plan precedes the building.

Remember that prosperity cannot flow into your life while your mind is filled with poverty thoughts and convictions. We go in the direction of our thought and our convictions. By no law can you expect to get that which you do not believe you will get. Prosperity can not come to you if, you are all the time driving it away from you by your poverty thought.

You must think in a positive determined way that you are going to succeed in whatever you desire to do or to be before you can expect success. That is the first condition by which you make yourself a magnet for the thing you are after. It doesn't matter whether it is work or money, a better position or health, or whatever else it is, your thoughts about it must be positive, clean cut, decisive, persistent. No weak, wobbly, "*Perhaps* I may get it," or "*Maybe* it will come, *sometime*," or "I *wonder* if *I* shall *get* this," or "if *I* can *do* that" sort of thought will ever help you to get anything in this world.

When young John Wanamaker started with a pushcart to deliver his first sale of clothing, he turned on a positive current toward a merchant princeship. As he passed big clothing stores he pictured himself as a great merchant, owner of a much bigger establishment than any of those he saw, and he did not neutralize or weaken this thought current by all sorts of doubts or fears as to the possibility of reaching the goal of his ambition.

Most people think too much about blindly forcing themselves ahead. They do not realize that they can, by the power of thought, make themselves magnets to draw to them the things that will help them to get on. Wanamaker attracted to himself the forces that make a merchant prince. Every step he took was forward, to match the vision of his advance with its reality.

Marshall Field projected himself mentally out of a little country store into a clerkship in Chicago. Then he thought and worked himself out of this clerkship into a partnership.

Still thinking and climbing upward, he next visualized himself at the head of the greatest merchandizing establishment in America, if not in the world. His mind always ran ahead. He was always picturing himself a little higher up, a little further on, always visualizing a larger business, and so making himself a magnet for the things he sought.

If John Wanamaker had been satisfied with himself at the start he would have remained in his first little store in Philadelphia, and thus cut off all possibility of becoming what he is—one of the greatest merchants the world has ever seen. If Marshall Field had stopped thinking himself higher up when the man he worked for in the little Pittsfield store predicted that he never would succeed as a merchant, he never would have been heard from But that man did not stop Marshall Field from thinking himself ahead. "On to Chicago, the City of Opportunity," he said to himself, and on and up he went until the little country merchant who predicted his failure was a Lilliputian by comparison.

The story of each of these men is, so far as the success principle is concerned, the story of every person who has ever succeeded in his undertakings. They may not have been conscious of the law underlying their methods, but they worked in unison with it, and hence succeeded.

The same thing is true of Andrew Carnegie, and of all the millionaires and self-made men and women among us who have raised themselves from poor boys to the ownership of colossal fortunes, or to commanding positions in some phase of the world's activities.

Any one who makes the accumulation of a fortune his or her chief goal, and who has grit, determination, willpower and sufficient faith in himself or herself to stick to his or her purpose, will get there. But sadly, long before many who have chosen such a goal have reached it, they will have dwarfed their ambitions and shriveled their souls.

To get away from poverty is one thing; to set one's heart on money as the ultimate good is another—and quite different—thing. There is a whole world of difference between so saturating one's mind with the thought of money and its acquisition that there is no room for any other aspiration, and the constant dwelling on the hopeless poverty thought, the incessant picturing yourself as a pauper until you are so convinced of poverty's hold on you that you destroy the very ability which should help you to get away from it.

People who are down and out financially are down and out mentally. They are suffering from a mental disease of discouragement and loss of hope. There ought to be institutions conducted by government experts for the treatment of these poverty sufferers, for they are just as much in need of it as are those in our hospitals. They need advice from mental experts. They have lost their way on the life path, and need to be shown the way back. They need to be turned about mentally, so that they will face the light instead of the darkness. They should be shown that they are stopping up their prosperity pipes, cutting off their source of supply by their pinching, poverty-stricken, limiting thought. Their whole mental attitude points toward failure, toward poverty, and by a natural law their outward conditions conform with the pictures they hold in mind.

What a revelation would come into your life if you will only eliminate from your mind for a single year the poverty thought; if you would erase from your mind poverty pictures and all the suggestions of grinding want that sadden and discourage; if, instead of expecting poverty, and all that the idea implies, you would go through one year expecting just the opposite—prosperity—visualizing, talking prosperity, thinking prosperity, acting as though you expected to be, as though you *were,* prosperous! Just this radical change of thought, this transposition of mental attitude; the persistent holding of the prosperous viewpoint for a year would not only change your whole outlook on life, but would revolutionize your material conditions.

Your ambition would grow; your new way of looking at life would give an upward tendency to your surroundings. Everything would take on a different appearance. There would-be a new light in your face; expectancy of better things would give a glow of cheerfulness to your countenance. There would be a light in your eyes which never was there before. Working in the spirit of hope and expectancy of better things instead of that of discouragement and the fears of even greater poverty, you would forge ahead in a way that would astonish yourself.

There is much talk about our not yet having come close to tapping the world's natural resources. But of even greater consequence is that we have not yet tapped even a fraction of possibilities of any part of the world's *human* resources. Every inhabitant of the earth today is treading on secrets which would emancipate humanity from drudgery and allow it to live happily, instead of merely to mostly eke out a wretched subsistence as he it has done up to the present. Hitherto, in the great majority of cases, we have barely been existing on the husks of things.

Now we are beginning to taste the kernel, because we are coming into a knowledge of the powers locked up within ourselves. Here and there, people are mastering the law of opulence. They are demonstrating that they can make themselves prosperity magnets, by thinking and working in conformity with the law of opulence, of abundance.

If every one of you reading these words who is suffering from the limitations and humiliations imposed by a grinding poverty would proceed to establish the prosperity habit along the lines suggested; if you would, by continually holding the prosperous thought, convince your subconscious self that you were made to be successful, that prosperity belongs to you; that it was never intended that you should live in poverty-stricken conditions, then you will have struck the very basic principle of prosperity.

Hold this victorious attitude toward life, and you will overcome all unfavorable conditions.

Eleven

HOW TO MAKE YOUR DREAMS COME TRUE

When Gordon H. Selfridge, former manager of the Marshall Field Company, went to London and there established a great department store of the Marshall Field type, he only took the final step in the realization of a dream which he had nursed for years. Long before he stepped foot on the shores of England, he had had the department store all worked out in his mind. He had built it mentally before he crossed the Atlantic, and already in his mind's eye, saw it a marvelous success. "I pictured the great crowds of customers headed toward my new store," he said, "and could see it full of eager buyers long before I went to England."

From the time that the idea of a department store in London took form in his mind, Mr. Selfridge kept visualizing the completed structure. He kept his dream alive and vivid by the determination to make it come true. He would not allow it to be shattered, or let his idea be driven out by doubts, fears, and uncertainties, or by the well-meant advice of his friends: to keep out of England because the English people were so slow to new ideas that he would fail if he went there. He didn't heed what they said, for he didn't believe that the English people were so unprogressive as they thought. He believed that they would respond to the American idea, the Marshall Field idea, and that the methods which had proved so successful in the United States would also be successful in England.

The amazing popularity of the Selfridge Department Store, which has long been one of the sights of London, is but another proof that the dreamer who dreams dreams and sees visions is always wiser than, and always ahead of, the so-called practical, wise ones who discourage them and try to turn them aside from their vision. The men and women who, in all ages, have done great things in the world have always been dreamers, and always pictured their dreams as realities; visualized themselves accomplishing the things they were ambitious to do long before they were able to work them out in the actual and make them realities.

Great discoverers, scientists, explorers, philanthropists, inventors, philosophers, who have pushed the world forward and done immeasurable service for humanity—such as Columbus, Stephenson, Charles Goodyear, Elias Howe, Robert Fulton, Cyrus W. Field, Edison, Bell—have visualized their dreams, nursed their visions through long years, many of them in the midst of poverty, persecution, ridicule, opposition, and contumely of all sorts, until they brought their dreams to earth and made them realities.

In making a study of the methods of successful men and women I have found that they are almost invariably strong and vivid visualizers of the things they are trying to accomplish. They are intense workers as well as dreamers, and nurse their vision tenaciously until they, match it with reality: They build castles in the air, but they put the solid foundation of reality under them.

When Lillian Nordica was a poor girl, singing in the little church choir in her native village in Maine. When even her own people thought it a disgrace for a girl to appear on the stage, to sing in public concerts or in opera, she was picturing herself a great prima donna singing before vast audiences in the United States, in foreign capitals, and before the crowned heads of Europe.

Young Henry Clay practiced oratory before the domestic animals in a Virginia barn and barnyard, visualizing himself swaying vast audiences by his eloquence.

When Washington was a lad of twelve he pictured himself as a leader, rich and powerful, a man of vast importance in the life of the colonies, and the ruler of a nation he would help to create.

When the young John Wanamaker was delivering clothing in a pushcart in Philadelphia, he saw himself as the proprietor of a much larger establishment than any then in that city. He saw beyond that and glimpsed the Wanamaker of later days, the great powerful merchant, with immense stores in the world's leading capitals.

Young Carnegie pictured himself a powerful figure in the steel world.

Now this sort of visualizing is not mere vanity, or petty egotism, it is the God urge in individuals men pushing them out beyond themselves, beyond what is visible to the physical eye, to better things. The Scriptures tell us that without a vision the people perish. I have never known anyone to do anything out of the common, who was never able to see beyond the visible into the vast invisible universe of the things that might be; who did not keep clearly in mind the vision of the particular thing he or she was trying to accomplish.

It is the person who can visualize what does not yet exist in the visible world about us and see it as a reality; who can see opportunities where others see no chance; who sees teeming cities, great populations on the prairies where others see only sagebrush, alkali plains, desolation; who sees power, opulence, plenty, success, where others see only failure, limitation, poverty, and wretchedness, who eventually pushes to the top and wins out.

Many people seem to think that the imagination, or visualizing faculty, is a sort of appendix to the brain, that it is not a fundamental or necessary part, and they have never taken it very seriously. But those of us who have studied mental laws know that it is one of the most important functions of the mind. We are beginning to discover that the power to visualize is a sort of advance courier, making announcement of the things that the Creator has qualified us to bring about. In other words, we are beginning to see that our visions are prophecies of our future; mental picture programs, which we are supposed to carry out, to make concrete realities.

For instance, a youth whose bent is entirely in another direction is not haunted by an architectural vision, an art vision, a mercantile vision, or a vision of some other calling for which he or she has no natural affinity. A girl does not dream of a musical career for years before she has the slightest opportunity for taking up music as a career if she has no musical talent, or if her ability in some other line is much more pronounced. Boys and girls, men and women, are not haunted by dreams to do what nature has not fitted them for. We dream a particular dream, see a particular vision, because we have the talent and the special ability to bring the dream, the vision, into reality.

Of course, I do not mean by dreams and visions the mere fantasies, the vague, undefined thoughts that flit through the mind, but our real heart longings, our soul yearnings, the mental pictures of a future which haunts our dreams, and the insistent urge which prods us until we try to match them with their reality, to bring them out into the actual. There is a divinity back of these visions. They are prophecies of our possible future; and nature is throwing up these pictures on our mental screen to give us a glimpse of the possibilities that are awaiting us.

One reason why most of us do such little, unoriginal things is because we do not sufficiently nurse our visions and longings. The plan of the building must come before the building. We climb by the ladder of our visions, our dreams. The sculptor's model must live in the sculptor's mind before it can be called out of the marble. We do not half realize the mental force we generate by persistently visualizing our ideal, by the perpetual clinging to our dreams, the vision of the thing we long to do or to be. We do not know that nursing our desires makes the mental pictures sharper, more clean cut, and that these mental processes are completing the plans of our future life building, filling in the outlines and details, and drawing to us out of the invisible energy of the universe the materials for our actual building.

There is no other one thing you will find so helpful in the attainment of your ambition as the habit of visualizing what you are trying to accomplish, visualizing it vividly, just as distinctly, just as vigorously as possible, because this makes a magnet of the mind to attract what one is after. All about us we see individuals focusing their minds with intensity and persistence on their special aims and attracting to themselves marvelous results.

There is a power which is creative and everywhere operative that is destined to lift every created thing up to the peak of its possibilities. This power is latent in you, awaiting expression, awaiting your cooperation to realize your ambition. The first step toward utilizing it is to visualize the ideal of what you want to make real, the ideal of the man or the woman you aim to be, and the things you want to do. Without this initial step the further process of creating is impossible.

Even if you are only a humble employee—an errand boy, a girl Friday, a sales clerk—visualize yourself as the person you long to be, see yourself in the exalted position you long to attain. There is nothing more potent in drawing your heart's desire to you than visualizing that desire, dreaming your dream, seeing yourself as the ideal of your vision, filling the position in which your ambition would place you.

No matter what happens, always hold fast to the thought that you can be what you long to be; that you can do the thing you want to do, and picture yourself always as succeeding in what you desire to come true in your life. No matter how urgent duties or obligations may for a time hold you back, how circumstances and conditions may contradict the possibility of your success; how people, even your own people, may blame or misunderstand you, may even call you a crank, crazy, a conceited egotist, hold fast to your faith in your dream, in yourself. Cling to your vision, nurse it, for it is the God-inspired model by which He is urging you to shape your life.

Do these things and work with all your might for the attainment of your object on the physical plane, and nothing can hinder your success.

Twelve

WHAT DISCOURAGEMENT DOES TO YOU AND HOW TO CURE IT

Someone said: "Discouragement hides God's means and methods." It does more. It hides God himself; it blots out of sight about everything that is helpful and friendly to us. It paralyzes our ability, our courage, our self-confidence; it destroys our efficiency and cuts down the effectiveness of every one of our faculties.

Every physician knows how discouragement affects the cure of a patient—delays it, and often makes it impossible. The sick person who is cheerful, hopeful of restoration to health, has ten chances to one for recovery compared with the one who is blue and despondent. Discouragement breaks the spirit: When one's spirit is broken, he or she has no heart for anything. He or she is beaten in life's battle. A broken spirit, the loss of hope and courage, causes more failures, more suicides, more insanity, than almost anything else.

Only a short time ago I read the story of a young man who had lost his job during a period of business recession. Every morning this man would start out every morning to hunt for another job, and every night he would come home disappointed. But, he was not discouraged, for he was always believing that he would ultimately get a job.

This went on for weeks, when one night he was late in returning, and his wife, watching at the window until it was too dark to see any more, drew down the shades and tried in busying herself with tasks to dispel the sudden feeling of anxiety that gripped her. When her husband came home an hour later, she noticed that some depressing influence seemed to have been working upon him; that he was not quite as hopeful as he had been. She gave him his supper, encouraged him in every possible way, and sent him to bed comforted. Next morning, he talked hopefully, and when he was ready to start for the city, assured her that he was going to do his best. But it was evident to her that he didn't feel quite as sure of himself, quite as self-confident, as he had been.

Watching at the window for his return that evening, the faithful wife was surprised to see that when her husband returned, he was not alone. A shadowy, sinister figure was at his side, talking very earnestly to him. It accompanied him to the gate and then suddenly vanished. The next evening the same sinister figure walked at his side, and the look of despair on the man's face frightened her. The third evening the wife waited and watched until long after dark, but no husband came. Numb with fear, she sat through the long night at the window, where she kept a light burning until daylight, but no husband, and no word from him, came to her.

As soon as life began to stir in the neighborhood in the morning, she went out for the paper, and the first item that caught her eye was the suicide of a man who had thrown himself into the river and was drowned. Filled with foreboding, she rushed to the morgue where the newspaper stated the body had been taken, and there her fears were verified. The body of the drowned man was that of her husband.

In his last days, discouragement was so persistently at the young man's side, telling him it was no use looking for a job, that he would never get one, that it was visualized by him as a reality, and actually became visible to the sensitive, sympathetic eyes of his wife.

Right now I know a number of people who are so depressed and demoralized by pessimistic, discouraged thinking, that they are seriously endangering their future success and the happiness of their whole lives. Because they are temporarily out of employment, discouragement has taken hold of them and filled their minds with such depressing pictures that they go about as do the insane in the beautiful grounds allotted to them. They see only the gloomy mental world their thoughts have constructed, and are unaware of the bright, cheerful, sunlit world all around them.

As Carlyle said, there are some who are "rich in the power to be miserable."

Yet, it is well known that worry and discouragement cause chemical changes in the body which actually produce chemical poisons. These poisons lower the resisting power of both body and mind and leave the sufferer a prey to all sorts of unfortunate results. There are multitudes of people today in poor health and in poor circumstances, plodding along in discontent and unhappiness, when they might be happy and doing superb things were they not the victims of discouraging conditions, conditions which are largely the result of their fear and worry. Their minds are out of joint, unhinged and unfit for the work of the day, because they are divided between looking forward to the future, anticipating all sorts of evils and misfortunes, and looking backward to the past, regretting whatever they have or have not done.

One of the saddest things in my work is the cry of unhappiness that comes to me from people who have lost their courage and ambition. They write me that they have ruined their careers, and that all they can do now is to live on in a very hopeless and unhappy way. "Oh, if I hadn't quit in a moment of discouragement!" they wail. "If I hadn't yielded to homesickness and left college!" "If I had only stuck to my trade, to my law practice, to my engineering work a little longer, until success came to me; if I had only kept on, how different things would be today! But I lost heart, got blue and discouraged and decided to try something easier. I have never been happy or satisfied with myself since I turned back, but it is too late to make a change."

But no matter what has happened, what obstacles or trials have pushed you back or for a time press you down, never lose hope or give way under disappointments and failures. It is not that you should never *feel* these things, but that you must make it your task to never allow them to turn you aside from your purpose, to defeat your ambition.

The greatest obstacles to our success are in our minds, and there are only a few who—because of problems in genetic development—cannot overcome their most destructive enemy thoughts by the application of mental chemistry—that is, by calling to their aid the antidotes for the enemy thoughts and training their minds to face the light instead of the darkness.

A discouraging, despondent thought can instantly be neutralized by a courageous, hopeful thought, just as an acid can instantly be neutralized by an alkali. The mental law is as scientific as the physical. We cannot hold two opposite thoughts in the mind at the same time, one neutralizes or drives out the other. We can always crowd out a negative, destructive fear thought, by persistently holding in mind its opposite—a positive, courageous, constructive thought.

"Whistling to keep up courage is no mere figure of speech," said William James, the great psychologist. "On the other hand, sit all day in a moping posture, sigh and reply to everything in a dismal voice and your melancholy lingers." That is, by our thoughts and acts we can draw to ourselves courage or discouragement. In other words, we can change our mental attitude as we will; and to change our thought is to change our condition.

For instance, if you are looking for a job and don't find one; if you have had reverses and don't know where your next dollar is coming from; if you feel that you are a round peg in a square hole; if you have made mistakes—if for *any reason* you are discouraged and tempted to retreat before the enemy—instead of going about with a defeated, gloomy, despondent air, turn about face at once and assume the attitude of a victor in life. Say to yourself: "I was not born to be a failure! I will now use the power within me to do the thing

I want to do; to get the position I desire; to satisfy all my needs. Failure cannot come near me. I am moving toward my success now, because I am doing something—and those steps that I am taking will lead me toward my goal."

Resolutely hold this mental attitude, and you will be surprised to find what courage it will give you, and how your difficulties will wilt before it.

All through history glorious victories have been won by individuals who had superb courage, a mighty faith in themselves and their undertaking, an unflinching determination to succeed. Innumerable instances abound where someone saved the day where his or her friends or colleagues had given up—because the friends and colleagues had seen nothing but defeat, where the person with the will to conquer saw victory.

French General Foch, who toward the end of World War I was given unified command of the British, French, and U.S. armies, said that a lost battle is a battle you think you can't win.

"*You* are beaten; this army is not beaten," has ever been the reply of great generals to the discouraged one who wanted to give up the battle as lost.

There is somebody not far from you at this moment, who could step into your place and command victory with the resources which you think so inadequate for the work you have to do. There is somebody who has no more ability than you have, who could see an unusual opportunity in the situation which you find so hopeless, so discouraging.

A great scientist said that when he encountered what seemed an unconquerable obstacle, he invariably found himself upon the brink of some important discovery.

The time above all others when it is most important for you to hold fast to your faith and courage is when the way is so dark that you cannot see ahead. If you push on toward your goal when everything seems going against you, when doubt and discouragement are doing their best to make you give up, turn back, turn coward and quitter, you will subsequently discover that it is at this time that you are closer to victory than you dreamed of.

If you never lose your conviction in your power to win out in spite of handicaps or any obstacles that may arise in your path, nothing can defeat you, because you are in conscious partnership with the Omnipotence of the universe, which always conquers.

I AM. . . .

I am the great paralyzer of ability, the murderer of aspiration and ambition, the destroyer of energy; the killer of opportunity.

I am the cause of more suffering, more human misery and loss, more tragedies and wretchedness than any other one thing.

I have cursed more human beings, arrested the development of more fine ability, strangled more genius, and stifled more talent than anything else in the world.

I have shortened vast multitudes of lives and sent more people to crime and suicide than any other cause.

I cause chemical changes in the brain which cripple efficiency and ruin careers.

I deprive human beings of more things that are good for them, things that fit their nature, and that they were intended to enjoy, than any other one agent.

I cause men and women to wear poor, shabby clothes, to look dejected and forlorn, when it is the right of every human being to look up, to be well-dressed, attractive, and happy.

I shut out the sun of hope and cause men and women to see everything in a distorted light, because I make them look on the shadow side of things.

I devitalize people and make chronic invalids of men and women who should be enjoying perfect health.

If I can get the barest suggestion of myself into the human consciousness at the right psychological moment, I can work destruction to the most ambitious, the greatest genius.

I starve and stunt minds, and keep vast multitudes of people in ignorance.

I usually attack when people are down, when they are tired, fatigued, devitalized. That is when I find an easy entrance to their minds, because then their courage is not so keen, their brains not so alert, and they have less dare in their natures.

I am the greatest human deceiver. Once I get into the mind, I can make a giant believe that he or she is a pygmy and of no account. I can cut down a person's self-respect until in his or her own estimation he or she is very ordinary.

I have a twin brother, Doubt, who is called the great traitor. He is always ready to help me to finish my little game. We work together, and when under our control it is impossible for a person to be resourceful, original, or effective.

I creep into people's minds after they have resolved to branch out in new lines, to step out from the beaten path and blaze their own way, and weaken their ardor, dampen their enthusiasm, and make them feel inefficient and helpless. I whisper in their ears, "Go slow; better be careful. Many more able than you have fallen down trying to do that very thing you are trying to do. It is not the time to start this thing; you had better wait, wait, wait."

I haven't a single redeeming thing in my nature, and yet I have more influence with the human race than have any one of the finer, nobler qualities which help to bring human beings up to the height of their possibilities.

I AM DISCOURAGEMENT.

Thirteen

HOW TO MAKE YOUR SUBCONSCIOUS MIND WORK FOR YOU

The mystery of mind is as yet but dimly understood. Very few have even a faint realization of its immense hidden powers.

The body becomes unconscious in sleep and all its voluntary activities cease. But the mind . . . What does it do when the body sleeps? We know it does not sleep, for when the body is wrapped in slumber the memory and imagination slip out of their house and go where they will. They wander in scenes of the past or they project themselves into the future. They certainly seem to be completely independent of the body during sleep.

That part of the mind which continues active when we sleep is that marvelous force in the great within of ourselves, which, understood and rightly used, can enable us to reach the heights of our possibilities.

When we can tap this source of power, we shall all be performing what hitherto have been regarded as miracles, shall accomplish things that will dwarf to insignificance achievements that now excite our wonder and admiration.

Everything, so far as results are concerned, depends upon the degree of intelligence and conscious purpose with which we use the subconscious mind, for it is forever occupied, registering on the invisible, creative substance our every thought, emotion, desire, wish, or feeling. It never sleeps, but is incessantly working on the suggestions it receives from the conscious or objective mind. Your habitual thought, your convictions, your visions, your dreams, your beliefs, are all impressed upon it, and will ultimately be expressed in your life. In other words, your subconscious mind is your servant and proceeds instantly, without quibbling, without questioning, to obey the order, to follow the suggestion, you give it—no matter whether it is a big thing or a little thing, whether it is right or wrong.

For instance, when you want to take an early train, or to get up in the middle of the night for some purpose, and you say to yourself, or hold the thought in mind before dropping to sleep, "I must wake up in time to get that train in the morning," or, "I must get up at one o'clock tonight," you are sure to awaken at almost the exact time you register, when, perhaps, you haven't been awake at that hour before in a year. You have no alarm clock; no one calls you. What is it that wakes you up at just the right time? Perhaps you never asked yourself the question, or thought about it. It was that little faithful subconscious servant who was on the watch for you while you slept.

A similar thing occurs regarding appointments. You agree to meet someone tomorrow or some day next week at a certain place and hour. You don't make any written record of it and the thing passes out of your mind. But when the time comes round you are reminded of your engagement.

From long experience, I know that something inside of me will bring to my consciousness every engagement I make, in time for me to attend it. I don't keep thinking of it all the time. Not at all. I file it away in the within of me as I would file a business letter in my office for future reference. Then I dismiss it from my thought, knowing that it will be taken care of at the proper time.

The trained person learns to commit all sorts of things to this subconscious secretary, knowing from experience that it will serve him or her faithfully, not only in comparatively small things, such as awakening one at any desired hour in the night or early morning, or constantly reminding one of engagements, but also in the big serious problems of life.

Indeed, wherever a man or a woman is accomplishing some great purpose, you will find someone who consciously or unconsciously is obeying the law, who is registering his or her tremendous intensity upon the subconscious, and is working so persistently, so confidently, along that line that his or purpose is unfailingly carried out.

Edison said that when he was right up against a great problem in his work and had no idea in the world how to solve it, he simply slept on it—and many a time he woke up in the morning to find his problem solved, worked out for him while he slept in ways which he never dreamed of. The details of various inventions were completed for him in this way.

And indeed, the interior creative forces are more active during the night than in the day time, and are especially susceptible to the suggestions they receive before we fall asleep. During sleep the conscious mind is not active, and consequently the subconscious mind operates uninterruptedly, without any of the objections or hindrances which it is constantly bringing up during the day. Therefore it is of the greatest importance that you give the subconscious the right message, the right model on which to work, during the night. Do this before you drop off to sleep and your subconscious mind will work for the attainment of your ambition, your desire, all night. Never, though, allow yourself to fall asleep in a doubting, despondent mood. Do not hinder the operation of the creative intelligence *at any time*—day or night, but especially before going to sleep—by doubt, or fear. Doubt is the great enemy which has neutralized the efforts and killed the success of multitudes of people.

When we each know how to make our subconscious work for us, there will be no poor people; no one in distress or suffering, in pain or ill health; no one unhappy, a victim of thwarted ambitions. We shall know then that all we have to do to make our dreams come true, to be prosperous and happy, is to give our invisible secretary the right instructions and follow this up with the necessary effort.

Establishing in your subconscious mind the things that you want to come true, that you are ambitious to attain; impressing upon it the ideal of the man or woman you long to be, is the first step toward achievement.

But, while the subconscious mind is all-powerful in working out the pattern or idea we give it, it, of itself, does not originate ideas, so it makes all the difference in the world what sort of material you give your subconscious mind to work on. You can make it an enemy or a friend, for it will do the thing which injures you just as quickly as the thing which blesses you. Not through malice, but because it has no discriminating power any more than the soil in which the farmer sows his seed.

If the farmer should make a mistake and sow thistle seed instead of wheat, the soil doesn't say to him, "My friend, you have made a mistake. You have been sowing thistle seed instead of wheat, so we will change the law so that you may get what you thought you were going to get." No, the soil will always give us a harvest like our sowing. If we sow thistle seed it, will be just as faithful in producing thistles as it will in producing wheat or cabbages or potatoes. We sow the seed and nature gives us a corresponding harvest; that is the law on the physical plane. It is exactly the same on the mental plane. The subconscious mind is like the soil, passive. The objective mind uses it, gives its commands or suggestions, and the subconscious carries them out according to the nature of the commands or suggestions. It is, in other words, the objective or conscious mind that sows the seed through words, motives, thoughts, or acts, and the subconscious mind then produces in us that which corresponds to what we have impressed on it.

The subconscious mind, then, has no choice but to follow the lead we give it. Hence, it is of great importance that your instructions to this invisible servant should be for your good and not for your harm; that you should saturate it not with the things you do not want, the things you hate and fear and worry about, but the things you long for and are striving to attain.

It is in your consciousness of the mighty possibilities of your subconscious mind that lies the secret of your creative, limitless opportunity for prosperity. There are powers in your subconscious mind which, if aroused and utilized, would help you do what others tell you is "impossible." Your ideal, your heart's desire, however unattainable it may seem at present, is a prophecy of what will come true in your life if you do your part.

The great trouble with most of us, even those who have studied along this line, is that our demands upon ourselves are so feeble, the call upon the great within of us is so weak and so intermittent, that it makes no vital or permanent impression upon the creative energies; it lacks the force and persistency that transmute desires into realities. Knowing that it is through our subconscious selves, the great within of us, that we make connection with all possible joy and satisfaction; that it is here the great creative processes which make our dreams come true are started, it seems strange that we don't use this great force to better advantage.

Work with the law by which the subconscious operates, instead of against it, and nothing can hinder your success. Let your subconscious mind help instead of hinder you. Give it the right thought, the right instruction, the right ideals to work on. Give it success thoughts instead of failure thoughts, bright cheerful, hopeful thoughts instead of gloomy discouraging ones. Never hold a thought that does not correspond with your ideal or ambition. No matter what conditions are, what obstacles stand in your way, persist in vividly visualizing your success, never letting a doubt or fear thought come between you and the confident belief that you will get the thing you long for and are working for with all your heart.

No more harbor a fear thought, a worry thought, a jealousy, envy or hatred thought, a selfish thought, than you would listen to the temptation to steal. These things rob you of your peace of mind, your power, force and vitality, your poise as well as your comfort.

You would not allow a thief to ramble through your home to steal. Why, should you allow your enemy thoughts to roam through your mind without a protest?

A dwarfed ideal means a dwarfed mind, a dwarfed future, a dwarfed career. Your conviction of yourself, your belief regarding yourself, your future, your ability, will all reappear in your career.

You must have faith in the thing you are trying to do or trying to get. Your hopes, confidence, expectations are powerful factors in the gaining of your prosperity. They are searchlights on the horizon, catching sight of opportunities from afar.

Live always in the consciousness that you are a success in whatever you are trying to do and the creative processes within you, faithfully working according to the model you give them, will produce whatever you desire.

Fourteen

HOW TO MAKE YOURSELF LUCKY

Nothing is so fatal to achievement of prosperity as the belief in a blind destiny, in the fallacy that an effect can be brought about without a sufficient cause. Yet how many able-bodied people are waiting around for luck to solve their problems, waiting to get a lift from that mysterious, indefinable something which helps one person and keeps another back, regardless of the efforts of each. One might as well wait for luck to solve mathematical problems as to wait for it to solve any of one's own life problems.

You are the master of your own destiny. The power to solve your problems is right inside of you. You make the fate which downs you or lifts you up. Life is not a game of chance.

There is within you that which is a great deal more than a match for anything that can try to down you. You have a power which more than matches any defect or deficiency you may think you have inherited, or any handicap in your environment.

No matter what happens to you, remember there is something in you bigger than any fate, something that can laugh at any cruel destiny—that you are your own fate, your own destiny.

"Luck is the ability to recognize an opportunity and take advantage of it," says Beatrice Fairfax, and if we accept her definition we must admit that there is such a thing as luck. But by "luck" we mean the following: It sometimes happens that in a railroad wreck or some other great catastrophe an unknown person leaps into notoriety by some simple act which thousands of others could have performed as well. This person's ability to seize the opportunity and do the needed thing promptly and accurately, however, was due not to "luck," but to that person's having cultivated his or her initiative.

What you may right now be calling your hard luck, may in truth be more the result of some weakness, some bad habit, which is thwarting your efforts, keeping from you the prosperity you desire. You may have peculiarities, objectionable traits, which are bars to your progress, stumbling-blocks in your path. Your "bad luck" may just be lack of preparation, a poor education, or insufficient training for your special work. It just may be that your foundation may not be large enough to support your ambition. Or, your "bad luck" may the result of the desire to have a good time first of all, no matter what happens.

Good luck is the very opposite of all this. Every prosperous person knows that good luck follows the strong will; the earnest, persistent endeavor; the good hard work and thorough preparation; the ambition to excel; a dead-in-earnest purpose.

Luck is like opportunity, it comes to those who work for it and are ready for it. Make the best possible use of your time, this will make you lucky.

If you are handicapped by the lack of an education you can get a fair equivalent of a college education, no matter how busy your life may be. Read and study during your spare moments. A multitude of men and women are educating themselves in this way every day, and are climbing up in the world in spite of a thousand obstacles and handicaps which you have never known.

If we should examine the careers of most of those who are called "lucky," we should find that their success has its roots way back in their lives, and that it has drawn its nourishment from many a battle in the struggle for supremacy over poverty and opposition. We should find that the "lucky" people are not believers in luck, but in themselves; that they have never waited for things to "turn up," or for luck to "come their way." They have gone to work and turned things up themselves, *made* luck come their way.

My experience has been that those who are made of winning material do not talk of hard luck or cruel fate; they do not talk of being kept back by others. Those who have yeast in them in them will rise; nothing can keep them back. Clear grit will attract more good luck than almost any other one thing I know of.

It is usually the unindustrious, the pleasure-loving, the feel-sorry-for-themselves who are the firmest believers in luck. Those who talk of their "hard luck" are invariably those who have not developed the strength of will, the mental fiber, which overcomes obstacles.

There is great benefit in forming the habit of thinking of yourself as lucky, of fortunate, of always seeing yourself as you would like to be rather than one who is inefficient and always blundering. Talk about yourself and of things as you wish they were, otherwise you will drive away what you long for and attract things which you wish to get rid of.

Multitudes of hard-working people who are continually driving away from them the very thing they are trying to get, because they do not hold the right attitude of mind. They lack the enthusiastic person's optimism, faith, and self-confidence—all friends of "good luck."

If you persist in looking and acting likes a failure, or a very mediocre or doubtful success; if you keep telling everybody how unlucky you are, and that you do not believe you will win out, because success is only for a favored few—those who have a pull, someone to boost them—you will be as much of a success as the actor who attempts to impersonate a certain character while looking, thinking, and acting exactly like the opposite.

Our thoughts and words are real forces which build or tear down. Who sees only failure is never a winner. It is the person who never sees anything but victory, who never acknowledges the possibility of defeat, who wins out. Those who excuse their failures on the grounds that they were doomed from the start by the bad cards fate dealt them and that they were obliged to play the game with them, and that no amount of effort on their part could have materially altered the results, deceives themselves.

Talking disparagingly about yourself, depreciating yourself, is self-deterioration. The constant suggestion of your inferiority, of your defects or weaknesses, will interfere with your success in anything. You can't be lucky, you can't be successful, if you are all the time talking against yourself, for this will not only undermine your confidence in yourself and in your efficiency, it will keep you from seeing opportunities that those without negativity blinders see.

Hold a good opinion of yourself. Think highly of yourself. Learn to appreciate your ability and to respect yourself, not egotistically or from a selfish standpoint, but because you appreciate your marvelous inheritance of divine qualities.

Remember that every time you talk depreciatingly of yourself—telling others of your hard luck, admitting that you cannot get along as do other people, that you cannot make money and save it, that you don't seem to have any money sense—you are lowering your estimate of yourself, your ideal of yourself, and this is the pattern for your life building. There is a sculptor in you who is working to the pattern which you hold up to it, and if you hold up a defective, weak, deficient, dwarfed, pattern, that's what will be built into the very structure of your being.

What you think of yourself will come to you; what you believe regarding yourself, your ability, your future, will tend to come to you. What you expect of yourself is this very instant being wrought into the texture of your being.

Always think of yourself as lucky. Never allow yourself to think of yourself in any other way. Say to yourself: "I *am* good luck. It is my nature to be lucky. I was made to be lucky. Nobody was born to lose. We are all born to win, and *I* was born to win."

Constantly meditate on what a marvelous thing it is to have a divinity within you which can never be lost, an omnipotence which can triumph over any handicap of earthly inheritance or accident.

Nothing can defeat you or rob you of success but *yourself*. No conditions, however inhospitable, can swamp you, or thwart your life aim—if you have a life aim. Only your own weakness can do that—your lack of determination, your lack of energy, your lack of confidence in yourself. Nothing in the world can make you a nonentity; no mischances, no conditions, no environment, nothing but yourself can do that. You can be a nobody if you will, or a somebody if you will; it is up to you. You can make a success of your life; you can send your influence down the ages, or you can go to your grave, without ever having made a ripple in the current of the life of your day. Your luck, good or bad, is in yourself.

Thinking of your misfortune or hard luck in not being as well placed or as well conditioned as others is fatal to success and happiness, because we must go in the direction in which we face, and we face the way we think, the way we talk, the way we act. We are like weather vanes and we turn this way and that way according as we think. Our thoughts, our emotions, our feelings are like the wind which turns the weather vane.

I know of no one thing that will have a greater influence upon your life than the forming of the habit of thinking of yourself as lucky, regarding yourself as fortunate in your ambition and in your chance in life to make good.

We are made, fashioned and molded by our thoughts, which are forces as real as is the force of electricity. Our thought is constantly shaping us to correspond with it. We are our own architects, our own sculptors. We are always reshaping, remolding ourselves to fit our thoughts and our emotions, our motives, our general attitude towards life. If we think of ourselves as being always lucky, we may not always be extraordinary examples of good luck, but we shall always be happy, smiling and contented, believing that everything that comes to us is the best that we could possibly attain.

WHERE LUCK HAS BEEN FOUND

In thrift and foresight.

In thorough preparation for one's life work.

In mental alertness.

In always being ready to lend a helping hand wherever and whenever needed.

In being tactful and a good mixer.

In holding the efficiency ideal of oneself and one's capabilities.

In downright, constant, hard work.

In being ready for the opportunity when it comes.

In courtesy, kindness, and consideration toward everybody.

In helping, oneself instead of looking to others for boosts, capital, or favors of any sort.

In doing one's work a little better than others do theirs.

In not being satisfied with anything but your best, never settling for second best or a botched job.

In always carrying some reading matter in your pocket, so that spare time can be utilized by reading for self-improvement while waiting for trains, buses, planes—or for those who are tardy for appointments.

In being cheerful, no matter how dark the outlook.

In trying to make good in every possible way, while never taking advantage of others.

In beginning the thing which something within you said you could and ought to do, no matter what obstacles stood in the way; by obeying your good impulses promptly, before they quit prodding one.

In never allowing yourself to believe that he was born to be poor, a failure, a mediocre sort of a man or woman.

In carrying the victorious attitude in everything: looking like a winner, talking like a winner, and radiating the confidence of a winner.

In holding that the good things of the world were not made for a favored few, but for all.

In substituting clear grit and persistency for the advantages which others may enjoyed from birth.

In indomitable perseverance, a determination which knows no give up or retreat; in everlastingly pushing ahead whether you can see the goal or not.

In choosing your company—associating only with people who were doing their best to get on and get up in the world.

In learning, through mental chemistry to neutralize the thoughts which kill your best efforts—fear, worry, anxiety, jealousy, envy, malice, touchiness, anger—and thus to keep your mind free for the larger things.

Fifteen

THE ATTITUDE OF EXPECTANCY

When I was graduated from a New Hampshire academy my greatest stimulus to further endeavor was my favorite teacher's belief in me. Taking me by the hand at parting, he said to me, "My boy, I expect to hear from you—that the world will hear from you—in the future. Don't disappoint me. I believe in you, and can see something in you that you do not see in yourself."

There is only one thing more stimulating, more helpful, in the struggle for success, than the knowledge that others—our teachers, our parents, our friends, and our relatives—believe in us and expect great things of us, and that is to expect great things of ourselves. The difference between what two people get out of life, what they accomplish, and what they represent to others, depends upon the difference in what they expect of themselves.

A general who goes into a battle expecting to be beaten will be beaten. His expectation of defeat communicates itself to his army, demoralizes it at the start, and makes it impossible for the men to do their best. It is the same in the battle of life. To enter it with the expectation of defeat, is to be defeated before you begin. If you desire to succeed you must show your confident expectancy of success in your very presence. You must also live day by day in the very soul of expectancy of splendid things which are coming to you.

Working for one thing and expecting the opposite can bring only one result-failure. Every time you say you don't expect ever to be anything, or to get anything, or to accomplish anything worth while, you are neutralizing the efforts you are making to be or to get or to do what you want. Our expectations must correspond with our endeavor. If we are convinced that we are never going to be really happy, that we are destined to plod along in discontent and wretchedness, to suffer all our lives, we shall tend to get what we expect. To be ambitious for happiness and yet always expect to be miserable, to continually doubt our ability to get what we long for, whatever it may be, is like getting on a train which is headed east when we wish to go west. We must *expect* to go in the direction of our desire, of our longing and effort. If you would succeed in what you are trying to do or to be, you must turn your back upon failure, blot out of your mind every thought, every picture, every suggestion of failure, and head toward success.

There is a tremendous power in the habit of expectancy—of believing that we shall realize our ambition; that our dreams will come true.

There is nothing else so helpful as the carrying of an optimistic, expectant attitude—the attitude which always looks for and expects the best, the highest, the happiest.

What we believe is coming to us, is a tremendous creative motive. The dream of home, of prosperity, the expectancy of being a person of influence, of standing for something, of carrying weight in our community—all these things are powerful creative motives. Yet how many take it for granted that there are plenty of good things in this world for others, comforts, luxuries, fine houses, good clothes, opportunity for travel, leisure, but not for them! They settle down into the conviction that these things do not belong to them, but are for those in a very different class.

But why are they not in that different class? Simply because they think themselves into another class. They think themselves into inferiority, because they place limits for themselves. By what philosophy can one obtain the good things of the world when thoroughly convinced that they are not for him or her?

If you go about with an apologetic air as though you would pick up anything that anybody else dropped and be glad to get it, but that you do not expect much for yourself; as though you do not believe that the grand things, the good things of the world were intended for you, you will get what you foresee.

We tend to get what we expect: If we expect nothing we get nothing. No one can become prosperous when who expects to remain poor.

I have just received some manuscripts accompanied by a letter, in which the writer says: "I know the enclosed are nothing like your articles, for I couldn't write like you no matter how hard I might try. I don't expect you will want to publish these, but thought I would send them along because of the possibility that you might."

Now, at the very outset, this writer prejudiced me against his articles by his self-expressed inferiority and the suggestion that they were not worth publishing, and would probably be returned. It was as though a young man should start out in a disheartened mood to look for a job, discouragement in his face and in his every action, and should say to a prospective employer: "I don't think you will hire me; I didn't expect any luck when I came in, but thought I would try. I haven't much confidence in myself, and don't know that I can do work along this line. I doubt very much if I should suit you. Still I will try my best if you want to give me a chance, though I don't believe you will, for I never have any luck in hunting jobs."

This may sound ridiculous, but it expresses the mental attitude which multitudes of people hold toward the thing they long for and are striving to attain. They never expect to succeed in anything they undertake, never expect to be comfortable—to say nothing of having the luxuries and refinements of life. They expect only failure and poverty, and do not understand that this very expectancy increases the power of their mental magnet to attract these things, even though they are trying to get away from them.

To be ambitious for wealth and yet always expecting to be poor, to be always doubting your ability to get what you long for, is like trying to reach East by traveling West.

There is no philosophy which will help a person to succeed who is always doubting his or her ability to succeed—and thus is attracting failure. Those who would succeed must expect success. They must think creatively, constructively, inventively—and, above all, prosperously.

It is fatal to work for one thing and to expect something else. No matter how much one may long for prosperity, a miserable, poverty-stricken mental attitude will close all the avenues to it.

Most people neutralize a large part of their effort because their mental attitude does not correspond with their endeavor, so that while working for one thing they are really expecting something else. They discourage, drive away, the very thing they are pursuing, by holding the wrong mental attitude towards it. They do not approach their work with that expectancy or assurance of victory which attracts, which forces results—that determination and confidence which knows no defeat.

"Whatever the soul is taught to expect, that it will build."

This can be seen most clearly when we keep in mind that we don't necessarily get what we work for—it is, instead, what we expect that comes to us. What you fear, as well as what you long for, is headed your way. All your fears, all your doubts, all your failure thoughts are taking shape in your life, molding conditions to their likeness. And no matter how hard you work for the thing you want, if you hold constantly in mind negative, discouraged thoughts; if you expect failure instead of success, evil instead of good, then it is what you expect that will come to you. Your thought, in other words, is the creative force that molds and determines the conditions of your life.

"You must have birds in your heart, Madam, before you can find them in the bushes," said John Burroughs, the great naturalist, to a woman who complained that no birds ever came to her orchard, while he counted a score or more there, even while she uttered her plaint.

It is what you hold in your heart, what you believe will manifest itself to you, that comes into your life. None can accomplish anything great in this world who are confident that they were made to do little things, and are satisfied with an inferior position, hopeless of being anything but an underling all their lives.

This perpetual expectancy of something which is going to make us suffer and finally kill us has a terribly depressing influence. It dries up the very source of life and vitality, and causes the victim to fail rapidly. It is hopeful expectancy, implicit faith, that can heal disease, and change habit and character. Expectancy of relief and unquestioned faith in the remedy or the physician are much more healing potencies than either the remedy or the physician.

The very habit of expecting that the future is full of good things for you, that you are going to be healthy, prosperous, and happy, will prove of more value to you than money capital in starting life.

No matter what the conditions of your birth, it is you who shape your career, fashion your life for happiness or unhappiness, success or failure. It is true of all men and women that "They themselves are makers of themselves."

Whatever you are trying to do, it is the hope and expectancy of success that compels success.

Most successful men and women I have known had the habit of expecting things to turn out right. No matter how discouraging the outlook, they held tenaciously to their faith in the final outcome. This habit of holding an expectant attitude attracts—in some mysterious way unknown to us—the thing for which we long, just as though it were always seeking us when we were seeking it.

Our various powers work under orders, and they tend to do or produce what is expected of them. If we expect a great deal, make a great demand of them, and insist on their helping us to carry out our ambition, they fall into line and proceed to help us.

The habit of expecting great things of ourselves calls out the best in us. It tends to awaken forces which, but for the greater demand, the higher call, would remain latent.

Believe with all your heart that you will do what you were made to do. Never for an instant harbor a doubt of it. Drive thoughts of doubt out of your mind, and entertain only the friend thoughts or ideals of the thing you are determined to achieve.

Live in the very soul of expectation of better things; in the conviction that something large, grand, and beautiful will await you if your habits and efforts are true to your aspirations, if your mind is kept in a creative condition and you struggle upward to your goal.

There is no more uplifting habit than that of bearing a hopeful attitude, of expecting that things are going to turn out well and not ill; that you are going to succeed and not fail; that, no matter what may or may not happen, you are going to be happy, prosperous.

Endow yourself with great expectancy and the determination to reach your goal. Let what will stand in your way, and by this very resolution you will get rid of the prosperity enemies that trip up the weak and the irresolute.

Sixteen

THE LAW OF OPULENCE

One of the most vicious ideas that ever found entrance into human brain is that there is not enough of everything for everybody, and that most people on the earth must be poor in order that a few may be rich.

The great fundamental principle of the law of opulence is that we each have an inseparable connection with the creative energy of the universe. When we come into full realization of this connection we shall never want again. It is our sense of separateness from the ongoing creative energy of the universe that makes us feel helpless.

As long as we limit ourselves by thinking that we are separate, insignificant, unrelated atoms in the universe; that the great supply, the creative energy is outside of us, and that only a little of it can in some mysterious way be absorbed by a few people who are "fortunate," "lucky," we shall never come into that abundant supply which is our birthright.

And where does the false idea of the absorption of all the good things by the few, of the necessity of competition, originate? It has its origin in the pessimistic notion of that there's a limitation to all the things which we most desire; and that there not being enough for all, *a few must fight desperately, selfishly for what there is*—and that the shrewdest will get the most of it.

There is nothing in this world which we desire and struggle for, and that is good for us, of which there is not enough for everybody.

Take the things we need most—food, clothing, and housing.

We have not begun to scratch the possibilities of the food supply in America. The most advanced agriculturists feel that they are but amateurs when it comes to the possibilities of mixing brains with the soil. Education and knowledge are enabling us to produce more from a few acres of soil than we formerly produced from hundreds of acres. Agriculture is still in its infancy. We know almost nothing as yet about the possibilities of getting nitrogen from the atmosphere, and of renewing the soil.

As for clothing, there is material enough in the country to clothe all its inhabitants in purple and fine linen. We have not begun yet to touch the possibilities of our clothing and dress supply. The same is true of all other necessities and luxuries. We are still on the outer surface of abundance, a surface beneath which there are kingly supplies for every individual on the globe.

And there is building material enough to give every person on the globe a mansion finer than any that a Vanderbilt or Rothschild possesses.

It was intended that we should all be rich and happy; that we should have an abundance of all the good things the heart can crave. We should live in the realization that there is an abundance of power where our present power comes from, and that we can draw upon this is great source for as much as we can use.

There is something wrong when the children of the King of kings go about like sheep hounded by a pack of wolves. There is something wrong when those who by their birthright have inherited infinite supply are worrying about their daily bread; are dogged by fear and anxiety so that they cannot take any peace; that their lives are one battle with want; that they are always under the harrow of worry, always anxious. There is something wrong when people are so worried and absorbed in making a living that they cannot make a life.

The trouble is not in the supply; there is abundance awaiting everyone on the globe. The trouble is that we do not trust the law of infinite supply, and in so doing, we close our natures so that abundance cannot flow to us. In other words, we do not pay attention to the law of attraction. We keep our minds so pinched, our hopes for ourselves and our faith in the universe so small, so narrow, that we strangle the inflow of supply.

With limitation thoughts, we create, see, and attract limitation.

Abundance follows a law as strict as that of mathematics: If we obey it, we get the flow; if we strangle it, we cut it off.

If we could only realize and feel our close, intimate connection with the creative energy of the universe, the Power of Infinite Supply, we could not want.

It is the feeling of separateness from this great Power that makes us fear, just as the child's separation from its mother fills it with fear and terror.

When we learn that it is not the universe but our wrong thinking that is the source of limitation, when we understand that it is our thinking that isolates us from abundance, we will know how to get in touch again with the great supplying Principle of the universe: feeling a sense of unity, an at-oneness with the universal creative principle, we cannot fear, we cannot want, because we understand that we are born in the very midst of the supply, in the very lap of abundance.

Prosperity is a product of the creative mind. The mind that fears, doubts, depreciates its powers, is a negative, non-creative mind—one that repels prosperity, repels supply. It has nothing in common with abundance, hence cannot attract it.

Of course, no one *means* to drive opportunity, prosperity, or abundance away from themselves. Nonetheless, we hold a mental attitude about life that is filled with doubts, fears, and lack of faith and confidence—which virtually does this very thing without our knowing it.

Oh, what paupers our doubts and fears make of us!

The opulent life stands ready to take us into it—and we starve ourselves in the midst of plenty because of our strangling thoughts. Our limited lives come not from some lack or shortage in the universe, but from our inability to unite in thought with the great Source of all supply.

Hence the life abundant, the river of plenty, flows past our doors, and we starve on the very shores of the stream which carries infinite supply.

All our limitations are in our own minds, the supply is there waiting in *vast abundance*.

The idea that riches are possible only to those who have superior advantages, more ability; or who have been favored by fate, is false and vicious.

People who put themselves into harmony with the law of opulence harvest a fortune, while those who do not do not, in many cases find enough to keep them alive.

There is everything in feeling opulent. I know a lady, who has such a wonderful appreciation of everything about her, who has such superb ideas of life and the grandeur of its meaning, that it makes one feel rich to converse with her. With her there is no such thing as commonness. When performed by her, the most ordinary duties are lifted into dignity and grandeur. Things come to her without worrying or anxious thought, She loves everybody and everybody loves her. She has no grudges against anybody, because her very nature is sunshine. There is no lack in her life, because she believes in and relies without doubt or shadow of fear on the Infinite Source of supply. She is rich, opulent in the truest sense of the word. Such people make others feel rich.

When we realize the fact that we do not need to look outside of ourselves for what we need; that the source of all supply, the divine spring which can quench our thirst, is within ourselves, then we shall not want—for we will know that we only have to dip deep into ourselves to touch the infinite supply. The trouble is that we do not abide in abundance, do not live with the creative, the all-supplying, source of things.

It is said of a remarkably successful man of our times that he is unable to see poverty. His mind is so constructed that he seems to see abundance everywhere, and believes so implicitly in the law of opulence that he demonstrates it easily. He has no doubts to paralyze his endeavor.

In the main we get out of life what we concentrate upon. If our thoughts are that the best things in the world were most likely not intended for us, then of course we shall get what we have concentrated upon.

If, on the other hand, we center our thoughts along the lines of prosperity, of abundance, if we believe that the best things in the world are for us, and that health, happiness, and prosperity are our birthright, and have done our best to realize our ideals, then our surroundings, our conditions will outpicture our thoughts.

Too many of us imprison ourselves in the narrow limited poverty thought, and then, like caged eagles trying in vain to get free, we beat out our wings against the bars we have ourselves put up.

When we have faith enough in the law of opulence to spend our last dollar with the same confidence and assurance that we would if we had thousands more, we have touched the law of divine supply. "Charity giveth itself rich. Covetousness hoardeth itself poor."

Train yourself to came away from the thought of limitation, away from the thought of lack, of want, of pinched supply. This thinking abundance, and defying limitation will open up your mind and set thought currents toward a greatly increased supply.

When you come into the full realization that you have been born into a creative universe—that your very birth is proof of the ongoing energy of creativity and that you *must* be a part, an *indestructible* part of this supply, you will never more know poverty or lack of any kind.

The plan of creation will have failed if every human being does not finally come into his and her own and participate fully in the always renewing, abundant, prosperous, creative force of life.

Seventeen

HOW TO ATTRACT PROSPERITY

A poor woman who had all her life previously lived in the back country, moved to a progressive little village where, to her great surprise, she found that her new home was lighted by electricity. She knew nothing about electricity, had never even seen an electric light before, and the little eight candle power electric bulbs with which the house was fitted seemed very marvelous to her.

Later, a man came along one day, selling a new kind of electric bulb and asked the woman to allow him to replace one of her small bulbs with one of his new style sixty candle power bulbs—just to show her what it would do. She consented, and when the electricity was turned on she stood transfixed. It seemed to her nothing short of magic that such a little bulb could give so wonderful a light, almost like that of sunlight. She never dreamed that the source of the new flood of illumination had been there all the time, that the enormously increased light came from the same current which had been feeding her little eight candle bulb.

We smile at the ignorance of this poor woman, but the majority of us are far more ignorant of our own power than she was of the power of the electric current. We go through life using a little eight candle power bulb, believing we are getting all the power that can come to us, all that we can express or that destiny will give us, believing that we are limited to being eight-candle-power bulbs. We never dream that an infinite current, a current in which we are perpetually bathed, floods our lives with light, with a light inconceivably brilliant and beautiful, if we would only put on a larger bulb, make a larger connection with the infinite supply current. The supply wire we are using is so tiny that only a little of the great current can flow through, only a few candle power, when there are millions flowing past our very door. An unlimited supply of this infinite current is ours for the taking, ours for the expressing.

Multitudes are getting no more from the vast resources at their command than this woman was getting from the electric current. They seem to think that if they are expressing four candle, or eight candle power, that it is all the infinite supply can give them, or all that they were intended to have. It never occurs to them that the trouble is not in the current itself, but in the small bulbs they are using.

But we must keep the current open or the supply will be cut off.

The law of supply is scientific. It will not act unless all the necessary conditions are fulfilled. Simply believing in a new philosophy and still keeping your old life doubts and fear habits, living in your old thought habits of lack and poverty, inefficiency, will not bring prosperity. If you don't believe you will prosper and you don't practice what you believe, you will get no results. If you would reap its fruits you must obey the law of supply, the law of abundance, the law of prosperity.

Prosperity never comes by merely wishing or longing for it. Keeping your mind fixed on it, simply thinking of prosperity, will never bring it to you. This is only the first step. You must cling to your prosperity thought, your prosperity ideal, but you must also back it up with scientific methods, the practical common-sense methods which all prosperous people employ.

You could dream of abundance and prosperity all your life and die in the poorhouse, if you do not back up your dream with efficient, business-like methods. That is, you must be methodical, orderly, systematic, accurate, thorough, industrious. You must do everything to a finish. You must fling your energy, your heart into your business, your profession, your work, whatever it is.

If you are determined to turn your back upon poverty and face toward prosperity, however your actual conditions may contradict this; if you really believe that you were not intended for poverty, but that on the contrary the good things, the beautiful things of life are for you, the life glorious and not the pauper or the drudge life; then you are opening your mind to the inflow of the prosperity current.

Imagine the entire universe, the great cosmic ocean of creative intelligence, packed with all the riches, all the glorious things, the magnificent possibilities the human mind can conceive, and then try to picture what it would mean to you if by some magic you could call out of this universal supply anything which would match your desires, your heart's longings.

You will say, doubtless, that such a thing is too silly to contemplate for a moment. Yet, haven't human beings been doing this very thing since the dawn of civilization, all up through the ages?

Every discovery, every invention, every improvement, every facility, every home, every building, every city, every source of transportation, every new technology, has been fashioned out of this vast cosmos.

How?

By thought force.

Everything we use, everything we have, every achievement is preceded by a mental vision, a plan. Someone's imagination first pictured the thing he or she wanted to do. He or she kept visualizing this mental conception, never stopped thinking about it, mentally creating and recreating it, until the efforts to match the vision with reality drew to that person the thing that he or she had been concentrating on.

We all imagine that we, of ourselves, create these things. We do not. We simply work in unison with the creative energy of the universe, drawing out of the vast invisible cosmic ocean of supply.

But we must do our part or there will be no realization for us. Just as the first step in an architect's building is the plan, so must we first make a plan or picture of the thing we desire.

The architect first sees in the mind's eye all the details of the building to be erected—even before drawing the plan on paper. He or she mentally sees the real building long before there are any materials on the spot for its construction. The plan has come out of the invisible, out of the fathomless ocean of possibilities which surrounds us.

In a like manner, all of our wants and desires can find their fulfillment in this unlimited supply.

This is a marvelous revelation, the significance of which most of us have not grasped. Only here and there are there those who utilize it in their daily daily living. But science is recognizing it. Edison says all scientists feel that *"about and through everything there is the play of an Eternal Mind."* They are recognizing that this is the first great Cause.

It is difficult to realize that every instant, under the impulse of Eternal Mind, miracles are leaping out from the cosmic ocean of energy into objectivity to meet our wants, to supply all our needs. Most of us are not able to grasp the idea that there is wealth and beauty and unthinkable luxuries waiting here. And because of this we do not materialize the things we desire.

It is one of the most marvelous things that we actually live, move, and have our being in this invisible ocean of limitless creative material, and that all we have to do to attract what we want is to hold the right mental attitude toward it and do our best on the physical plane to match it with its reality.

Do you doubt it?

Consider the following then: Noah might have lighted the Ark had he known enough. The force was there just as today.

When we once get it firmly fixed in our minds that in this invisible world of possibilities is everything which matches every legitimate desire and ambition, and that our own will come to us if we visualize it intensely enough, persistently enough, and do our best to make it real, we will no longer live in poverty and misery.

The idea of opulence, however, must be implanted firmly in the subconscious mind—just as everything else which we desire to bring about, to draw out of the universal supply, must be impressed upon our subconscious minds by registering in them our vow, our determination—until our unwavering dedication to our goal becomes a fixed motive or actuating principle.

Whatever we wish to bring about in the actual, we must first establish in the subconscious mind by the constant, positive, affirmative attitude toward our desire.

With such resolve, and hope, and expectation, and confidence, poverty is still, admittedly, not a very comfortable state, but there is no despair in it, there is no real pain in it, there is not much real distress, because hope sees the goal beyond the darkness—it gives a light that dispels the gloom of limitation by showing a vista of good things in process of realization. It is the poverty which is accompanied by despair, which sees no light ahead and forces men and women to drudge on day after day without prospect of relief or hope of betterment that grinds the life out of its victims. This is the poverty that kills the spirit, that destroys the buoyancy of life, the gladness and the joy, which are the birthright of every human being.

What a pity it is that in this land of opportunity and plenty that our government should not have institutions conducted by experts for the treatment of poverty sufferers—those who are obsessed with the idea that their poverty is unavoidable. These people are just as much in need of prosperity treatments as the patients in hospitals are in need of health treatments. They have only lost their way on the life path and are facing the darkness instead of the light, facing towards the poverty goal instead of the prosperity goal. Their mental attitude needs changing so it will point toward success instead of toward failure, toward comfort and plenty, opulence, instead of poverty and limitation. Mental prosperity treatments would kindle a new hope in their discouraged minds, and expectancy of good things would take the place of despair. A new light would come into the eyes of those poor people; and if these prosperity treatments were administered to poverty sufferers in every country of the globe the world would take on a different appearance.

But there is no need for those of you now suffering from poverty to wait for the coming of that time to be cured. Anyone can apply the law and treat himself or herself for prosperity.

Mental laws are clear and simple. We know that the fear thought attracts more fear, the worry thought more worry, the anxious thought more anxiety, the hatred thought more hatred, the jealous thought more jealousy, and the poverty thought more poverty. This is the law of attraction. Like every other law, it is unalterable.

The poverty disease can be cured only by its antidote—the prosperity thought. You carry within you this antidote to the poison of poverty, of lack, of pinching, dwarfing limitation. It is the prosperity thought. Use it, and cure yourself. Kill the poverty germ.

Picture yourself as prosperous. Obey the law of opulence by holding the ideal of opulence in your mind. Saturate yourself with the prosperity thought, the thought of abundance.

I was recently talking with a man who only a few years ago was so poor that he and his wife and children were reduced to a diet of bread and crackers without butter. They couldn't pay even the cheapest rent or buy themselves comfortable clothing. In fact, they were rapidly heading toward the ranks of the "down and outs." Today they are living in luxury, in a sumptuous hotel. They own a beautiful car, and have all they need to make life comfortable. They do not appear like the same people who but a comparatively short time ago were in a condition of semi-starvation.

Whence the change? Did some one leave them a fortune, or did they find a gold mine? No, nothing of that sort at all. They simply realized that their poverty was of their own making, that the cause of their miserable condition was entirely mental. And there and then they turned their backs on their despair environment and resolved that, no matter what appearances were, they would face the light and struggle toward it. As a result they began in a very short time to attract better things.

The whole family has now taken a new lease of life. The expression of despair and misery has gone out of their faces, and is replaced by the light of hope and joy. There is just the difference in their appearance and condition between despair and gladness, between the hope and expectation of more of the good things which belong to them, and the fear of want, the misery of grinding limitations.

Psychology is teaching us that all forms of discouragement, despondent thoughts, thoughts of doubt, of fear, of worry, must be kept out of the mind, for the mind cannot create while these enemies are in possession of the mental kingdom. We are finding that in order to create, to build, we must bold a constructive mental attitude all the time, that we must keep all negatives, all thoughts of discouragement, despondency, of possible failure out of the mind. We are learning through psychology that we can produce only that which we concentrate upon, that which we constantly think of; that only that which is dominant in our mind, whether it is beneficial or injurious, will be reproduced in our lives.

Your mental attitude will lead you into the light or hold you in darkness. It will lead you to hope or despair, to a glorious success or a miserable failure, and it is entirely within your own power to choose which it shall be.

Successful people are—and perhaps without always consciously being aware of it—constantly giving themselves prosperity treatments, success treatments, by encouraging themselves, by making their minds positive, so that they will be immune from all negative, discouraging, poverty, thought currents.

Holding the success thought, the prosperity ideal, constantly dwelling upon one's successful future, expecting it, working for it, these are, whether you know it or not, prosperity treatments.

Every time you indulge in discouraging and gloomy, despondent thoughts, every time you allow yourself to get down in the dumps or in the blues, you are tearing down what you have been trying to build up by your success treatments, by holding the prosperous thought. Your attitude is hostile to prosperity, and your very atmosphere blights and strangles it. It is as if you are saying to yourself, "I long to have you, Mr. Prosperity, but I don't believe I ever will. You were evidently not intended for me, for everything I do ends in failure. There must be some strange fate that is keeping me from the success and prosperity I want. I really never expect to be prosperous, although I am working hard to get you, Mr. Prosperity."

When we get lost in the woods, we cannot tell the direction in which we are facing, because we have lost the points on the compass. Unless we can see the sun and recover our bearing, we will walk around in a circle, thinking we are going in a straight line in the right direction. But we make no advance, because we aren't facing our goal. After a while, when we find that we are not getting toward any opening and don't know how long we will wander about in a circle, we get discouraged.

Millions of us are lost in the dense woods of wrong thought. We are not traveling toward the goal of prosperity. We see no light, no way out of the woods, and we lose courage. We are turned about mentally, and don't know it.

Eighteen

HEART-TO-HEART TALKS WITH YOURSELF

My words are spirit and they are truth; and they shall not return to me void; but shall accomplish that whereunto they were sent." How many of us grasp the real significance of this Biblical utterance? Or of this other: "And the word was made flesh and dwelt among us"? How many of us ever think that our own words, our uttered thoughts are living forces and are made flesh? Yet it is literally true that they are being outpictured in our body, are chiseling our physique, shaping our faces, molding our expression to their likeness. What we think and say reappears not only in our expression, but also in our physical condition, in our health, good or bad, according to the nature of our thoughts and words. Every word we speak is an indestructible force, because it affirms a thought, a sentiment, an emotion, a motive, which never ceases to exert its power.

Jesus evidently recognized that words are real forces, for He said, "Heaven and earth shall pass away, but my word shall not pass away." Material things might pass away, but His word was a force which could never cease to exercise its power.

All through the Bible the power of the word is emphasized. "The Word was made flesh and dwelt among us," "The Word was with God, and the Word was God," "He sent His Word and healed them."

There is a mysterious power in the spoken word, in the vigorous affirmation of a thought, which registers a profound impression on the subconscious mind, and the silent forces within us proceed to make the word flesh, to make the thing we affirm a reality. There is a tremendous constructive power in registering your vow, in vigorous, determined affirmation, backed by a persistent, dogged endeavor to bring about the thing we desire.

A very striking proof of this was afforded in the European war, in the awful conflict at Verdun in 1916. As stated in a telegraphed report from a high French officer, the fundamental secret of French resistance to the terrific German onslaught was psychological. It was, he said, autosuggestion on a vast scale. General Petain replaced doubt and discouragement with iron determination when throughout the entire army flashed his expressed resolution that the Germans should not get through the French lines—*"Ills ne passeront pas."* (They shall not pass.) All of the soldiers were so hypnotized by the constant repetition of the phrase *"Ills ne passeront pas"* that no idea save that of resistance could enter their heads.

There is no doubt that it trebled and quadrupled the resisting power of the army. The mighty suggestion of invincibility in the words was literally the decisive factor in the battle. The repetition of "They shall not pass," was what enabled the infantry to undergo unexampled bombardment and then rush forward with the bayonet as eagerly as fresh troops. The confidence of victory seen even in captured Frenchmen amazed their German captors.

The French officer's report further stated that a surgeon in the dressing station close to the front said that the most remarkable thing about the wounded was their general attitude of determination. In some cases, the surgeon said, the faces seemed fixed with an expression of ferocious resolution. Many of those suffering from shell shock and those only partially conscious would repeat at intervals of their delirium, *"Passeront pas, passeront pas."*

All of the soldiers at Verdun were obsessed by this one dominating idea to the exclusion of everything else. "The Germans shall not pass." A correspondent at the front said: I saw a regiment coming back to rest after six days in the trenches. The soldiers all seemed animated by a spirit of intense determination and iron resolution. When asked their opinion of the battle, the general reply was just this: *"The Germans shall not pass."*

And the Germans did not pass.

Suppose you should instill in your subconsciousness regarding the entrance into your mind of destructive thoughts, motives and emotions—those bitter enemies of your prosperity and happiness—a grim resolution such as the French soldiers at Verdun registered regarding the Germans? What would happen? If whenever enemy thoughts or emotions tried to get entrance to your mental kingdom you said grimly to them, "You shall not pass. I will not allow in my mind any enemies of my success and happiness," do you think it would be possible for them to get by? Why, of course they couldn't. It would be impossible. And if you should iterate and reiterate the same grim resolve—"You shall not pass"—regarding hindering habits, regarding every temptation that makes an appeal to you, why, my friend, this would revolutionize your life.

Words are the clothes of our thoughts. Every word we speak, even uttered thought, is power for good or ill. We must remember that it is what we put into the word that gives it its meaning, and determines its quality and its force.

Your words are messengers of life or death to yourself and to others.

We can take a word and think love into it, think service into it, think friendliness into it, and it will create a corresponding feeling in the one it is addressed to. Or we can take the same word and think hatred into it, think jealousy into it, think envy into it, and hurl it out and arouse antagonism, jealousy, hatred or envy in another mind.

Everything depends upon the thought behind the word. It is the mental attitude that gives the word its real meaning.

Words have put civilization where it is today. The word wedded to the thought has built everything that we have achieved.

There is a force in spoken words which is not stirred by going over the same words mentally. Words spoken aloud arouse slumbering energies within us which thinking does not stir up; when vocalized they make a more lasting impression on the mind—just as we are so much more impressed and inspired by listening to a great lecture or sermon than we would be if we read the same words in print; or how *seeing* things in nature makes a more lasting impression upon the mind than *thinking* about them. A vividness, a certain force, accompanies the spoken word—especially if earnestly, vehemently uttered—which is not conveyed in merely thinking about what words express. If you repeat to yourself aloud, vigorously, even vehemently, a firm resolve, you are more likely to carry it to reality than if you merely resolve in silence.

We can talk to our inner self and know from experience that it will listen to and act on our suggestions. After all, we are constantly sending suggestions or commands to this inner self. We may not do so audibly, but we do so silently, mentally. Unconsciously we advise, we suggest, we try to influence it in certain directions.

Now, by consciously, audibly addressing it, in heart-to-heart talks with ourselves, we will equally find that we can very materially influence our habits, our motives, our methods of living. In fact, the possibilities of influencing the character and the life by this means are practically limitless.

Many people have killed character enemies, peace and happiness enemies, have doubled and quadrupled their self-confidence, have strengthened tremendously their initiative, their executive ability, have literally made themselves over, by heart-to-heart talks with themselves.

I know a man who has so completely changed his timid, self-effacing nature by talks with his inner self that no one would dream that only a few years ago he was so shy, so extremely sensitive, that he would blush scarlet if attention were called to him in any gathering, and he would avoid people in every possible way.

Five years ago no amount of money would have induced this man to get up in a public meeting, even to put a motion or to make the simplest statement. I think he would have fainted away at the mere calling of his name in a public place. Not only had he no confidence whatever in himself, but he had a haunting obsession that he was a fraud. Although a perfectly honest, earnest, hard-working man, with good intentions toward all, he could not help feeling that in some way he was not genuine, and that sometime something would happen to show him up in his true light.

For years he suffered untold tortures from his foolish imaginings about himself. Conscious that he had ability, but cursed with weaknesses that made it in many ways unavailable, his life was headed towards failure, when he accidentally came across a which told him of the miracles possible through the practice of audible self-encouragement. He began immediately to carry out the suggestions of the book and made a daily habit of heart-to-heart talks with himself. In a very short time he was conscious of a great improvement in his feelings, his mental attitude, and his spirits. Others soon began to notice an improvement in his manner and bearing. Now, he presides at public meetings without the slightest feeling of self-consciousness. His painful shyness has vanished; he can stand any amount of criticism and denunciation without a sign of sensitiveness or embarrassment.

There is no fault, no weakness, great or small, which will not succumb to persistent, audible auto-suggestion. Not only this, but it tends to arouse slumbering qualities within us which mere thinking does not stir up or waken.

We all need stirring up. There is gunpowder enough in us to make a tremendous explosion if we could only get the spark to the giant powder that is sleeping within us.

If you are doubting, fearful of failure, or poverty, you can reinforce your courage and strengthen your confidence in yourself by daily heart-to-heart talks with your inner self, by the frequent affirmation of the positive assertions "I must," "I can," "I will." There is no better suggestion than Emerson's for stiffening the will and the power to do: "Nerve us with incessant affirmatives." And incessant affirmatives will nerve us.

The perpetual affirmation of the power to achieve one's ambition, of one's grim determination to win out in life at any cost; the affirmation of prosperity, of success, the constant assertion of confidence in one's self, of the belief in one's ability to do the thing that one has set one's heart on, will nerve a weak will and brace up a wavering purpose as nothing else can.

If you are not satisfied with your progress so far, if you are not growing bigger and broader, something is holding you back, hindering you from making your ideal real. Find out what it is and then remove it by audible self-treatments.

The best way to find what is your stumbling block is to have a frequent heart-to-heart talk with yourself. Look into your own soul and take an account of your personal stock, your success and failure qualities. Analyze yourself as you would a friend you were anxious to help—whose strong and weak points you could see clearly.

Get by yourself where you can be absolutely alone and examine yourself something after this fashion, putting the questions aloud, and addressing yourself by name:

"Now (James or Ann, or whatever your name is) what is the trouble with you? Why do you not get along faster? Are you locking up your ambition or has it not yet been awakened? Why are you not doing as well as you would like? Why are you plodding along in mediocrity while those all about you with no better chances, perhaps infinitely poorer chances than yours, are getting on by leaps and bounds? There, must be some reason for this? Do you lack vitality, energy, or are you not using what you have? Have you some weakness, defect or peculiarity which is holding you down? Are you the victim of a weak link in the chain of your character which is nullifying all your efforts in other directions? Where is the trouble? You must do all you can to put your finger on it and correct it."

Write out a list of the qualities that make a strong, courageous, successful character and their opposites—those that make a weak, timid, unsuccessful one—and examine yourself to see what is your rating in the list. Call them off aloud—faith, courage, self-confidence, ambition, enthusiasm, perseverance, concentration, initiative, cheerfulness, optimism, thoroughness, etc. Ask yourself if you possess these splendid qualities, or if you incline to their opposites.

Don't be afraid to face your weak points, to call your faults by their right names. Bring them into the light, see them for what they are, and then grapple with them. *You cannot afford to be less than you feel that you should be and can be, to have your life spoiled by some defect which you can overcome.*

When you have gone over the specific character qualities ask yourself these broader questions; always visualizing and addressing yourself by name:

"What are you here for? What do you mean to the world? What message does your life bring to it? What do you stand for? What do you represent? Do you realize that you were sent here with a message for humanity? Are you delivering it—persistently, determinedly, without grumbling, whining, or shirking? *What are you giving to the world?* Are you dreaming of the big thing you *might* do tomorrow, or are you doing the little things which you *can do today*, giving *yourself* as you go along—giving, if you have nothing else to give, encouragement, inspiration, helpfulness to those on the way with you?"

Probe yourself in this manner until you get a good line on yourself, a fair estimate of yourself; until you know both your strength and your weakness; until you can see with clear eyes the things that are keeping you back, the lack in your nature that is handicapping you, the weakness that is cutting down the average of your ability by ten, twenty, fifty or even seventy-five percent. Then vigorously attack your enemies—the enemies of your success, of your efficiency, of your happiness. Constantly stoutly affirm your complete mastery over them, their powerlessness to dominate your life and ruin your career.

By heart-to-heart talks of this sort with yourself you can change your whole nature, revolutionize your career. Whether it is faith, courage, initiative, cheerfulness, whatever it is you lack, assume the quality you wish to possess, affirm positively that it is already yours, exercise it whenever possible, concentrate on it, and you will be surprised how quickly you can acquire the desired.

A prominent music master in New York who trained opera singers advised a girl with great musical ability—but who lacked self-confidence and self-assertion—to stand before a mirror every day and, assuming a magnificent pose, say to herself, "I, I, I," with all the emphasis and power she could muster. He coupled this by telling her to simultaneously imagine that she was the then leading singer of the day. He told her that as she affirmed herself and constantly played the role, she would acquire the habit of self-confidence, which would be worth everything to her. "Assume your art boldly and fearlessly," he told her, "and hold yourself with a dignity and power corresponding with the character." She followed his advice literally, and it proved to be worth more to this timid girl than scores of music lessons—increasing her confidence in herself wonderfully, and curing her of her shyness and timidity.

I am a great believer in the building power of affirmation; in the possibilities in persistently affirming the thing I am determined to do, in strengthening qualities in which I am weak, in building character, in making life noble.

The habit of *claiming as our own, as a vivid reality that which we desire*, has a tremendous magnetic power. There is a mysterious power in the spoken word, in the stalwart affirmation of a thought, which registers a profound impression on the subconscious mind—where the silent forces within us proceed to make the word flesh, to make the thought we affirm a reality.

"As the rain cometh down, and the snow from heaven, and returned not hither," says Isaiah, "but watered the earth and maketh it bring forth and bud, that it may give seed to the sower, and bread to the eater: So shall my word be that goeth out of my mouth: it shall not return unto me void, but it shall accomplish that which I please, and it shall prosper *in the thing* whereto I sent it."

Great things are done under our repeated conviction of our ability to do whatever we undertake. But many of us seldom ever give thought to the words we utter, to the reality that our uttered thoughts are living forces and are made flesh. Yet those words are continually being manifest in our bodies, shaping our faces and expressions, and molding our destinies to their likeness.

Those immersed in material things and who live only to make money, for example, *believe* they will make it—*know* that they can make it; *affirm* that they will make it. They do not say to themselves every morning, "Well, I do not know whether I can make anything today. I will try. I may succeed and I may not." They simply and positively asserts that they can do what they desire—and then start out to put into operation plans and forces which will bring it about.

When you assert yourself, assert the spiritual "I," the divinity in you, not the physical "I," the flesh of you. This would be mere egotism, and it is not asserting your egotism that will benefit you. This will only hurt you. But asserting the reality, the divinity of yourself will do everything for you.

Remember: "And the word was made flesh." First comes the spirit—then the flesh.

Your divine is your creative self, and when you assert the reality of this self, not the outward or bodily personality, you are asserting omnipotence, omniscience—you are asserting a power that can do things.

If we could only realize the creative power of affirmation, of assuming that we are the actual embodiment of the thing we long to be or to attain—not that we simply possess all the qualities of good, but that because the thought of them has arise from within us, because our thought of them are the expressions brought to consciousness of our inherent aspirations, we *are* these qualities—what lives we would live!

Affirmation is a living, vital force. The Bible owes much of its strength to this force. It is a book of affirmations, of strong, positive statements. But for this fact it would long ago have lost its power.

There is no parleying, no arguing, no attempt by the sacred writers to prove the truth of what they say. They merely assert, affirm dogmatically that certain things happened, and that certain other things would happen. Had they attempted to prove the authenticity of what they wrote, endeavored to convince the reader that they were honest men making genuine statements, they would have aroused doubts. But there is no appeal to sympathy, no appeal to the readers' credulity, no appeal for confirmation, no posing for effect, only unrelenting positiveness, persistent affirmations. They simply state facts and affirm principles. Every line breathes dominance, superiority and confidence. In this lies their tremendous power. There is no sentimental imploring even in the Lord's Prayer. It demands. It is "give us," "lead us not," forgive us," etc.

In your talks with yourself, be like the Biblical writers. Don't wobble, or "think," or "hope." Say stoutly, "I am," "I can," "I will," "It is." Constantly, everlastingly affirm that you will become what your ambitions indicate as fitting and possible. Do not say, "I shall be a success *sometime*" say "I am a success now. Success is my birthright." Do not say that you are going to be happy in the future. Say to yourself, "I was intended for happiness, made for it, and I am happy now." Say with Walt Whitman, "'I, myself, am good fortune.'" Assert your actual possession of the things you need; of the qualities you long to have. Force your mind toward your goal; hold it there steadily, persistently, for this is the mental state that creates. This is what causes the word to be made flesh. The negative mind, which doubts, wavers, fears, creates nothing. It cannot send forth a positive, confident assertion.

We are constantly letting loose mighty thought forces, emotion forces, word forces which are forever multiplying and expressing themselves in the universal energy, which are forever fashioning our conditions. We are rich or poor, successful or unsuccessful, happy or unhappy, noble or ignoble, according to our use of our thought and word forces. The outer registration in the flesh, in *all* material circumstances and things, corresponds with the inner thought and the decisive positive word.

But remember it is the life, the driving power of the spirit, that gives the word its power. If you don't mean what you say, if you don't live the meaning into your words, they are mere idle breath.

You must *believe* what you affirm. If you affirm "I am health; I am prosperity; I am this or that," but do not believe it, you will not be helped by affirmation.

Remember, it is the life in your affirmations—your heart-to heart talks—the *spiritual life*, that does the healing through the words which the intellect suggests. Just as faith without good works is of no avail without the spirit, your words, without the life behind them, are cold and ineffectual.

People who affirm by saying that "If God willing," or "If Providence so wills" they will then do this or that, little realize how the doubt expressed by the "if" takes the edge from their positiveness, and tends to produce negative minds.

The intensity of your affirmation of your confidence in your ability to do what you attempt is definitely and directly related to the degree of your achievement. To confront life's vicissitudes, we often need great projectile—power. It is easier to force a huge shell through the steel plates of a ship when projected with lightning speed from a cannon than to try to push it through slowly.

When you long for anything that it is right for you to have, affirm in perfect confidence that the thing is already yours; claim it as a reality. No matter whether you feel like it or not, affirm that you *must* feel like it, that you *will* feel like it, that you *do* feel like it—that whether you are doing so now or not, you have it within your capacity to do your best.

Then, do what you can on the material plane to make it yours, and soon you will reap what you have sown in thought and in positive creative affirmation.

Make your affirmations again and again, and do not wait for an opportunity to begin the thing you want to do. Make your opportunity. The power of affirmation will work miracles for you.

You will find that, just in proportion as you increase your confidence in yourself by the affirmation of what you are determined to be and to do, your ability will increase. No matter what other people may think or say about you, never allow yourself to doubt that you can do what you will to do. Boldly, confidently assert that there is a special place for you in the world, an individual role which only you can fill, and that you are going to fill it. Train yourself to expect great things of yourself. Never admit, even by your manner, that you think you are destined to do little things all your life.

Stoutly, constantly, everlastingly affirm that you will become what your ambitions indicate as fitting and possible. Do not say "I shall be a success sometime," say, "I *am* a success. Success is my birthright." Do not say that you are going to be happy *in the future.* Say to yourself, "I was intended for happiness, made for it, and I am happy."

Always stoutly affirm your ability to conquer.

Resolve every morning that you will be prosperous, that your destiny is prosperity.

The following strong, positive affirmations by C. D. Larson, are very suggestive and would make a splendid daily exercise:

"I will become more than I am."

"I will achieve more because I know that I can."

"I will recognize only that which is good in myself; that which is good in others."

"When adversity threatens, I will be more determined than ever in my life to prove that I can turn all things to good account."

"I will wish only for that which can give freedom and truth, which can add to the welfare of others."

"I will always speak to give encouragement, inspiration and joy."

"I will work to be of service to an ever-increasing number; and my ruling desire shall be to enrich, ennoble and beautify existence for all who may come my way."

Every day, impersonate someone you admire for his or her prosperity thinking. No matter if you make mistakes at first, stick to your resolve to be prosperous once and for all. Continually reinforce yourself throughout the day with positive affirmations.

But remember, if you do not act with the same grim resolution in making good your words as the French soldiers did at Verdun, they will be worse than useless. If you don't mean what you say, if you don't live the meaning into your words, they are mere idle breath. You might just as well be saying "I'm a successful playwright," yet not even be writing a play; or having written one, leave it in your desk drawer.

Give people the suggestion of invincibility. This will be worth more to you than a large amount of money without it.

Deciding to talk to yourself may at first seem silly to you, but you will soon get accustomed to it and feel its beneficial effects. Remember, you are already talking to yourself every minute of the day. Now you want to control the words you are telling yourself. Now you want to practice prosperity-empowering affirmations faithfully every day, throughout the day, and just before retiring at night. They will, if backed up by earnest effort to make your words true, do wonders in bringing about the desired results.

You will think more highly of yourself, you will have more self-respect, more self-confidence; you will believe more in yourself, you will have more assurance, more confidence in your ability, you will stand higher in your own estimate in every way. This does not mean that you will become egotistical or conceited, but simply that you will know yourself and your possibilities better, and be able to use to better advantage all the power and talent within you.

We all have the power to be prosperous. We were not born to be anything less. Does not every child come into this world eager to embrace it? experience it? be filled by it?

Don't be disappointed if you do not get immediate relief. Continue to talk to yourself in a confident manner, especially upon retiring, always affirming your ability to overcome your weakness, whatever it may be, and you will conquer it. Your will power will assist you, but conviction is a thousand times stronger than will power, and the constant affirmation of the ability of the power within you to overcome the thing which handicaps you will finally help you to conquer.

Always encourage yourself; always talk up, never down. In every possible way establish confidence in yourself, because a great self-faith is a powerful force, a creative force.

"According to thy faith be it unto you."

Nineteen

SUCCESS AND HAPPINESS ARE FOR YOU

There is plenty of evidence that we were made for grand things, sublime things: for abundance and not for poverty. *Lack and want do not fit our divine nature.* The trouble, though, is that we do not have half enough faith in the good that is in store for us. We do not dare fling out our whole soul's desire, to follow the leading of our divine hunger and ask without stint for the abundance that is our birthright. Instead, if we ask at all, we ask little things, and we expect little things, pinching our desires and limiting our supply. Not daring to ask to the full of our soul's desire, we do not open our selves sufficiently to allow a great inflow of good things. We think in terms of limitation. We do not fling out our soul's desire with that *abundant* faith that trusts implicitly—and that receives accordingly.

The rose does not ask the sun for only a tiny bit of its light and heat, for it is the sun's nature to throw itself out to everything which will absorb it and drink it in.

The candle loses nothing of its light by lighting another candle.

We do not lose but increase our capacity for friendship by being friendly, by giving abundantly of our love.

One of the great secrets of life is to learn how to transfer the full current of the universal creative force to ourselves, and how to use this force effectively. If each of us will understand—grasp—this law of transference, we will multiply our efficiency a millionfold, because we will then be a co-operator, co-creator with the great creative force of life.

When we recognize that everything comes from the great Infinite Supply and that it flows to us freely, when we get in perfect tune with the Infinite, then all of the good things in the universe will flow to us spontaneously.

The trouble is that we restrict the inflow by wrong acts and wrong thoughts.

Do not be forever apologizing for your lack of this or that. Every time you say that you have nothing fit to wear, that you never have things that other people have, that you never go anywhere or do things that other people do, you are simply etching a despairing picture deeper and deeper. As long as you recite these unfortunate details and dwell upon your disagreeable experiences, your mentality will not attract the thing you are after, will not bring that which will remedy your hard conditions.

Your mental attitude, your mental picturing, must correspond with the reality you seek.

When you learn the art of seeing opulently, instead of stingily; when you learn to think without limits; when you learn how not to cramp yourself by limiting thought; when unfairness, a desire to take advantage of your brothers and sisters, is removed from your life; then you shall find that the thing you are seeking is seeking you—and that it will meet you half way.

Prosperity begins in the mind, and is impossible with a mental attitude which is hostile to it. We can not attract opulence mentally by a poverty-stricken attitude which is driving away what we long for. It is fatal to work for one thing and to expect something else. No matter how much one may long for prosperity, a poverty-stricken mental attitude will close all the avenues to it.

Opulence and prosperity can not come in through poverty-thought and failure-thought channels, for the weaving of the web is bound to follow the pattern.

We must think prosperity before we can come to it. It must be created mentally first.

How many of us take it for granted that there are plenty of good things in this world for others—comforts, luxuries, fine houses, good, clothes, opportunity for travel, leisure—but not for us? We settle down into the conviction that these things do not belong to us. And so, we put up bars between ourselves and plenty. We cut off abundance; we make the law of supply inoperative for ourselves by shutting your mind to it.

The limitation is in ourselves, not in life.

One of the greatest curses of the world is the belief in the necessity of poverty. Most people have a strong conviction that some must necessarily be poor—and many believe that *they* were made to be poor. But there need not be a poor person on the planet. The earth is full of resources which we have scarcely yet touched. We have been poor in the very midst of abundance, simply because of our own limiting thoughts.

We are discovering that thoughts are things, that they are incorporated into life and form part of the character, and that if we harbor the lack thought, if we are afraid of poverty, of coming to want, this poverty thought incorporates itself into our very life texture and makes us the magnet to attract more poverty like itself.

It was not intended that we should have such a hard time getting a living, that we should just manage to squeeze along, to get together a few comforts, to spend about all of our time making a living instead of making a life. The life abundant, full, free, beautiful, was intended for us.

If we held the abundance thought that is our birthright, that we possess as children, then just as children, our living-getting would be a mere incident in our life-making.

Resolve that you will turn your back on the poverty idea and that you will vigorously expect prosperity; that you will hold tenaciously the thought of abundance, the opulent ideal, which is befitting your nature; that you will try to live in the realization of plenty, to actually feel rich, opulent. This will help you to attain what you long for. There is a creative force in intense desire.

The fact is that we live in the world of our making: We are creations, the results, of our own thoughts. We each build our own world by our thought habits. We can surround himself with an atmosphere of abundance, or of lack; of plenty, or of want.

We were made to aspire; to look up, not down. We were made for grand things, not to pinch along in poverty.

It is not life or circumstances, but the poverty attitude, the narrowness of our thought, that has limited us.

If we learn to trust implicitly that life is a source of Infinite Supply which always brings seed time and harvest, we shall never know what want is.

But most of us do not have half good enough opinions of our possibilities; do not expect half enough of ourselves. We do not demand the abundance which belongs to us, hence the leanness, the lack of fullness, the incompleteness of our lives. We do not demand *royally*, enough. We are content with too little of the things worth while. *It was intended that we should live the abundant life*, that we should have plenty of everything that is good for us. No one was meant to live in poverty and wretchedness. *The lack of anything that is desirable is not natural to the constitution of any human being.*

Hold the thought that you are one with what you want, that you are in tune with it, so as to attract it. Keep your mind vigorously concentrated upon it. Never doubt your ability to get what you are after, and you will move toward it.

Poverty is most often a mental disease. If you are suffering from it, if you are a victim of it, you will be surprised to see how quickly your condition will improve when you change your mental attitude. Instead of holding a limited, poverty image, turn about and face towards abundance and plenty, towards freedom and happiness.

Prosperity comes through a perfectly scientific mental process. Those who become prosperous *believe* that they are going to *be* prosperous. They have faith in their ability to make money. They do not start out with a mind filled with doubts and fears—all the time talking poverty, thinking poverty, walking like a pauper, and dressing like a pauper. They turns their faces towards the thing they are trying for and are determined to get, and will not admit its opposite picture in their minds.

There are multitudes of people in this country who work hard, but they have lost the hope, the expectation, of prosperity.

Some keep themselves poor by *fear* of poverty, allowing themselves to dwell upon the possibility of coming to want, of not ever having enough.

The terror of poverty, the constant worry about making ends meet, the fear of that awful "rainy day," not only will make you unhappy, it actually disqualify you from putting yourself in a better financial condition. In carrying around such thoughts, you are simply adding to a load which is already too heavy for you.

No matter how dark the outlook or how seemingly limited your environment, positively refuse to see anything that is unfavorable to you, any condition which tends to enslave you, anything that could keep you from expressing the *best* that is in you.

By what philosophy can we expect poverty thoughts, thoughts of lack and want, to produce prosperity? Our conditions will correspond to our attitudes and ideals. We tend to get what we expect, and if we expect nothing we get nothing. The stream cannot rise higher than its fountainhead; no one can become prosperous who expects, or half expects, to remain poor.

Do not say to yourself, "What's the use? The great business combinations are swallowing up the chances. Before long the multitude will have to work for the few. I do not believe I shall ever do anything more than make just a plain living in a very humble way. I shall never have a home and the things that other people have. I am destined to be poor and a nobody." You will never get anywhere with such ideals.

Those who expects prosperity *are constantly creating money in their minds, building their financial structure mentally.* There must be a mental picture of prosperity first. The building, after all, is first completed in all its details in the architect's mind. The contractor merely puts the stones, the brick and other material around the idea.

We are all architects. Everything we do in life is preceded by some sort of a plan.

It does not take as great a person to place the material around the idea as it does to *create* the idea, the mental picture.

This is not idle dreaming. It is mental planning, mental construction. The *true* dreamer is the believer, the achiever.

The poor man person is not the one who has little or no property, but the one who is poverty-stricken in ideas, in sympathies, in power of appreciation, in sentiment. The truly poor are those who are poverty-stricken in their opinions of themselves, of their own destinies, of their abilities to reach up—who commit the crime of self-depreciation.

It is *mental* penury that makes us poor.

The great achievers do comparatively little with their hands—they build with their thought. They are practical dreamers. Their minds reach out into the infinite energy ocean and create their opportunities—just as the seed reaches out into the infinite fertile soil around it and brings forth the tree.

To be prosperous we must put ourselves in the prosperous attitude. Parsimonious saving by cheese-paring efforts does not compare in effectiveness with the results of obeying the laws of opulence. We must think opulently. Our mental attitude towards the thing we are striving for and the intelligent effort we put forth to realize it will, in the final analysis, be the measure of our attainment.

We must feel opulent in thought. We must exhale confidence and assurance in our very bearing and manner.

We go in the direction of our concentration. If we concentrate upon poverty, if want and lack predominate in our thought, poverty-stricken conditions must result.

Before we can conquer outward poverty, then, we must conquer inward mental poverty.

PART III
The Prosperity Habit

Twenty

GETTING AWAY FROM POVERTY

The struggle to get away from poverty has been the human race's great character and progress developer. Had all human beings been born with a silver spoon in their mouths—had there been no necessity put upon them to work—the race would still be in its infancy. Had everybody in this country been born wealthy, ours would be one of the dark ages. The vast resources of our land would still be undeveloped, the gold would still be in the mines, and our great cities would still be in the forest and the quarry. Civilization owes more to the perpetual struggle of the individual to get away from poverty than to anything else. We are so constituted that we make our greatest efforts and do our best work while struggling to attain that for which the heart longs. It is practically impossible for most people to make their utmost exertions without imperative necessity for it. It is the constant necessity to improve their condition that has urged individuals onward and developed the stamina and sterling character of the whole race. History abounds in stories of failures of men and women who started with wealth—and it is illuminated with examples of those who owe everything to the spur of necessity.

A glance at the history of our own country will show that the vast majority of successful men and women in every field were poor at the start: Benjamin Franklin, Alexander Hamilton, Andrew Jackson, Henry Clay, Daniel Webster, Abraham Lincoln, Horace Mann, George Peabody, Ulysses S. Grant, James A. Garfield, Charlotte Bronte, Lillian Nordica, Louisa Alcott—to mention but a few of the great names of past generations—rose to distinction from an iron environment and direst poverty.

Greatness has, for the most part, been pushed forward by the goad of necessity—by the desire to make the most of oneself.

"Those who have the misfortune to be rich parents' children are heavily weighted in the race," said Andrew Carnegie. "The vast majority of rich parents' children are unable to resist the temptations to which wealth subjects them, and they sink to unworthy lives. It is not from this class that the poor beginner has rivalry to fear. The partner's sons or daughters will never trouble you much. Bu look out that some boy or girl poorer, much poorer, than yourselves, whose parents cannot afford to give them any schooling, do not challenge you at the post and pass you at the grandstand. Look out for the child who has to plunge into work directly from the high school, and who begins by sweeping out the office. He or she is the probable dark horse that will take all the money and win all the applause."

A youth, born and bred in the midst of luxury, who has always leaned upon others, who has never been obliged to fight his or her way up, who has been coddled from his infancy, rarely develops great stamina or staying power. He or she is often like the weak sapling in the forest compared with the giant oak which has fought every inch of its way up from the acorn by struggling with storms and tempests.

Those who are conscious that they have a fortune awaiting them, too often say to themselves, "What is the use of getting up early in the morning and working one's life out? I have money enough coming to me to take care of me as long as I live." So they turn over and take another nap, while the those who have nothing in the world but their own selves to depend on, feel the spur of necessity forcing them out of bed in the morning. They know that there is no other way open for them but the way of struggle. They have nobody to lean on—nobody to help them. They know that it is a question either of being a nobody or getting up and hustling for dear life.

Power is the result of force overcome. The giant is made strong in wrestling with difficulties. It is impossible for one who does not have to struggle and to fight obstacles to develop fiber or stamina. "To live without trial is to die but half a person."

Strength of character is a thing which must be wrung out of obstacles overcome. Life, is a great gymnasium, and no one who sits in a chair and watches the parallel bars and other apparatus ever develops muscles or endurance.

And yet how many parents try to do the exercises for their sons and daughters, while the children sit on soft benches or easy chairs, watching the process!

Isn't it strange that so many prosperous people who take pride in having made themselves, who consider it the most fortunate thing in the world that they were thrown upon their own resources, who put great value on the fact that they were obliged to develop their independence and stamina and self-reliance, should then work so hard to keep their children from having the same experience? Isn't it strange that they should provide crutches so that it will be all the more difficult for their children to walk alone? That they should take away the strongest possible motive for the development of power by making it unnecessary for their children to strive, by providing for every want and guarding them on all sides by wealth?

A famous artist, who was asked if he thought a young man who was studying with him would make a great painter, replied, "No, never. He has an income of six thousand pounds a year." This artist knew how the great struggle against thwarting difficulties brings out power—how hard it is to develop a strong fiber in the sunshine of wealth.

How many young immigrants have come to this country uneducated, ignorant of our language, friendless and penniless, and yet have risen to positions of distinction and wealth, putting to shame tens of thousands of native-born youths who possessed every advantage of wealth, education, and opportunity, but who have never been heard from!

I am no advocate of the blessings of poverty, considered as a finality. Poverty is of no value except as a vantage ground for a starting point. It is only good as is the apparatus in the gymnasium—to develop the individual. In itself, poverty is a curse—a slavery. The great thing is in the *getting away* from it. It is the getting away from it—if honestly and conscientiously done—that calls out the individual, that develops the human giant.

We do not always see at the time that what we get incidentally on the way up from poverty is infinitely better and more precious than the thing we were aiming for—that the development of a strong character in the mighty struggle with necessity is a thousand times more valuable than the lifestyle, the money, or the property gained.

Former U.S. President Grover Cleveland, who was once a poor clerk at a salary of fifty dollars a year, in speaking of poverty as a developer, said: "There is surely no development of mental traits, and no stimulation of the forces of true character so thorough and so imperiously effective as those produced by the combination of well-regulated ambition with the healthful rigors of poverty."

It is the student who has to struggle hardest to obtain an education that gets the most discipline and good out of it. Those who are "born scholars," and who only need to read a lesson over to know it and to be able to pass an examination upon it, do not derive half so much from their college course as do those who have to fight hard for everything they get. It is not, as a rule, the youth who has a regular income and every want supplied by indulgent parents who makes the most of the opportunities at college, but the one who has to work his or her way through, who has to toil and make his or her expenses, or else go without an education.

What would the average person do if not compelled by necessity to work—if not obliged to exert themselves in order to get the things they want? Not one in ten thousand would go through the struggle with poverty—the wrestling with necessity—just to produce character and make themselves a stronger person.

Thus, shrewd Nature, in making us get that which we want most by way of necessity, achieves her great ends of both civilization-development and character-development. She does not care a fig for money prosperity, it is the prosperity of the race and civilization that she is after. The property, the position that mean so much to us, are of no consequence to her. She is after the *individual of character*. And so, in order to perfect her work, she puts us through the hardest school of discipline and train us for years in the great university of experience.

Twenty One

ONE UNWAVERING AIM

To succeed, to attain prosperity, you must concentrate all the faculties of your mind upon one unwavering aim, and have a tenacity of purpose which means death or victory. Every inclination which tempts you from your aim must be suppressed.

New Jersey has many ports, but they are so shallow and narrow that the shipping of the entire state amounts to but little. On the other hand, New York has but one ocean port, and yet it is so broad, deep, and grand, that it leads America in its enormous shipping trade. She sends her vessels into every port of the world, while the ships of her neighbor are restricted to local voyages.

One person may starve on a dozen half-learned trades or occupations, while another may grow rich and famous upon one trade thoroughly mastered, even though it be the humblest.

Success is noted for its power of concentration, its single-mindedness, which makes it oblivious of everything outside its aim.

"Why do you lead such a solitary life?" asked a friend of Michelangelo. "Art is a jealous mistress," replied the artist. "She requires the whole man." During his labors at the Sistine Chapel, according to Disraeli, he refused to meet any one, even at his own house.

In answer to an advertisement, a New York sportsman sent in twenty-five cents for a sure method to prevent a shotgun from scattering. He received the following: "Dear Sir: To keep a gun from scattering, put in but a single shot."

Victor Hugo wrote his "Notre Dame" during the revolution of 1830, while the bullets were whistling across his garden. He shut himself up in one room, locking his clothes up, lest they should tempt him to go out into the street, and spent most of that winter wrapped in a big gray comforter, pouring his very life into his work. Adam Smith spent ten years on the *Wealth of Nations*. Gibbon gave twenty years to his *Decline and Fall of the Roman Empire*. Hume worked thirteen hours a day on his *History of England*. Webster devoted thirty-six years to his dictionary. Cyrus Field, crossed the Atlantic Ocean fifty times to lay a cable, while the world ridiculed. Newton wrote his *Chronology of Ancient Nations* sixteen times. General Ulysses Grant said he proposed "fight it out on this line if it takes all summer."

The weakest, by concentrating their powers upon one thing, can accomplish something; the strongest, by dispersing theirs over many, may fail to accomplish anything. Drop after drop of water, continually falling, wears a passage through the hardest rock, while the hasty tempest, as Carlyle points out, rushes over it with hideous uproar—but leaves no trace behind.

A one-talent person who decides upon a definite object accomplishes more than the ten-talent people who scatter their energies and never knows exactly what they will do.

A great purpose is cumulative; and, like a great magnet, it attracts all that is kindred along the stream of life.

Scientists estimate that there is energy enough in less than fifty acres of sunshine to run all the machinery in the world, if it could be concentrated. But the sun blazes upon the earth without setting anything on fire. When focused by a magnifying glass, however, it can melt solid granite or even change a diamond into vapor.

Chiseled upon the tomb of a disappointed, heartbroken king, Joseph II of Austria, in the Royal Cemetery at Vienna, a traveler tells us, is this epitaph: "Here lies a monarch who, with the best of intentions, never carried out a single plan."

In Paris, a certain Monsieur Kenard announced himself as a "public scribe, who digests accounts, explains the language of flowers, and sells fried potatoes."

A wavering aim, a faltering purpose, has no place in life. "Mental shiftlessness" is the cause of many a failure. The world is full of unsuccessful people who spend their lives letting empty buckets down into empty wells.

"Mr. A. often laughs at me," said a young American chemist, "because I have but one idea. He talks about everything, aims to excel in many things; but I have learned that, if I ever wish to make a breach, I must play my guns continually upon one point." Not many years later, he was performing experiments in electromagnetism before English earls, and subsequently he was at the head of one of the largest scientific institutes of this country. This man was the late Professor Henry, of the Smithsonian Institution, Washington.

We should guard against a talent which we cannot hope to practice in perfection, says Goethe.

George Eliot said of the years of close work upon *Romola*, "I began it a young woman, I finished it an old woman."

It is the single aim that wins.

The world always makes way for those with a purpose in them.

This age of concentration calls not for those who are merely educated, not for geniuses, not for jacks-of-all-trades, but for those who know to do one thing as well as it can be done.

Constant and steady use of the faculties under a central purpose gives strength and power, while the use of faculties without an aim or end only weakens them. The mind must be focused on a definite end, or, like machinery without a balance-wheel, it will rack itself to pieces.

Find your aim and stick to it.

Drifting around from one kind of employment to another, learning part of each, but all of none, will never give a good living, much less a competency—and wealth will absolutely be out of the question.

To be prosperous is to *find your sphere and fill it, to get into your place and master it.*

And yet, despite the fact that nearly all prosperous people have made a life work of one thing, we see hundreds of men and women flitting about from occupation to occupation, trade to trade, in one thing today and another tomorrow—just as though they could go from one thing to another by turning a switch, as if they could run as well on another track as on the one they have left. This fickleness, this disposition to shift about from one occupation to another, seems to be peculiar to American life, so much so that, when two people meet who have not seen one another for some time, the commonest question asked is "What are you doing now?"—showing the improbability or uncertainty that either is doing today what he or she was doing when they last met.

But simply "keep everlastingly at it" is not the measure of success or prosperity. Those who succeed have a program. They fix their course and adhere to it. They lay their plans and execute them. They are not pushed this way and that every time a difficulty is thrown in their path. If they can't get over it, they go through it.

"That day we sailed westward, which was our course," were the simple but grand words which Columbus wrote in his journal day after day. Hope might rise and fall, terror and dismay might seize upon the crew at the mysterious variations of the compass, bat Columbus, unappalled, pushed due west and nightly added to his record the above words.

Working without a plan is as foolish as going to sea without a compass. A ship which has broken its rudder in the middle of the ocean may "keep everlastingly at it," may keep on a full head of steam, driving about all the time, but it never arrives anywhere, it never reaches any port unless by accident; and if it does find a haven, its cargo may not be suited to the people, the climate, or conditions among which it has accidentally drifted.

The ship must be directed to a definite port, for which its cargo is adapted, and where there is a demand for it, and it must aim steadily for that port through sunshine and storm, through tempest and fog.

So too, if you would find your prosperity, you must not drift about rudderless on the ocean of life. You must not only steer straight toward your destined port when the ocean is smooth, when the currents and winds serve, but you must keep his course in the very teeth of the wind and the tempest, and even when enveloped in the fogs of disappointment and mists of opposition.

On the prairies of South America there grows a flower that always inclines in the same direction. If travelers lose their way and have neither compass nor map, by turning to this flower they will find a guide on which he can implicitly rely; for no matter how the rains descend or the winds blow, its leaves point to the north. Similarly, the needle of your compass must always point to the North Star of your hopes. Then, whatever comes, your life will not be purposeless: A wreck that makes it to port is a greater success than a full-rigged ship with all its sails flying, with every mast and rope intact, which drifts into an accidental harbor.

Admittedly, to fix a wandering life and give it direction is not an easy task, but a life which has no definite aim is sure to be frittered away in empty and purposeless dreams.

Mere energy is not enough; it must be concentrated on some steady, unwavering aim. What is more common than "unsuccessful geniuses," or failures with "commanding talents"? Indeed, "unrewarded genius" has become a proverb.

Every town has unsuccessful educated and talented citizens. But education is of no value, talent is worthless, unless it can do something, achieve something.

What this age wants is men and women who can do one thing without losing their identity or individuality—without becoming narrow, cramped, or dwarfed. Nothing can take the place of an all-absorbing purpose; education will not, genius will not, talent will not, industry will not, will-power will not. The purposeless life must ever be a failure.

What good are powers, faculties, unless we can use them for a purpose? What good would a chest of tools do a carpenter unless the carpenter can use them? A college education, a head full of knowledge, are worth little to those who cannot use them to some definite end.

Those who would prosper in this short life must apply themselves with such a concentration of their forces as, to idle spectators who live only to amuse themselves, looks like insanity.

Christ knew that one affection rules in life when he said, "No man can serve two masters."

One affection, one object, must be supreme in us. In every great painting of the masters there is one idea or figure which stands out boldly beyond everything else. Every other idea or figure on the canvas is subordinate to it, but pointing to the central idea, finds its true expression there

One may have subordinate plans, but only but one supreme aim. And from this aim, all other aims we might have will take their character.

"Try and come home a somebody," said the fond mother of Léon Gambetta as she sent him off to Paris to school. Poverty pinched him hard in his little garret study and his clothes were shabby. But what of that? He had made up his mind to get on in the world. For years he was chained to his desk and worked like a hero. At last his opportunity came. Jules Favre was to plead a great cause on a certain day, but, being ill, he chose this young man, absolutely unknown, rough and uncouth, to take his place. For many years Gambetta had been preparing for such an opportunity, and he was equal to it, for he made one of the greatest speeches that up to that time had ever been made in France. That night all the papers in Paris were sounding the praises of this ragged, uncouth Bohemian, and soon all France recognized him as the Republican leader. This sudden rise was not due to luck or accident. He had been steadfastly working and fighting his way up against opposition and poverty for just such an occasion. Had he not been equal to it, it would only have made him ridiculous. What a stride: yesterday, poor and unknown, living in a garret; today, deputy elect, in the city of Marseilles, and the great Republican leader! The gossipers of France had never heard his name before. He had been expelled from the priest-making seminary as totally unfit for a priest and an utterly undisciplinable character. In two weeks, this ragged son of an Italian grocer arose in the Chamber, and moved that the Napoleon dynasty be disposed of and the Republic be declared established.

When Louis Napoleon had been defeated at Sedan and had delivered his sword to William of Prussia, and when the Prussian army was marching on Paris, Gambetta went out of the besieged city in a balloon barely grazed by the Prussian guns, landed in Amiens, and by almost superhuman skill raised three armies of 800,000 men, provided for their maintenance, and directed their military operations. A German officer said, "This colossal energy is the most remarkable event of modern history, and will carry down Gambetta's name to remote posterity." This youth who was poring over his books in an attic while other youths were promenading the Champs Élysées, although but thirty-two years old, was now virtually dictator of France, and the greatest orator in the Republic. Yet he did not lose his head in his quick leap into fame. He still lived in the upper room in the musty Latin quarter, and remained a poor man, without stain of dishonor, though he might easily have made himself a millionaire. When Gambetta died, the *Figaro* said, "The Republic has lost its greatest man." It the great purpose which gives meaning to life. It unifies all our powers, binds them together in one cable, and makes strong and united what would otherwise be weak, separated, scattered.

It is what lays the path to success and prosperity.

Twenty Two

CONQUERING THE ULTIMATE PROSPERITY OBSTACLE

The first essential of prosperity is to *expect* it.

Upon entering a New York office once, I was struck by their business motto: "We talk abundance here." These people are prosperous because they expect prosperity, I said to myself; they do not recognize poverty or admit lacking all they need.

As the way to make the ideal the real is to persistently hold the thought of its identity, the way to demonstrate abundance is to hold it constantly in the mind. Thousands of people have *thought* themselves away from poverty by getting a glimpse of this great principle: *We tend to realize in the life what we persistently hold in the thought and vigorously struggle toward.*

Never allow yourself to dwell on the bleak side of anything. Refuse to talk about depressed markets or hard times.

Learn to talk up, not down. Many are chronic grumblers and fault-finders: times are always hard with them; they get into a pessimistic rut and never see brightness or success in anything. It is impossible for such people to prosper. Success is a delicate plant, and requires encouragement and sunshine.

We tend to become and to grow more and more like that which we cherish, harbor, and constantly long for, and we tend to lose or become unlike that which we hate, despise, and habitually deny. The latter gradually loses its grip upon our lives, releases its hold upon character, and finally vanishes.

The persistent denial of the belief that you are a victim of limitation and the stout affirmation of your attainment of prosperity will not only bring out the richer part of your character, but that for which you aspire. That which you are constantly and persistently refusing to give voice to will ultimately fade out of your consciousness and go out of your life.

If you are like the sundial and face toward the light and follow the sun, you will never be in darkness. Shadows will always fall behind you.

Nothing will so completely paralyze the creative power of the mind and body as a dark, gloomy, discouraged, hopeless mental attitude.

The assumption that there is not enough for all, that a few must fight desperately, selfishly, for what there is, is fatal to all individual and race betterment.

The Creator never put vast multitudes of people in the world to scramble for a limited supply, as though He were not able to furnish enough for all. There is nothing on this earth which we desire and struggle for, and that is good for us, of which there is not supply enough for everybody. Yet, we find that wherever we go, the fear-ghost, the terror-specter of coming to want, stands between so many and their goal. No one is in a position to be prosperous while haunted by it.

Half the battle is in the conviction that we can do what we undertake. There can be no great courage where there is no confidence or assurance.

We cannot accomplish great work unless the banner of hope goes in advance of us. If it is always before us, will follow to our success even when money, friends, reputation, and everything else has gone.

Nevertheless, some people seem pitched to a minor key. There is a downward tendency in their thought and conversation. Everything is down: business poor, prospects dark, there are snags ahead, nothing is as it used to be when they were young, they cannot get any more decent help, everything is in a deplorable condition. They see tendencies in American life which are sure to undermine our democracy and end in revolution.

Such people go through life like a tornado—uprooting the foundation of their own works, assuring the disaster they predict wherever they go.

And all the while, next door to these calamity howlers we find others who see challenges in seeming failure, and who are increasing in prosperity.

Someone has defined worry as "spiritual nearsightedness; a fumbling way of looking at little things, and of magnifying their value. True spiritual vision," he said, "sweeps the universe and sees things in their right proportion. Seen in its true relations, there is no experience of life over which one has a right to worry."

The mind that is obsessed with fear or worry cannot see anything in its true light. It is at a disadvantage in waging the battle of life.

Our thought creates our atmosphere, and we live in discord or harmony according to the quality of the thoughts and moods which we harbor. Doubts, fears, worry, anxiety, self-depreciation are all disturbing elements in our atmosphere that deprive us of the good things of life which are our legitimate birthright—peace, happiness, prosperity, success in life making as well as in living making.

Of all our mental enemies, fear is the worst. It is always the biggest obstacle in our path. All the victims of discouragement, those who are suffering from despondency, those who are going through life disheartened, hopeless, despairing, are the authors of their own misery. They persist in killing the very thing they are pursuing, in queering their own quest by the poison of fear—which is forever holding them back from doing the things they can and ought to do.

If we only realized that every anxious, fear-burdened thought hampers self-development and dwarfs success possibilities, we would avoid such thought as we would avoid taking poison. If they truly understood that fear and worry have wrought more destruction in human lives than all the wars that have decimated the world since the birth of the race, we would no more allow them to enter our mental dwelling than we would admit a thief to our house to rob us of our most valued possessions.

No one can estimate the havoc these happiness killers, these efficiency destroyers, play in our lives. They chill the heart, whiten the hair, wrinkle the face, take the elasticity out of the step, blight ambition, kill courage, strangle hope, and leave their victim only the wreck of his or her former self.

There are thousands of perpetual clerks in ordinary positions because they listened to the voice of fear. They were once ambitious to climb to the heights, and never dreamed that they would always remain in such ordinary positions. When they started out, they thought they were going to be something very unusual, but fear clutched them, and paralyzed their initiative, their courage. Whenever they thought of going into business for themselves, it cautioned them to be careful, that it was no time for any one without capital, without a lot of friends and backers, to start out on one's own. It whispered that they would only fail if they did, and that then they would be laughed at for their conceit and rashness.

Then Doubt, the child of Fear, asked if they were sure they had the ability to start out for themselves. It suggested that the vision of their ambition might be a mere fantasy of the imagination, that there might be no prophecy of fulfillment in it. So many, it urged, had tried and failed because they were incompetent.

Most of us are held down by the mortal enemy Fear and its relatives: Doubt, Worry, Hopelessness. We are handicapped all our lives by fear suggestions: fear of heredity, fear of disease, fear of accident, fear of death, fear of fire, fear on land and on sea, fear of failure, fear of the disappointment of our hopes and plans, fear of the failure of our lives through inefficiency.

How seldom we see one who really enjoys the present moment! Some anxiety, some fear, some foreboding is forever making a note of discord in our lives. Something which we think is likely to happen, or something that has happened, contrary to our wishes and plans, is constantly haunting us and pushing us backward on the path of life.

We civilized people pity ignorant savages who live in terror of their gods, cruel demons of their own creation, who keep them in abject slavery—but we ourselves are the slaves of a demon which blasts our hopes, blights our happiness, casts its hideous shadow across all our pleasures, destroys our sleep, mars our health, and keeps us in misery most of our lives. This fear demon of ours not only keeps the body in bondage, but creates mental currents which tend to turn the soul back on its voyage to perfection. As the Theosophists tell us, anything which fills the mind with gloom and fear retards the spiritual growth in a corresponding degree.

Fear-laden souls, habitual worriers, are constantly depleting their powers and working against their own interests and happiness.

When you worry, you maim and defraud yourself.

No one who is a victim of fear can ever be really efficient or successful on any plane. They never can do their best, never can be serene, poised, healthy or happy. They can never get into the success current, the current of abundance; they can never follows the law of opulence.

You can cure yourself of fear, worry, habitual discouragement and all other destructive emotions. You can make your life a grand success.

Through the exercise of mental alchemy you can change your thoughts from lead to gold. Quit fearing things just as you would quit any bad practice which has caused you suffering. Fill your mind with the opposite thoughts to those that terrify you.

No discouragement, no anxiety, no gloom or despondency—none of the enemies of your happiness—can possibly enter your mind while it is filled with friend thoughts: good cheer, kindness, beauty, truth, harmony, love. Giving expression to courage thoughts will be a great help in driving out fear. Fear in any of its expressions—worry, anxiety, lack of faith, self-depreciation—cannot live an instant in your mind in the presence of thoughts and images of courage, fearlessness, confidence, self-assurance, self-reliance.

Whenever fear or worry tries to take possession of you say, "I was never made to cower, to slink, to be afraid. Fear is not an attribute mine. I am a conqueror of fear, not its slave."

The next time something whispers in your ear and tries to shake your confidence in yourself, to keep you from beginning the things which you long to do and feel that you have the ability to carry through, remember that something that is speaking is fear.

The next time you cower before some unusual difficulty and think of turning back, remind yourself that that is your worst enemy again trying to influence you.

When you are tempted to worry about something that has happened, or that you think may happen; when you doubt your ability to do this or that, and think you would better not undertake anything that is not perfectly sure to come out all right, remember it is fear again trying to fool you. Don't listen to its suggestions, for it is the greatest of all liars, the greatest of all deceivers and misrepresenters.

Thrust it out of your mind. Say to it: "You have no power over me; I will not allow you to destroy my peace and thwart my career; you are not the truth of my being; the reality of me is capability. I can and I will rise above all my troubles, make good all my mistakes and errors. I will not be overcome by any enemy. I will overcome."

If things are not presently going well for you, be careful of whom you tell that to—so that you will be spared the influence of the unfortunate suggestions which your hard luck stories may make upon other people's minds who may echo sentiments that all is in vain.

Remind yourself that every time you repeat the story of your misfortunes, your troubles, your trials, your failures, you etch the picture a little deeper in your own mind—making a little more real to you what you ought to erase forever.

Conquer fear and worry and all their evil progeny, and you will conquer all the enemies of your success and happiness—and you will live in harmony with the law of opulence.

Twenty Three

USES OF OBSTACLES, OR ATTAINING PROSPERITY UNDER DIFFICULTIES

"What does one know," said a sage, "who has not suffered?"

Prosperous men and women have ever had the mettle to turn disappointments into helps, as the oyster turns into pearl the sand which annoys it.

"Many and many a time since," said Harriet Martineau, referring to her father's failure in business, "have we said that, but for that loss of money, we might have lived on in the ordinary provincial method of ladies with small means, sewing and economizing and growing narrower every year; whereas by being thrown, while it was yet time, on our own resources, we have worked hard and usefully, won friends, reputation, and independence, seen the world abundantly, abroad and at home; in short, have truly lived instead of vegetating."

"I do believe God wanted a grand poem of that man," said George Macdonald of Milton, "and so blinded him that he might be able to write it."

Two of the three greatest epic poets of the world were blind—Homer and Milton—while the third, Dante, was in his later years nearly, if not altogether, blind. It almost seems as though some great characters had been physically crippled in certain respects so that they would not dissipate their energy, but concentrate it all in one direction.

A distinguished investigator in science said that when he encountered an apparently insuperable obstacle, he usually found himself upon the brink of some discovery.

"Returned with thanks" has made many an author. Failure often leads one to success by arousing latent energy, by firing a dormant purpose, by awakening powers which were sleeping. Thousands with great native ability have been lost to the world because they have not had to wrestle with obstacles—to struggle under difficulties sufficient to stimulate into activity their dormant powers.

Poverty and obscurity of origin may impede our progress, but they are not insurmountable obstacles. The can become a stimulus—developing a firmer fibre of mind, a stronger muscle and stamina of body.

During the ten years in which he made his greatest discoveries, Isaac Newton could hardly pay two shillings a week to the Royal Society of which he was a member. Some of his friends wanted to get him excused from this payment, but he would not allow them to act.

As a child, Emerson was unable to read the second volume of a certain book, because his widowed mother could not afford the amount (five cents) necessary to obtain it from the circulating library.

Swedish botanist and taxonomist Carolus Linnaeus was so poor when getting his education, that he had to mend his shoes with folded paper, and often had to beg his meals of his friends.

The Reverend Eliphalet Nott, a pulpit orator, was especially noted for a sermon on the death of Alexander Hamilton, who was shot in a duel by Aaron Burr. Nott was so poor after he entered the ministry that he could not buy an overcoat. His wife sheared their only cosset sheep in January, wrapped it in burlap blankets to keep it from freezing, carded and spun and wove the wool, and made it into an overcoat for him.

When Michelangelo was at work on his colossal bronze statue of Pope Julius II, he was so poor—as we discover in his correspondence now in the British Museum—that he could not have his younger brother come to visit him at Bologna, because he had but one bed in which he and three of his assistants slept together.

"I was always at the bottom of my purse," said great French novelist Émile Zola, when describing the struggles of his early years of authorship. "Very often I had not a sou left, and not knowing, either, where to get one. I rose generally at four in the morning, and began to study after a breakfast consisting of one raw egg. But no matter, those were good times. After taking a walk along the quays, I entered my garret, and joyfully partaking of a dinner of three apples, I sat down to work. I wrote, and I was happy. In winter I would allow myself no fire; wood was too expensive—only on fête days was I able to afford it. But I had several pipes of tobacco and a candle for three sous. A three-sous candle—only think of it! It meant a whole night of literature to me."

When Elias Howe, harassed by want and woe, was in London completing his first sewing-machine, he frequently had to borrow money to live on. He also borrowed money to send his wife back to America. He sold his first machine for five pounds, although it was worth fifty, and then he pawned his letters of patent to pay his expenses home.

A young widow in Philadelphia sat wondering how she could feed and clothe three little ones left dependent by the death of her husband, a naval officer. Happening to think of a box of which her husband had spoken, she opened it, and found therein an envelope containing directions for a code of colored light signals to be used at night on the ocean. The system was not complete, but she perfected it, went to Washington, and induced the Secretary of the Navy to give it a trial. An admiral soon wrote that the signals were good for nothing, although the idea was valuable. For months and years she worked, succeeding at last in producing brilliant lights of different colors. She was paid $20,000 for the right to manufacture them in our navy. Nearly all the blockade runners captured in the Civil War were taken by the aid of the Coston signals, which are also considered invaluable in the Life Saving Service. Mrs. Coston introduced them into several European navies, and became wealthy.

If the seed has to struggle to push its way up through the stones and hard sod, to fight its way up to sunlight and air, and then to wrestle with storm and tempest, with snow and frost, the fibre of its timber will be all the tougher and stronger.

The success that leads to prosperity never waits for opportunities; it makes them. Nor does it wait for facilities or favoring circumstances. It seize upon whatever is at hand, works out the problem, and masters the situation.

"Do you wish to live without a trial?" asks a modern teacher. "Then you wish to die but half a person. Without trial you cannot guess at your own strength. We do not learn to swim on a table. We must go into deep water and buffet the waves. Hardship is the native soil of selfhood and self-reliance. Trials are rough teachers, but rugged schoolmasters make rugged pupils. One who goes through life prosperous, and comes to his grave without a wrinkle, is not half a person. Difficulties are God's errands. And when we are sent upon them we should esteem it a proof of God's confidence. We should reach after the highest good."

Perhaps no one ever battled harder to overcome obstacles which would have disheartened most men than the Greek orator Demosthenes, known as the greatest of Greek orators. He had such a weak voice, and such an impediment in his speech, and was so short of breath, that he could scarcely get through a single sentence without stopping to rest. All his first attempts were nearly drowned by the hisses, jeers, and scoffs of his audiences. His first effort that met with success was against his guardian, who had defrauded him, and whom he compelled to refund a part of his fortune. He was so discouraged by his defeats that he determined to give up forever all attempts at oratory. One of his auditors, however, believed the young man had something in him, and encouraged him to persevere. He accordingly appeared again in public, but was hissed down as before. As he withdrew, hanging his head in great confusion, a noted actor, Satyrus, encouraged him still further to try to overcome his impediment. He stammered so much that he could not pronounce some of the letters at all, and his breath would give out before he could get through a sentence. Finally, he determined to be an orator cost what it might. He went to the seashore and practiced amid the roar of the breakers with small pebbles in his mouth, in order to overcome his stammering, and at the same time accustom himself to the hisses and tumults of his audience. He overcame his short breath by practicing speaking while running up steep and difficult places on the shore. His awkward gestures were also corrected by long and determined drill before a mirror.

Opposition develops in us the very power by which we overcome it. Without opposition, we would never learn to brace, anchor, and fortify ourselves—as the oak is braced and anchored for its thousand battles with the tempests. Our trials, our sorrows, and our griefs develop us in a similar way.

The great men who have lifted the world to a higher level were not developed in easy circumstances, but were rocked in the cradle of difficulties and pillowed on hardships.

The best tools receive their temper from fire, their edge from grinding; the noblest characters are developed in a similar way. The harder the diamond, the more brilliant the lustre, and the greater the friction necessary to bring it out. Only its own dust is hard enough to make this most precious stone reveal its full beauty.

The spark in the flint would sleep forever but for friction; the fire in us would never blaze but for antagonism. The friction which retards a train upon the track, robbing the engine of a fourth of its power, is the very secret of locomotion. Oil the track, remove the friction, and the train will not move an inch. The moment person is relieved of opposition or friction and the track of his or her life is oiled with inherited wealth or other aids, that moment that person often ceases to struggle and therefore ceases to grow.

The huge truck's wheels were sliding uselessly in the mud until someone tossed a shovelful of sand under the heavy wheels—then the truck lumbered on its way. "Friction is a very good thing," remarked an onlooker.

The philosopher Kant observed that a dove might suppose that if only the air were out of the way it could fly with greater rapidity and ease—inasmuch as the only obstacle it has to overcome is the resistance of the air. Yet if the air were withdrawn, and the bird should try to fly in a vacuum, it would fall instantly to the ground unable to fly at all. The very element that offers the opposition to flying is at the same time the condition of any flight whatever.

Nearly every great discovery or invention that has blessed humanity has had to fight its way to recognition, even against the opposition of the most progressive men.

Sir Charles Napier fiercely opposed the introduction of steam power into the Royal Navy. In the House of Commons, he exclaimed, "Mr. Speaker, when we enter Her Majesty's naval service and face the chances of war, we go prepared to be hacked in pieces, to be riddled by bullets, or to be blown to bits by shot and shell. But Mr. Speaker," he added with great emphasis, "we do not go prepared to be boiled alive."

When life wants to educate us, it does not send us to school to the Graces, but to the Necessities.

"I once knew a little colored boy whose father and mother died when be was but six years old," said Frederick Douglass, addressing a school of black students not long before he died. "He was a slave and had no one to care for him. He slept on a dirt floor in a hovel, and in cold weather he would crawl into a meal bag, head foremost, and leave his feet in the ashes to keep them warm. Often he would roast an ear of corn and eat it to satisfy his hunger, and many times he has crawled under the barn or stable and secured eggs which he would roast in the fire and eat.

"That boy did not wear pantaloons, as you do, but a tow-linen shirt. Schools were unknown to him, and he learned to spell from an old Webster's spelling-book, and to read and write from posters on cellar and barn doors, while boys and men would help him. He would then preach and speak, and soon became well known. He became a presidential elector, United States Marshal, United States Recorder, United States Diplomat, and accumulated some wealth. He wore broadcloth, and didn't have to divide crumbs with the dogs under the table. That boy was Frederick Douglass."

"What was possible for me, is possible for you. Don't think because you are colored, you can't accomplish anything. Strive earnestly to add to your knowledge. So long as you remain in ignorance, so long will you fail to command the respect of your fellow-men."

"Galileo with an opera-glass," said Emerson, "discovered a more splendid series of celestial phenomena than any one since with the great telescopes. Columbus found the new world in an undecked boat."

Through the pit and the dungeon, the biblical Joseph came to a throne.

We are not conscious of the mighty cravings of our half divine humanity; we are not aware of the god within us, until some chasm yawns which must be filled, or till the rending asunder of our affections forces us to become conscious of a need.

Two highwaymen chanced once to pass a gibbet. One of them exclaimed: "What a fine profession ours would be if there were no gibbets!" "Tut, you blockhead," replied the other, "gibbets are the making of us; for, if there were no gibbets, every one would be a highwayman." Just so with every art, trade, or pursuit; it is the difficulties that scare and keep out unworthy competitors.

"Success grows out of struggles to overcome difficulties," wrote the great, English motivational author Samuel Smiles. "If there were no difficulties, there would be no success. In this necessity for exertion we find the chief source of human advancement—the advancement of individuals as of nations. It has led to most of the mechanical inventions and improvements of the age."

"Stick your claws into me," said composer Felix Mendelssohn to his critics when entering the Birmingham orchestra. "Don't tell me what you like, but what you don't like."

John Hunter said that the art of surgery would never advance until professional men had the courage to publish their failures as well as their successes.

"Seldom does one reach a position with which he or she has reason to be satisfied," said Dr. Elizabeth Peabody, American educator, lecturer, and founder of one of the first kindergartens in the United States, "without encountering difficulties and what might seem discouragements. But if they are properly met, they are not what they seem, and may prove to be helps, not hindrances. There is no more helpful and profiting exercise than surmounting obstacles."

It was in the Madrid jail that Cervantes wrote *Don Quixote*. He was so poor that he could not even get paper during the last of his writing and had to write on scraps of leather. A rich Spaniard was asked to help him, but the rich man replied: "Heaven forbid that his necessities should be relieved; it is his poverty that makes the world rich."

The prison has roused the slumbering fire in many a noble mind. *Robinson Crusoe* was written in prison. The *Pilgrim's Progress* appeared in Bedford Jail. The *Life and Times* of Baxter, Eliot's *Monarchia of Man*, and Penn's *No Cross, No Crown* were written by prisoners. Sir Walter Raleigh wrote *The History of the World* during his imprisonment of thirteen years. Luther translated the Bible while confined in the Castle of Wartburg.

For twenty years Dante worked in exile, and even under sentence of death. His works were burned in public after his death; but genius will not burn.

Said a great musician of a promising but passionless cantatrice, "If I were single, I would court her; I would marry her; I would maltreat her; I would break her heart; and in six months she would be the greatest singer in Europe."

"He has the stuff in him to make a good musician," said Beethoven of Rossini, "if he had only been well flogged when a boy; but he is spoiled by the ease with which he composes."

We do our best while fighting desperately to attain what the heart covets. Martin Luther did his greatest work, and built up his best character, while engaged in sharp controversy with the Pope. Later in life his wife asks, "Doctor, how is it that whilst subject to Papacy we prayed so often and with such fervor, whilst now we pray with the utmost coldness and very seldom?"

"Drudgery, calamity, exasperation, want, are instructors in eloquence and wisdom," wrote Emerson. "The true scholar grudges every opportunity of action passed by as a loss of power."

As soon as young eagles can fly, the old birds tumble them out and tear the down and feathers from their nest. This rude and rough experience of the eaglet fits it to become the bold king of birds, fierce and expert in pursuing his prey.

Those who are bound out, crowded out, kicked out, usually "turn out," while those who do not have these disadvantages frequently fail to "come out."

Almost from the dawn of history, oppression has been the lot of the Hebrews, yet they have given the world its wisest proverbs, its noble examples of faith, its greatest literature.

In one of the battles of the Crimea a cannon-ball struck inside the fort, crashing through a beautiful garden. From the ugly chasm, however, there burst forth a spring of water which ever afterward flowed a living fountain.

From the ugly gashes which misfortunes and sorrows make in our hearts, perennial fountains of rich experience and new joys often spring.

Don't lament and grieve over lost wealth. The Creator may see something grand and mighty which even He cannot bring out as long as your wealth stands in the way. God may see a rough diamond in you which only the hard hits of poverty can polish. He knows where the richest melodies of your life is and what drill and what discipline are necessary to bring them out.

Many have never found themselves until they have lost their all. Adversity stripped them only to discover them. Obstacles, hardships are the chisel and mallet which shape the strong life into beauty. The statue would have slept in the marble forever but for the blasting, the chiseling, and the polishing. The angel of our higher and nobler selves would remain forever unknown in the rough quarries of our lives but for the blastings of affliction, the chiseling of obstacles, and the sand-papering of a thousand annoyances.

How many people in business have made their greatest strides toward prosperity, have developed their greatest virtues, when the reverses of fortune have swept away everything they had in the world; when disease had robbed them of all they held dear in life?

Many have been ruined into salvation.

At the age of fifteen, famed circus man P.T. Barnum was obliged to buy on credit the shoes he wore at his father's funeral. At fifty years of age, he was ruined—worse than ruined, for he was heavily in debt besides. Yet on the very day of his downfall, he began to rise again, wringing victory from defeat by his indomitable persistence.

"Under different circumstances," says Castelar, "Savonarola would undoubtedly have been a good husband, a tender father, a man unknown to history, utterly powerless to print upon the sands of time and upon the human soul the deep trace which he has left; but misfortune came to visit him, to crush his heart, and to impart that marked melancholy which characterizes a soul in grief, and the grief that circled his brows with a crown of thorns was also that which wreathed them with the splendor of immortality. His hopes were centered in the woman he loved, his life was set upon the possession of her, and when her family finally rejected him, partly on account of his profession, and partly on account of his person, he believed that it was death that had come upon him, when in truth it was immortality."

Adversity exasperates fools, dejects cowards, draws out the faculties of the wise and industrious, puts the modest to the necessity of trying their skill, awes the opulent, and makes the idle industrious. Uninterrupted success and prosperity seldom qualify individuals for usefulness and happiness. Like the storms of the sea, the storms of adversity rouse the faculties, and excite the invention, prudence, skill, and fortitude of the voyager. Those upon whom continuous sunshine falls are like the earth in August: they becomes parched and dry and hard and close-grained.

Beethoven was almost totally deaf and burdened with sorrow when he produced his greatest works. Schiller wrote his best books in great bodily suffering. He was not free from pain for fifteen years. Milton wrote his leading productions when blind, poor, and sick. "Who best can suffer," said he, "best can do."

"Do you know what God puts us on our backs for?" asked. Dr. Payson, smiling, as he lay sick in bed. "No," replied the visitor. "In order that we may look upward." "I am not come to condole but to rejoice with you," said the friend, "for it seems to me that this is no time for mourning." "Well, I am glad to hear that," said Dr. Payson, "It is not often I am addressed in such a way. The fact is I never had less need of condolence, and yet everybody persists in offering it; whereas, when I was prosperous and well, and a successful preacher, and really needed condolence, they flattered and congratulated me."

Not ease, but effort, not facility, but difficulty, makes greatness, success, and prosperity. Toilsome culture is the price of great success, and the slow growth of a great character is one of its special necessities.

This is the crutch age. "Helps" and "aids" are advertised everywhere. Our thinking is done for us. Our problems are all worked out in books whose sole purpose is to render simple the complex. Ingenious methods are used everywhere to get the drudgery out of the college course. Newspapers give us our politics, and preachers our religion. Self-help and self-reliance are getting old fashioned.

Even Nature, as if conscious of our pursuit of delayed blessings, seems to have rushed to our with her wondrous forces—undertaking to do the world's drudgery and emancipate us from Eden's curse. But do not misinterpret her edict. She emancipates from the lower only to call to the higher. She does not bid the world go and play while she does the work. She emancipates the muscles only to employ the brain and heart.

As the sculptor thinks only of the angel imprisoned in the marble block, so Nature cares only for the man or woman shut up in the human being. The sculptor cares nothing for the block as such, and Nature has little regard for the mere lump of breathing clay. The sculptor will chip off all unnecessary material to set free the angel. Nature will chip and pound us remorselessly to bring out our possibilities. She will strip us of wealth, humble our pride, humiliate our ambition, let us down from the ladder of fame, discipline us in a thousand ways, if she can develop a little character. Not ease, not pleasure, not happiness, but character is Nature after. Everything must give way to that: In the strength of character lies the way to success and prosperity.

In 1813, when it was expected that New York would be attacked by British ships, all the boatmen except the young Cornelius Vanderbilt put in bids to convey provisions to the military posts around New York, naming extremely low rates, as the contractor would be exempted from military duty.

"Why don't you send in a bid?" asked his father.

"Of what use?" replied young Vanderbilt. "They are offering to do the work at half price. It can't be done at such rates."

"Well," said his father, "it can do no harm to try for it."

So, to please his father, but with no hope of success, Cornelius made an offer fair to both sides, but did not go to hear the award. When his companions had all returned with long faces, he went to the commissary's office and asked if the contract had been given. "Oh, yes," was the reply. "That business is settled. Cornelius Vanderbilt is the man."

Then, seeing that the youth was apparently thunderstruck, the commissary asked, "What? Is it you?"

"My name is Cornelius Vanderbilt," said the boatman.

"Well," said the commissary, "don't you know why we have given the contract to you?"

"No."

"Why, it is because we want this business done, and we know you'll do it."

Character gives confidence, success, and prosperity.

"Observe yon tree in your neighbor's garden," says Zanoni to Viola, in a novel by the English writer Bulwer. "Look how it grows up, crooked and distorted. Some wind scattered the germ, from which it sprung, in the clefts of the rock. Choked up and walled round by crags and buildings, by nature and man, its life has been one struggle for the light. You see how it has writhed and twisted—how meeting the barrier in one spot, it has labored and worked, stem and branch, towards the clear skies at last. What has preserved it through each disfavor of birth and circumstances—why are its leaves as green and fair as those of the vine behind you, which, with all its arms, can embrace the open sunshine? My child, because of the very instinct that impelled the struggle—because the labor for the light won the light at length. So with a gallant heart, through every adverse accident of sorrow and of fate, to turn to the sun, to strive for the heaven. This it is that gives knowledge to the strong and happiness to the weak."

Those who survive their blighted hopes and disappointments, who take these just for what they are—lessons, and perhaps blessings in disguise—are truly the prosperous.

Only the muscle that is used in effort is developed in beauty.

Twenty Four

THRIFT AND CHARACTER

Benjamin Franklin is one of the most inspiring examples of what the practice of thrift can do. Son of a poor tallow chandler and soap boiler, the fifteenth child in a family of seventeen, he began at the age of ten to earn his living by working in his father's shop. From these humble beginnings he succeeded, entirely by his own efforts, in becoming one of the world's greatest men—a distinguished patriot, scientist, statesman, inventor, diplomat, philosopher, author, and, last but not least, a noted humorist.

All this he accomplished by the practice of thrift. That does not mean merely economy in financial matters, the wisest expenditure of his income, but the wisest expenditure of his time and efforts in all the business of life. For to him thrift meant not only prudence in business and money spending, but the conservation of health, of energy, of life capital, and the utmost development of all his natural resources. As well as being the most thrifty, Franklin was the most generous of men, and would share his last cent with one who needed it.

One of Franklin's favorite maxims—one that he literally lived by himself—was "God helps those who help themselves." And the first lesson for those to learn who wish to help themselves is the one that he constantly taught: Thrift.

Thrift is measured not by the pound but by the penny, not by the dollar but by the cent. Thus any person in receipt of an income or salary, however small, has it within his or her power to practice thrift and to lay the foundation of prosperity.

The word "thrift" in its origin means the grasping or holding fast the things that we have. It implies economy and carefulness, as opposed to waste and extravagance. It involves self-denial and frugal living for the time being, until the prosperity which grows out of thrift permits the more liberal indulgence of natural desires.

One of the primary elements of thrift is to spend less than you earn, to save something however small from the salary received, to lay aside at regular intervals some part of the money earned or made, as provision for the future.

And yet, how many there are who have received a comfortable salary for five or ten years and then suddenly find themselves out of a position and without any money saved up. Quite likely, they blame their luck, instead of looking at the matter with a dispassionate mind and realizing that experience is putting before them, in the most convincing manner, a lesson which they need to learn by heart.

If, instead of bemoaning our "luck" we will listen, a still, small voice will whisper to us of nickels, dimes, and even dollars we foolishly squandered; nickels, dimes, and dollars spent which did not yield their value in enjoyment. Money spent on legitimate pleasures need never be regretted: such pleasures as those which bestow delightful memories that no amount of hardship can deprive one of.

The author knows of a person whose income had unexpectedly been cut off, leaving him quite unprepared. For years he had lived up to the limit of his salary, giving no thought to the future. "Think of it," he remarked, desperately, "had I but saved only ten cents a day for the last fifteen years, and I could have done so without ever missing it, I should now have five hundred and forty-seven dollars and fifty cents, not allowing for, accrued interest! And I might have saved a great deal more than that, without foregoing any real pleasures. It is maddening to think of such folly, and I deserve the hard time I am having."

But perhaps you think that the family of a laboring man could not save ten cents a day without a great deal of self-sacrifice. It is certainly no over-statement of fact to assume that the average workingman in this country might save five cents a day without undergoing deprivations. The amount is too small to be worth while? Let us see.

Suppose that a person should make a vow to put away just five cents a day, each day in the year, and not to touch it for ten years. Do you realize that, at the end of that time, there would be one hundred and eighty-two dollars and fifty cents saved—not counting interest—as a result of putting away an amount so small that he or she would never miss it? Not a king's ransom admittedly, but many enormous fortunes have grown from a smaller capital than this.

And the examples was only five cents a day. What if it were ten cents? Or a quarter? Is there truly anyone who cannot set aside a quarter a day?

The power of small things is one of the most important facts of life, and too much stress cannot be laid upon it. It is absurd and illogical to think that little of pennies, dimes, or quarters, when there can be no tens and hundreds without them.

Here's an analogy: A person alone may be puny and insignificant, but multiplied, he or she constitutes the power which dominates the earth.

Likewise, one penny may seem to you a very insignificant thing. But the small seed is the source from which all fortunes grow—just as it is the tiny acorn from which the great oak grows.

The penny is the seed of that wonderful growth which the best of us cannot help admiring, and for which all of us long: the fortune plant. If you would have one of these wonderful plants for your own, if you dream of sitting at ease under its branches in your old age, go about it in a rational way. From this moment, treat that little disk of copper, with the head of an Indian on one side and "ONE CENT" on the other, with the respect that a fortune seed deserves. Don't scatter and waste seeds so valuable, but plant them in the soil which will foster them—first a savings bank; then a sound investment.

There is hardly anyone who might not become financially independent if he or she would but carefully guard against the little leaks of needless expense. But, unfortunately, this is the one thing which many of us find the hardest to do. Instead of hoarding a small percentage of our receipts, so as to provide against sickness, want of employment, meager retirement or the like, we eat and drink up our earnings as they come, and thus, in the first financial crash many of us are unable to weather the storm. So many of us, by setting aside nothing, by taking what little extra we may have and spending it on some pleasure whose joy is short lived, thus live "from hand to mouth," never keeping more than a day's march ahead of actual want—making ourselves for all our efforts, little better off than slaves.

If you want to make your dreams of a prosperous future come true, you will enter into a pact with yourself to save a certain amount every week from your salary.

"Provided one has some ability and good sense to start with," said Philip D. Armour, "there is no reason why anyone is thrifty, honest, and economical should not accumulate money and attain so-called success in life."

When asked to what qualities he attributed his own success, Mr. Armour said "I think that thrift and economy had much to do with it. I owe much to my mother's training and to a good line of Scotch ancestors, who have always been thrifty and economical."

"Everyone should realize, in starting out, that one can never accumulate money unless one acquires the habit of saving," said Russell Sage. "Even if you can save only a few cents at the beginning, it is better than saving nothing at all. And you will find, as the months go on, that it becomes easier for you to lay by a part of your earnings. It is surprising how fast an account in a savings bank can be made to grow, and those who starts one and keep it up stand a good chance of spending a prosperous old age. Those who spend every cent of their income on their living expenses are always bewailing the fact that they have never become rich. They pick out those who are know to have made a fortune and speak of them as being 'lucky.' There is practically no such thing as luck in business, and those who depend upon it to carry them through are very likely not to get through at all."

"The first thing that one should learn to do," said Andrew Carnegie, "is to save money. By saving money, you promote thrift—the most valued of all habits. Thrift is the great fortune-maker. It draws the line between the savage and the civilized man. Thrift not only develops the fortune, but it develops, also, one's character."

"One should cultivate the habit of always saving something," said the late Marshall Field, "however small one's income." It was by living up to this principle that Mr. Field became the richest and most successful merchant in the world. When asked by an interviewer whom I sent to him on one occasion, what he considered the turning point in his career, he answered, "Saving the first five thousand dollars I ever had, when I might just as well have spent the modest salary I made. Possession of that sum, once I had it, gave me the ability to meet opportunities. That I consider the turning point."

"You may have many friends," said Sir Thomas Lipton, "but you will find none so steadfast, so constant, so ready to respond to your wants, so capable of pushing you ahead, as a little leather-covered book, with the name of a bank on the cover. Saving is the first great principle of success. It creates independence, it gives you standing. It fills you with vigor, it stimulates you with proper energy. In fact, it brings to you the best part of any success—happiness and contentment."

"Economy is wealth." This proverb has been repeated to most of us until we are either tired of it or careless of it. But it is well to remember that a saying becomes a proverb because of its truth and significance.

Professor Marshall, the noted English economist, estimated that $500,000,000 is spent annually by the British working classes for things that did nothing to make their lives nobler or happier.

At a meeting of the British Association, the president, in an address to the economic section, expressed his belief that the simple waste of food alone could well account for the above-mentioned estimate.

It has been estimated that in the United States, the waste from bad cooking alone is over a hundred million dollars a year!

The lack of thrift is one of the greatest curses of modern civilization. Extravagance, ostentatious display, a desire to outshine others, is a vice of our age, and especially of our country. "If you know how to spend less than you get," said Benjamin Franklin, "you have the philosopher's stone." The great trouble with many, however, is that they don't learn to spend less than they get. They do not acquire the saving habit and never find the "philosopher's stone."

John Jacob Astor said it cost him more to get the first thousand dollars than it did afterwards to get a hundred thousand—but that if he had not saved the first thousand, he would have died poor.

The majority of people do not even try to practice self-control; are not willing to sacrifice present enjoyment, ease, for larger future good. They spend their money at the time for transient gratification, for the pleasure of the moment, with little thought for tomorrow, and then they envy others who are more successful, and wonder why they do not get on better themselves. They store up neither money nor knowledge for the future.

Squirrels know that it will not always be summer. They store food for the winter, which their instinct tells them is coming. But multitudes of humans' store nothing, consume everything as they go along, so that when sickness or old age come, there is no reserve, nothing to fall back upon, They have sacrificed their future for the present.

The facility with which loose change slips away insidious. How many of us have not found ourselves wondering aloud at the end of a day, "Where has all the money gone?" We seldom keep any account of it, and rarely restrain a desire. We do not realize that when we fling out a nickel here and a dime there, pay a quarter for this and a quarter for that, that in a week it counts up. And in a year it can amount to a considerable sum—a sum which at the end of the year, during the holiday season, most of us are looking for.

Thrift is not only one of the foundation-stones of a fortune, but also of character. The habit of thrift improves the quality of the character.

There is an noteworthy description the Gospel story of the Prodigal Son. We are told that the younger son "wasted his substance in riotous living." This means more than that he wasted his funds; it implies that he wasted himself.

The most serious aspect of all waste is not the waste of substance, but the waste of self—of one's energy, of one's character, of one's self-respect, which thrift encourages and promotes.

The saving of money usually means the saving of character. It means cutting off indulgences or avoiding vicious habits which are ruinous. It often means health in the place of dissipation.

Furthermore, the saving habit indicates an ambition to get on and up in the world. It develops a spirit of independence, of self-reliance. Saving means hope, it means ambition—a determination to "make good."

A snug little bank account will to your self-respect and self-confidence. You will be able to look the world in the face with assurance that you know that there stands between yourself and want, a little ready money or a safe investment of some kind.

The very consciousness that there is something back of you that will prove a barrier to the wolf which haunts so many human beings, and which is a terror and an efficiency destroyer to so many, will strengthen and buttress you at every point. It will relieve you from worry and anxiety about the future; it will unlock your faculties, release them from the restraint and suppression which uncertainty, fear, and doubt impose, and leave you free to not only do your best work, but to risk taking steps to move ahead.

Among the sworn enemies of thrift may be named going into debt, borrowing money, keeping no itemized account of daily expenditures, and buying on the installment plan.

The temptations to go into debt are increasing rapidly. On every hand we are presented with such advertisements as "Your Credit is Good With Us," "No Payment For 90 days," and the like. And with these inducements come offers of clothing, furniture, and what-not "on easy payments"—easy payments take all the ease and comfort out of life.

Beware, too, of the temptations of buying on the installment plan. There are thousands who buy all sorts of things which they might get along without, because they can pay for them a little at a time—but in this way they keep themselves poor and own possessions whose allure has soon faded.

As far as borrowing money is concerned the bitter experience of countless men and women is crystallized in that old saying: "He that goes a borrowing goes a sorrowing." There is a world of safety for the man who follows Shakespeare's advice: "Neither a borrower nor a lender be."

But let it be remembered that thrift is not parsimony not miserliness. Remember, thrift is first ans foremost a virtuous character trait, and parsimony and miserliness are not admirable traits.

Thrift, as a character trait and means of prosperity is a perpetual protest against putting the emphasis on the wrong thing.

No one should make the mistake of economizing to the extent of planting seeds, and then denying liberal nourishment to the plants that grow from them; of conducting business without advertising; or of saving a little extra expense by pinching on one's table or dress.

"A dollar saved is a dollar earned," but a dollar spent well and liberally is often several dollars earned. And a dollar saved is often very many dollars lost.

Hoarded money is of no more use than gold so inaccessible in the earth that it will never feel the miner's pick.

Imagine everybody in the world stingy, living on the principle of "We can do without that." Or "Our grandfathers got along without such things, so I guess we can, too." We would still be reading by candlelight, traversing the continent on foot or horse, waiting days and weeks to communicate to one another by letter or messenger rather than telephone.

Thrift is the beginning of prosperity and the development of character. The lesson of character development, then, is the lesson of thrift: be not profligate, but be not pinching. For each of us, the balance between those two may well require different measures, different expressions of self-discipline.

You will know when you have reached that balance, because in your character and in your life, you will experience prosperity—the freedom from want; the confidence to do.

Headed with a picture of Benjamin Franklin, a calendar, issued by the Y. M. C. A. in New York had this slogan—"Make Your Money Mean More." Then, it gives the "Ten Commandments for a Young Man's Financial Life."

1. Work and Earn.
2. Make a Budget.
3. Record Your Expenditures.
4. Have a Bank Account.
5. Carry Life Insurance.
6. Own Your Own Home.
7. Make a Will.
8. Pay Your Bills Promptly.
9. Invest in Reliable Securities.
10. Share With Others.

If you "forge these links of success into your character," as the calendar suggests, you will not only develop a self-reliant, vigorous type of manhood or womanhood, but you will also be laying the foundation of enduring prosperity, contentment, and happiness.

I AM. . . .

I am stored-up happiness.

I lead the way to peace, power, and plenty. I bring you freedom from anxiety and worry over the living problem.

I am a friend alike of the rich and the poor.

I am common sense applied to life in all sorts of ways.

I am a tower of strength in youth and a staff in old age.

I increase hope, confidence, assurance, certainty as to the future.

I am the best form of insurance against poverty and failure. I remove the shadow of the poorhouse.

I make for health, for efficiency, for the highest possible welfare of the individual.

I kill that "rainy day" dread; in fact, I do away with the "rainy day" altogether.

I put hope into the heart of a person—light into human eyes that was never there before.

I put people in a position to take advantage of all sorts of opportunities for advancement—to take advantage of chances that, but for me, would be lost.

I make possible a needed vacation, rest, recreation and travel. I mean leisure, more living with natural art and with the beautiful things in the world.

I mean better opportunities for your children, better schools, better clothing, a more refining environment, greater security for their future.

I show you how to make the most of your income; how to expend the margin to the best advantage; how to make the wisest investments of your time, your strength and your ability as well as your money.

I safeguard the future; I enable you to work with confidence, to look up and not down, to rise superior to your surroundings.

I keep thousands of people out of the penitentiary; prevent them from committing theft and other crimes.

I am a symbol of character, of stability, of self-control; a proof that a person is not a victim of his or her appetites and weaknesses, but their master.

I am the enemy of that great curse of humanity—debt—which wrecks multitudes of homes, causes divorce, blasts love, and destroys all peace of mind.

I am that which helps people to lift their heads above the crowd; to be independent, self-reliant, and to stand for something in the world.

Multitudes of families are homeless, moneyless, and are enduring all sorts of hardship, privation, and humiliation because they never took me into partnership.

I am the best friend of woman. I make her a better business woman. I help her to make herself independent, self-reliant, and finance herself.

However you make your living, whether by the work of your hand or of your brain, in a trade or in a profession, at home or in the shop, whether your income be small or large, you will always be placed at a disadvantage, will always be taking chances with your future security and happiness, unless you have me as a working partner.

I am the beginning of real success; that which puts a foundation under your air castles, that which makes your dreams come true, which builds that "home of my own" to which every ambitious person looks forward as the culmination of his or her hopes.

I AM THRIFT.

Twenty Five

FINANCING YOURSELF

There is no other one thing which will mean quite so much to you as learning the art of handling money and knowing how to finance yourself wisely—for on this depends your power to make yourself independent, and, consequently, to do your best work in the world.

Every child should be taught how to handle money, how to save money, how to spend it wisely for personal enlargement and for life enrichment.

Every child should be trained in thrifty habits, should learn the true value of money and should be able to feel the backaches in every dollar. If we do not teach our children to know what money means, how can we expect them to show wisdom in handling money in their maturity?

Sadly, however, when it comes to spending or investing money, the average person, by the time he or she becomes and adult, does not use anything like the good judgment that he or she does in earning it. Multitudes of people live, retired, and die without ever achieving financial independence, without ever having been able to truly support themselves.

I am constantly running across people in middle life or later who have worked hard for many years and tried to get on, but they have nothing to show for it—they have nothing laid by; they have no good, solid investments; they have no ready cash to enable them to avail themselves of opportunities and no good, solid investments. They have never made any headway because they never learned how to finance themselves. They are like the frog in the well, which keeps jumping up only to fall back again to the bottom from where it started.

Money is the slipperiest stuff in the world. The majority of people can't hold on to it any more than they could hold on to an eel or a greased pig. It slips through their fingers and disappears through all sorts of leaks of the pocketbook. Scores of people can *make* money, while only here and there can one person hold on to it.

One of the first steps in financing yourself properly is to keep a personal cash account. This is one of the best educators and teachers of economy and system. If the habit is formed when you are young in years it will never be broken. It will mean a competence in later life when otherwise there would have been none.

The world demands that we each know how to take care of ourselves—how to be independent, self-reliant, finance ourselves wisely, make the most of our incomes.

However you make your living, whether by the work of your hand or of your brain, in a trade or in a profession, at home or in the shop, whether your income be small or large, you will always be placed at a disadvantage, unless you know how to finance yourself successfully. This is not to be stingy, but to know how to make the most out of your income; not to expend the margin you save in silly extravagances or foolish investments.

The tragic consequences of debt, of not being able to finance oneself, should be indelibly impressed upon every one's from childhood on up. It has ruined many of the most promising careers.

If you have not already, begin now to train yourself that under no condition will you be induced to complicate your life by financial obligations. Know that your success in life, the realizing of your ambition, will depend very largely upon keeping your abilities free from any sort of entanglement, and that you must keep this freedom at all costs. Your unencumbered enthusiasm and zeal are precious assets, and nothing will kill these more effectively than the consciousness of being tied hand and foot by the curse of debt. No one can be happy, no matter how optimistic, who is forever in the clutches of poverty, of harassing debt.

Ever remind yourself that to mortgage your future prospects is fatal.

I have known quite a number of promising people to run in debt for automobiles. Many have even mortgaged their homes in order to get an automobile, trying to justify themselves by what it would mean to the health and pleasure of their spouses and children, or to their prestige in the world.

And, yes, quite likely it *would* mean a lot to them. But on the other hand, the purchasing of that which you cannot afford may handicap you—and your family—for years. As the late Marshall Field said, "The present day tendency to live beyond their incomes brings disaster to thousands."

Many people live beyond their means because they cannot bear to have other people think that they cannot afford this and cannot afford that, that they cannot keep up appearances, their social standing. But it is better to be unpopular than to be in a hole.

I AM....

I am your best friend in time of need.

I can do for you what those who love you most are powerless to do without my aid.

I am the oil that smooths the troubled waters of life. I straighten out difficulties and remove obstacles that will yield to nothing else.

I am a supporter of faith, a spur to ambition, a tonic to aspiration, an invaluable aid to people who are struggling to make their dreams come true.

I give you a fine sense of independence, a feeling of security in regard to the future, which increases your strength and ability and enables you to work with more vigor and spontaneity.

I am a stepping-stone to better things; a hope builder; an enemy of discouragement, because I take away one of the greatest causes of worry, anxiety, and fear.

I increase self-respect and self-confidence, and give a feeling of comfort and assurance that nothing else can give. I impart a consciousness of power that makes multitudes, who otherwise would cringe and crawl, hold up their heads and carry themselves with dignity.

I have enabled tens of thousands who made sacrifices to get me to take advantage of splendid opportunities—in self-development as well as business development—which those who did not have me were obliged to let go by.

I increase your importance in the world and your power to do good. I make people think well of your ability, increase their confidence in you; give you standing, capital, an assured position, influence, credit, and many of the good things of life that without me would be unattainable.

I am a shock-absorber for the jolts of life, a buffer between you and the rough knocks of the world.

Millions of households have suffered all sorts of hardships and humiliations because they lacked me, which having me would have saved them so much suffering and misery.

Multitudes have spent their declining years in homeless wretchedness, or eked out a miserable existence in humiliating dependence on the charity of relatives—sometimes grudging—while other multitudes have died in the poorhouse, because they failed to make friends with me in their productive years.

I am one of the most reliable aids in the battle of life, the struggle for independence; ever ready to help you in an emergency in your family, or a crisis in your business. You can always rely on me to step into the breach and do my work quietly, effectively, without bluster.

I AM . . . A LITTLE READY CASH.

Twenty Six

SELF-FAITH AND PROSPERITY

"According to your faith be it unto you" (Mat. 9:29), is just as scientific in the world of affairs as in the world of religion. Whether your ambition be to build up a great business, to accumulate a fortune, to win political power and influence, to make a great name in science—in whatsoever field your bent inclines—a superb faith in yourself is the imperative price.

Most people fail because they lack faith in themselves. They doubt their power to make good. They do not believe enough in themselves, while they believe too much in circumstances and in help from other people. They wait for luck, for outside capital, for a boost, for influence, for a pull, for some one or something outside of them to help them. They depended too much upon everything else but themselves. And now they remain short of their goals because they are not willing to pay the price for what they want, or they haven't the courage to try again.

Self-confidence has ever been the best substitute for friends, pedigree, influence, and money. It is the best capital in the world; it has mastered more obstacles, overcome more difficulties, and carried through more enterprises than any other human quality. It has made more millionaires than any other human force or quality.

If you do not learn to decide firmly and finally and then act on your decision; if you waver and dilly-dally, allow yourself to be carried this way and that by conflicting circumstances, your life ship will always be adrift; you will never be anchored. You will always be at the mercy of storms and tempests, and will never make the port of prosperity.

When someone asks my opinion of his or her chances for success in life, I try to find out something about that person's ability to decide things. If one can do this quickly, firmly, and finally, I am very sure he or she will win out. There is no other one quality which plays such an important part in business careers especially as the ability to decide things wisely, quickly, firmly, and finally.

Those made of winning material do not hesitate and dawdle and waver and balance on the fence. They jump in and tackle the hardest things first—and go through with it.

We are just beginning to learn that we can not only control our moods and all of our thoughts, but that we can also control our immediate circumstances, because our immediate circumstances are largely our objectified thoughts, feelings, emotions, and mental attitude. We make much of our own world by our thoughts, our motives.

As long as you keep your mind positive and creative you will have courage, initiative, and sound judgment—you will be a producer. But the moment you become discouraged and blue, your ability is diminished, your decision wobbles, your judgment is weak and uncertain, and your whole mental kingdom is demoralized. Keep your mind positive by refusing to admit to it such traitors as doubt, discouragement, fear or worry. They are your fatal enemies. You can never succeed while you entertain them. Drive them out. Don't leave the doors of your mind open to them.

Never fear failure; don't visualize it; don't picture poverty or have a horror of it, for this tends to make it a reality and keeps away from you the very things you desire.

It is perfectly possible to make our mentality so vigorously positive that, no matter what conflicting currents or vibrations from other negative, discordant minds strike us, they find no response. Then we are immune to all negativeness; we can walk through all sorts of adverse conditions about us without responding, because we do not vibrate to the negative thought and the negative condition, and we can still keep our robust, positive poise.

Making yourself positive to everybody and everything you contact with in life is what counts. This is the key to mastership, to success and prosperity.

Indeed, it was the ambition to succeed, backed by the "I can and I will" spirit of self-confidence that enabled a poor boy, after repeated and disheartening failures, to give New York City its most beautiful business structure—the Woolworth Building. Foreign architects have pronounced this one of the most beautiful in the world, "a dream in stone."

The man who brought it into being was Frank W. Woolworth. Born on a small farm in New York State, this man had no other heritage than a sound body and the native grit and self-reliance which have carried so many to their goal.

He began his career in a little grocery store, in the corner of a freight shed, owned by the station-master at Great Bend, N. Y. There he acted as grocery clerk and assistant station-master without pay. His first salary in a larger store was $3.50 a week. In spite of persistent hard work for years, disappointment and failures were the only visible results of his efforts. But in spite of desperate poverty, he hung on until fortune smiled, and then he began to establish the Woolworth five-and-ten-cent stores, with the result that before his death, he had built the great Woolworth Building and had over a thousand stores with a capital of $65,000,000, providing employment to many thousands of people.

Henry Ford is another American who started in life with nothing but brain power and a belief in his ability to do the thing he wanted to do. After many ups and downs, working first as a youth on the home farm near Detroit, later as a machinist, and as chief engineer of the Edison Illuminating Company, always plugging away in his spare time, developing the invention on which he began to work as a small boy, his farm tractor, he had passed the age of forty before he made acquaintance with success. Indeed, at forty he was supposed by those who could not gauge his character, his indomitable will, his faith in himself and his power to wring victory from defeat, to be a failure. But he was even then engaged in organizing the Ford Motor Company and well started on the way to the phenomenal success that has made his name and his automobiles known all over the world.

It is those with one hundred per cent of faith—who kill their doubts, strangle their fears, get up every time they fall and push to the front regardless of obstacles—who win out in life.

As long as you live in an atmosphere saturated with failure thought you cannot do the biggest thing possible to you, because you cannot have a hundred per cent of faith—and, remember, that your achievements, your success, will depend upon the percentage of your faith in yourself and in what you are trying to do.

A great many of those who fail in life, or who attain only mediocre positions, keep themselves back by self-depreciation, by a lack of faith in their own powers, the suggestion of their own inferiority. Nothing is more detrimental to success than this sort of mental attitude. It would take the stamina out of a Napoleon. The instant you acknowledge that you are incapable of doing the thing you attempt to do, or that anything can permanently block the way to the goal of your ambition, you set up a barrier to your success that no amount of hard work can remove.

Those can who think they can, holds true in every situation of life.

When some one asked Admiral Farragut if he were prepared for defeat, he said: "I certainly am not. Any man who is prepared for defeat would be half defeated before he commenced."

Dr. William F. Warren, a former president of Boston University, in an address to the students said: "No command or entreaty occurs so many times in the Bible as this emphatic one, 'Fear not!' I once thought to prepare a sermon on it, but it proved too fruitful for me. From Genesis to Apocalypse 'Fear not' seemed an unending refrain. I began to count the occurrences; soon I had twenty, then thirty, then forty, then fifty. Glancing from fifty to seventy I noticed that other words, like those of our Lord, 'Let not your heart be troubled, neither let it be afraid,' meant exactly the same thing; so that my count, however complete, never represents the true total."

Yet there are millions of people in America, in every part of the world, whose minds are constantly filled with the fear of something. From the cradle to the grave, fear throws its shadow over many, marring and stunting vast multitudes of lives, making people wretched, keeping them in poverty and inferiority—even driving many to insanity and death.

Not long ago a girl in New York slipped on an icy pavement and fell to the street. At that moment, an approaching horse-drawn truck passed so close to her that the wheels almost touched her. Terror-stricken at the thought of her danger, the girl imagined that the horses and the truck had actually passed over her. When picked from the street and taken in an ambulance to a nearby hospital, she was raving about the horses and the truck running over her, and finally became insane.

This tragedy was purely the result of imagination, for there was not a scratch of any kind on the girl's body, not even her clothes had been touched. Like the fears and worries that make the lives of so many people wretched failures, the thing that drove away her reason had no reality.

Consider just the fear of poverty. Consider the misery it has caused. Who can ever estimate what havoc this single fear has played in the race history—the fear of coming to want, the torture of visualizing the wolf approaching the door; the agony of possible suffering for our loved ones if we cannot provide for their needs! Oh, this terrible fear of want! We read it in the faces of multitudes of people who never have learned to demonstrate supply, who know nothing of the law of prosperity and never dream that holding in mind this fear of want, this horror of poverty, having the conviction that they are doomed to be poor all their lives, is driving away from them the supply, the opulence they long for. They do not know that it is only by holding the prosperity thought, the thought of abundance; by picturing themselves in connection with limitless supply, visualizing what they want instead of what they don't want, that they will get away from the poverty they hate and connect with the very fountainhead of supply.

How many men and women deplete their strength and thus lessen their earning power by lying awake nights worrying over their business problems, their home problems, the expanding needs of their growing families, and wondering where their supply is coming from! Has this fear and worry ever added to their income, to their health, to their comfort or your happiness?

The great secret of prosperity and of happiness, too, is to have faith; to face life with courage and confidence, and not to anticipate trouble. Yet the majority of us don't face life in the right way; we fear and worry. The Public Health Service in Washington realizing this, and knowing the evil effects of such a mental attitude in breeding nervous diseases and other life stranglers, once issued a bulletin in which was written the following:

> So far as is known, no bird ever tried to build more nests than its neighbor. No fox ever fretted because he had only one hole in which to bide. No squirrel ever died of anxiety lest he should not lay by enough nuts for two winters instead of for one, and no dog ever lost any sleep over the

fact that he did not have enough bones laid aside for his declining years.

Might we not, then, take a lesson from what we call the "lower animals" in not worrying about our future supply, which is one of the chief sources of our anxiety.

"But," we say in response, "they cannot reason."

But that is not the message. The message is that even amidst the most dire drought and famine, the animals continue to venture forward in hope, until every resource is exhausted, while we so quickly lose the hope the faith, that the Christ so constantly tried to implant in his disciples:

> Therefore take no thought [that is, be not anxious], saying What shall we eat? or What shall we drink? or, Wherewithal shall we be clothed? . . . For your heavenly Father knoweth that ye have need of all these things. . . . Take therefore no thought for the morrow; for the morrow shall take thought for the things of itself. Sufficient unto the day *is* the evil thereof. (Mat. 6:31)

Now, the man or the woman who is constantly afraid of some impending evil, always dreading, anticipating something that will work to his or her injury, or who is worrying about something that has already happened, is lacking in the most essential character and success elements—courage, self-confidence, and faith in the great within of themselves, which makes them greater than anything that can happen to them.

Worry, anxiety, lack of faith, self-depreciation, timidity, lack of self-confidence, these are all expressions of fear, and cannot exist in your mind for a moment in the presence of the courage, thought, the mental suggestion of fearlessness, self-confidence, self-reliance. Instead of picturing trouble and misfortune ahead, brooding over the difficulties that confront you, and fearing you will never be able to get past them, flood your mind with triumphant thoughts, with the thought of the power that is stored in the great within of you, always wanting to be used, always more than a match for the giant fear that tries to frighten you with scarecrows, with unrealities that most often have no existence outside of your troubled imagination.

You will find it a great help in driving out fear and worry to express strong, courageous sentiments aloud. The next time that something which you feel is holding you back whispers to you, "Don't do that; you'll make a fool of yourself. Many a stronger, abler man than you are has failed in trying to do that same thing. Many with more ability, in more favorable circumstances, with more influence, and with outside help, have failed in the ambitious undertaking you are going to attempt, poor and ill-equipped as you are. You had better be careful; make sure that you are going to succeed before you begin"—don't listen to the evil thing, for it is fear that is whispering to you. And it is lying as it has lied to millions who came before you, as it will lie to millions who come after you. Those who listen to it will never enter into their birthright of peace, power, harmony, success, and abundance.

It makes a great difference whether you go into a thing to win, with clenched teeth and resolute will; whether you are prepared at the very outset to make your fortune, to succeed in your business or profession, to put through the thing you have set your heart on—or whether you start in with the idea that you will begin and work your way along gradually, and continue if you do not find too many obstacles, but that if all doesn't go well there is always a way to back out. To go into a thing determined to win, to feel that self-assurance, that inward sense of power that makes one master of the situation, is half the battle; while, on the other hand, to be prepared for defeat; to anticipate it is, just as Admiral Farragut said, to be half defeated before one commences. You must burn all your bridges behind you, leaving no temptation to retreat when things look uncertain ahead.

All the people who have done and are doing big things in the world not only had the faith which does the "impossible" but they have been exacting trainers of themselves. They do not handle themselves with kid gloves. They hold themselves right up to stern discipline. They do not allow dawdling, idling; they put a ban on laziness, indifference, vacillation; they fix their eye on the goal and sacrifice everything which interferes with their ambition, everything which stands in the way of the larger success. They know that the person who is too enamored of the easy chair, who thinks too much of comfort and ease, of good times with companions in the evenings, who thinks too much of the pleasures of the senses, will never get anywhere.

There is no possible way of defeating a human being who is victory organized. If he or she has the faith that moves mountains, has winning stuff within, he or she is going to win, no matter what stands in the way. There is no holding such people down, because, in addition to their unswerving belief in themselves, they are ready to pay to the last cent the price that even the most gifted must pay for success.

Nothing can be denied to you if you are willing to pay the price for it. Only your own inertia, your own lack of faith in yourself, your own lack of push and determination, can thwart your ambition. Your longings are the proofs that you can back them up with realities.

Faith makes light of obstacles, because it increases ability and multiplies power. Joan of Arc multiplied herself ten thousand times by her faith; multiplied her ability a million times by her conviction that she was God-ordained to restore the throne of France and drive the enemy from her soil. She was ready to make any sacrifice to save her country—and every sacrifice she made, every obstacle she overcame, made her stronger to accomplish the great task she had undertaken.

"But wilt though know . . . that faith without works is dead?" (James 2:20).

Without work we know that faith is of no avail. Everything depends on the "hustle" with which we back it. The only real power one ever gains is won in the struggle to overcome obstacles. It is the effort of brain and muscle put forth in the actual doing of the thing, the downright hard working, the vigorous thinking and planning that make the strong individual—the one who reaches the goal of his or her ambition.

It was everlasting hustling, added to his indomitable self-confidence that made Alfred Harmsworth, now Lord Northcliffe, one of the wealthiest men in England, and one of the most successful publishers in the world. In an interview he said, "I feel that whatever position I have attained is due to focusing my energies and time. When I went into journalism I made up my mind that I would master the business of editing and publishing. This is a vast specialty, but then I was very young and had a good deal of self-confidence." This self-confidence was one of his most marked characteristics even as a boy. When only fifteen, while attending an English grammar school, he started a little school paper in which he said: "I have it on the best authority that this paper is to be a marked success." And a marked success it proved. At twenty-three, Harmsworth started in the regular publishing business with a little weekly called *Answers to Correspondents*, increasing its circulation to over a million in five years. Before he had reached the age of thirty he was a millionaire publisher and at forty-three, he was the head of the largest publishing business in the world—a publishing business whose newspaper campaigns had a significant influence in England's activities in Word War I.

We get in this life whatever we concentrate upon with all our might and main. Our success or failure is in our own hands. Many who are complaining that the door to success is locked and barred against them because they are too poor to get an education, or they have no one to help them to get the position they desire, are in actuality not succeeding, not getting the thing they want, because they are not willing to make the necessary effort to succeed. They are not willing to do the hard work. They may have faith in their ability, but they aren't exerting the unwavering energy to put the ability to work and make it do things for them. They want someone else to do the pushing, to make things happen for them—but no one ever climbed to success on another's back. Each of us must hustle, make things happen ourselves, or fail.

Joseph Pulitzer, a young boy who came to America from Germany, was so poor when he landed he had to sleep on the benches in City Hall Park, New York, in front of the space now occupied by the World Building, which he built later. This poor youth had so much faith and so much energy that he made millions out of a paper which was pretty nearly a failure in the hands of the people from whom he bought it.

No matter how humble your position, though you be but a section hand on a railroad, a street cleaner, a day laborer or a messenger boy, if you have faith in yourself, in your vision, and back up your faith with hard work, nothing can keep you from realizing your vision. A fortune is accumulated by the same means that makes one a successful musician, or politician, or inventor: faith and persistent work.

Faith and work have magic in them. It is faith that leads the way in all undertakings. It is the divine faculty which connects a person with the great Source of all supply, the Source of all intelligence, the Source of all power, of all possibilities. If you have faith—one hundred per cent faith in yourself, in your life work, in anything you undertake—and you back your faith with equal tenacity in your work, you cannot fail. You cannot help but be prosperous

I AM. . . .

I am that which is back of all achievement, which has led the way to success, to happiness, through the ages.

I crossed an unknown ocean with Columbus, who without me would never have discovered America.

I was with Washington at Valley Forge; and but for me he would not have succeeded in liberating the American colonies and making them a nation.

I went through the Civil War with Lincoln, and guided his pen when he wrote the Emancipation Proclamation that freed millions of human beings from slavery.

I was with the English patriots who forced King John to sign that great charter of human rights—the Magna Charta.

I was back of those who signed the American Declaration, of Independence.

I crossed the ocean with Cyrus W. Field fifty times before his great undertaking, the ocean cable, was perfected. I was on the ship with him when the cable parted in mid-ocean, after the first message had passed over it, and gave him courage to persist when the work had to be done all over again.

I am the locksmith who can unlock all doors, whom no obstacle can hold back, no difficulty or disaster dishearten, no misfortune swerve from my purpose.

I am a friend to the down-and-outs, the unfortunates, those to whom life has been a great disappointment. If these people would take hold of me I would turn them around so that they would face their goal and go toward it instead of turning their back on it and going in the opposite direction; they would face the sun and let the shadows fall behind instead of in front of them.

I am a booster, an optimist, one who always sees something of hope in every human being, for I know that there is a God in every one; that men and women are gods in the making; that they are all capable of doing infinitely more, infinitely better things, than they have yet done.

No matter how bad the conditions which confront me, I wear a smile, for I know that the sun is always behind the clouds and that after a time the storm will pass and the sun will shine again.

I see triumph beyond temporary defeat. I look past obstacles which discourage most people, for I know that obstacles become smaller as one approaches them; and experience has shown me that but a very small fraction of the things which people dread, fear, and worry about ever happen.

If you know me, if you believe in me, work with me, cling to me, no matter how full of failures and disappointments your past has been, I will help you to overcome adverse conditions and I will crown you with success, for I conquer all difficulties.

I AM FAITH.

Twenty Seven

"TIME IS MONEY" . . . AND MUCH MORE

I have never known of anyone to make life worthwhile in any direction until he or she came to the realization of the immense value of time. Time is our most precious asset, our greatest riches; because in it lives our success, our happiness, our destiny.

Yet multitudes are engaged in killing time. Their chief aim in life is to fritter it away as rapidly as possible. They do not realize that this is infinitely more wasteful than it would be for a rich man to throw hundred dollar bills or valuable diamonds into the sea.

One's success can be gauged quite accurately by the value he or she puts upon time, especially spare time.

"I have in my time known many famous in war, in statesmanship, in science, in the professions, and in business," said the late U.S. Senator Hoar of Massachusetts. "If I were asked to declare the secret of their success, I should attribute it, in general, not to any superiority of natural genius, but to the use they made, after the ordinary day's work was over, of the hours which other's throw away or devote to idleness, or rest, or society. The great things in this world have been done by individuals of ordinary, natural capacity who have done their best. They have done their best by never wasting their time."

The only reason why many remain common, ordinary employee, doing routine work and drawing a small salary, is not because they don't have the ability to rise higher, but because they are not awake to the possibilities in their spare time.

"One is so tired after a day's work one does not feel like studying," is an excuse often urged by many when reminded that they are not doing anything to advance themselves. It is only the excuse of those who lack the ambition to climb—and then point to others who have used their time well as having more "luck."

In fact, it is well known that a change of occupation in the evening—the bringing into play of a different set of muscles, brain tissues, ideas, and thoughts—generally rests rather than tires one. Of course every one should allot a proper amount of time for needed recreation, exercise and rest; but very often those who claim they are too tired to study evenings waste more energy in foolish dissipation or dawdling aimlessly around doing nothing than they would spend in reading or study.

Only a short time ago I read of a young school teacher who learned six or seven languages in her spare time, and who managed, by earning some extra money evenings in teaching private pupils, to save enough money to go to Europe and perfect herself in these languages. The enjoyment and breadth of culture she got out of her travels in the different European countries would no doubt have been a great reward for the sacrifices she made; but she got much more than that, for she advanced rapidly in her profession, and is now an instructor in French, German, and Italian in a high school for girls.

There is no magic which can give a person a golden future who is allowing wasted hours to enter into the fabric of the day. Persevering in the pursuit of self-improvement in your spare time is the ingredient required to make your future golden—to bring you wealth, knowledge, wisdom, power, fame . . . whatever you set your heart on.

If you would succeed in any adequate way, in a way at all commensurate with your possibilities, you must not only shut off all time leaks, but you must also repair every leak in your mental and physical system, and stop every output of energy that does not tell in rendering you more fit to make your life the great success it is possible for you to make it.

How often we are reminded of the value of time by the expression, "Time is money." But time is more than money, it is life itself—for in each separate moment it flies away, it takes with it a part of our life span.

Time is opportunity. Time represents your success capital, your achievement possibilities. Everything you hope for, everything you dream of accomplishing, is dependent on it.

"Short as life is," said Victor Hugo, "we make it still shorter by the careless waste of time."

Put that sentence up on the wall over your desk or work bench, where it will constantly remind you of the immense possibilities stored in the minutes and hours of every single day. Resolve to make good every minute of every day and live up to your resolution—and nothing will then be able to keep you from not only being a successful man or woman, but a superb character.

You are the architect of your fate, the master of your destiny, and right now you are shaping your future. Every day is a step nearer to, or farther from, the goal of your ambition. The precious hours of your days are invaluable. The realization of all your dreams lives in them.

No matter how limited your time, or how exacting your daily work, you can cultivate yourself by reading and study in your spare moments and give yourself an infinitely greater earning capacity.

The bigger the person, the greater value they put upon time. They regard it as a great asset, as the most precious capital which can enrich life. Whether their ambition is to acquire a fortune or to achieve success in some other direction, they know that everything depends on what they do with their spare time.

Others, on the other hand, never regard time as a precious asset until it is too late. They cannot resist the lure of pleasure, and so postpone the pursuit of their ambition. They practice no more thrift in the use of their time than they do in the use of their money. They kill a lot of time without realizing that in doing this they are killing their prospects, killing their future, killing themselves.

When you awake in the morning, when you start to work, and many times during the day, say to yourself: "I will make this day worth while." If you do this every day you will be surprised at the wonderful effect it will have upon your whole life. It will lift it to the highest point of your possible efficiency and effectiveness. It will mean everything to you both in character and financial returns.

Each of us has the same number of hours in the day, the same number of days in the year. The chief difference between the success and the failure lies in the use to which the hours in those days are put.

It is what we put into the passing moment, just that and nothing more, that makes up all of life, all of character, all of success. The harvest of our tomorrows will be like the seed we sow today. If we do not put that quality into the present moment which we expect in our success, in our character, in our life as a whole, it will not be there. If there is not energy, initiative, and industry in your today, the results of these cannot appear in your future. It is the daily goal to not to let the hours slip through one's fingers until one has wrung from them their utmost possibility, that makes the successful day. And it is the accumulation of such daily successes that enables us to realize our ambitions.

Twenty Eight

MAKING YOUR DREAMS COME TRUE

Washington, in a letter written when he was but twelve years old, said: "I shall marry a beautiful woman; I shall be one of the wealthiest men in the land; I shall lead the army of my colony; I shall rule the nation which I help to create."

General Grant, in his *Memoirs*, says that as a boy at West Point, he saw General Scott seated on his horse, reviewing the cadets, and something within him said, "Ulysses, some day you will ride in his place and be general of the army."

Every one knows how those boyish visions were realized by the mature men.

The late J. Pierpont Morgan's fortune was built largely by the dynamic forcefulness of his thought, of his mental visualizing, the nursing of his youthful visions. He was a man of varied and aesthetic tastes, but he concentrated upon finance and he became the world's master in its science.

Ancient Greece concentrated on beauty and art, and she became the great beauty model and art teacher of the world. The Roman Empire concentrated upon power—and became mistress of the world. England concentrated on the control of the seas and commerce, and she became the ruler of the seas and the greatest commercial nation in the world.

Whatever you concentrate upon you tend to get, because concentration is just as much of a force as is electricity. The person who concentrates upon law, thinks law, dreams law, reads everything he or she can get hold of relating to law, steals into courts listens to trials at every chance he gets, is sure to become a lawyer.

It is the same with any other vocation or art—medicine, engineering, literature, music; any of the arts or sciences. Those who concentrate upon an idea, who continue to visualize their dreams, to nurse them, who never lose sight of their goal, no matter how dark or forbidding the way, get what they concentrate on. They make their minds powerful magnets to attract the thing on which they have concentrated. Sooner or later they realize their dreams.

If you can concentrate your thought and hold it persistently, work with it along the line of your greatest ambition, nothing can keep you from its realization. But spasmodic concentration, spasmodic enthusiasm, however intense, will peter out. Dreaming without effort will only waste your power. It is holding your vision, together with persistent, concentrated endeavor on the material plane, that wins.

There are thousands of devices in the patent office in Washington which have never been of any use to the world, simply because the inventors did not cling to their vision long enough to materialize it in perfection. They became discouraged. They ceased their efforts. They let their visions fade, and so became demagnetized and lost the power to realize them. Other inventors have taken up many such "near" successes, added the missing links in their completion and have made them real successes,

Everywhere there are disappointed men and women who have soured on life because they could not get what they longed for—a musical or art education, the necessary training for authorship, for law or medicine, for engineering, or for some other vocation to which they felt they had been called. They are struggling along in an uncongenial environment, railing at the fate which has robbed them of their own. They feel that life has cheated them, when the truth is they have cheated themselves. They never got the spindle and distaff ready that would have drawn to them the flax for the spinning of a happy and complete life web. They did not insistently and persistently send out their de- sires and longings; they did not nurse them and positively refuse to give them up; above all, they did not put forth their best efforts for their realization.

Three things we must do to make our dreams come true:

Visualize our desire;

Concentrate on our vision;

Work to bring it into the actual.

The implements necessary for this are inside of us, not outside. No matter what the accidents of birth or fortune, there is only one force by which we can fashion our life material: mind.

Of two boys or two girls in the same wretched environment, one picks up an education, trains himself or herself for place and power, while the other grows up a nobody. It is all in the boy or the girl. Each has similar material to work in. One transmutes it into gold; the other into lead.

Two sailors force the same breeze to send their boats in opposite directions. It is not the wind, but the set of the sail that determines the port.

The power that makes our desire, our vision, a reality is not in our environment or in any condition outside of us, it is within us.

There is some unseen, unknown, magnetic force developed by a long-continued concentration of the mind upon a cherished desire that draws to itself the reality which matches the desire. We cannot tell just what this force is that brings the thing we long for out of the cosmic ether and objectifies it, shapes it to correspond with our longing. We only know that it exists. The cosmic ether everywhere surrounding us is full of undreamed of potencies and the strong, concentrated mind reaches out into this ether, this sea of intelligence, attracts to it its own, and objectifies the desire.

All human achievements have been pulled out of the unseen by the brain, through the mind reaching out and fashioning the wealth of material at its disposal into the shapes which matched the wishes, the desires, of the achievers.

All the great discoveries, great inventions, great deeds that have lifted us up from our animal existence have been wrought out of the actual by the perpetual thinking of and visualizing of these things by their authors. These grand characters clung to their vision, nursed it until they became mighty magnets that attracted out of the universal intelligence the realization of their dreams.

Most revolutionary inventions have evolved from a flash of thought. The sewing machine, for example, started with a simple idea, which the inventor held persistently in his mind until through his efforts the idea materialized into the concrete reality. Elias Howe used to watch his wife making garments, sewing, sewing far into the night, and it set him thinking, questioning whether such: drudgery was really necessary. As he watched her busy needle fly back and forth, he began to wonder if this same work which it took his wife so long to do could not be done with less labor and in half the time by some sort of mechanical contrivance. He kept nursing his idea, thinking what a splendid thing it would be if some one could relieve millions of women from this toil, which frequently had to be done at night after a day of hard work. He began to experiment with crude devices, clinging to his vision through poverty and the denunciation of friends, who thought the man must be crazy to spend his time on "such a fool idea." But at last his vision materialized into a marvelous reality, a perfected machine which emancipated the world from infinite drudgery.

The idea of the telephone was flashed into the mind of Professor Alexander Bell by the drawing of a string through a hole in the bottom of a tin can, by means of which he found that the voice could be transmitted. The idea took such complete possession of the inventor that it robbed him of sleep and, for a time made him poor. But nothing could rob him of his vision or prevent him from struggling to work it out of the visionary stage into the actual

I lived near Professor Bell, in the next room, indeed, while he worked on his invention. I saw much of his struggle with poverty, heard the criticisms and denunciations of his friends, as he persisted in his visionary work until the telephone became a reality—a reality without which modern life could not be conducted.

All of Edison's inventions, those of every inventor, have been wrought out on the same principle that gave us the sewing machine and the telephone. They all started in simple ideas, in dream visions which were nursed and worked into actualities.

The brain cells grow in response to desire. Where there is no desire there is no growth. The brain develops most in the direction of the leading ambition, where the mental activities are the most pronounced. The desire for a musical career, for instance, develops he musical brain cells. Business ambition develops that part of the brain which has to do with business, the cells which are brought into action in executive management, in administering affairs, in money making. Wherever we make our demand upon the brain by desire that part responds in growth.

For years a poor country boy builds air castles of his future. He visualizes the great mercantile establishment over which he is to preside. The ridicule of his family and of young companions cannot daunt him or blur the bright vision he sees away in the distance. He continues to nurse his vision, and behold, out of the unknown, unexpected resources come, and soon he finds himself an office boy in a great mercantile house in the city of his dreams. He watches everything with an eagle eye; he absorbs information and ideas; he is alert, active, energetic, resourceful, and in a few months he is promoted, and then again, promoted. He attracts the attention of the head of the establishment, who calls him into his private office, tells him that he has had his eye on him for many months and that he believes he is the youth he has been looking for to manage the business. He gives him a little stock; the business prospers still further under his management, and in a few years the new manager is made a full partner in the house which he entered as an office boy. This is the flowering out of his dream, the objectifying of his vision, the matching with reality his youthful longings. His brain has been continually developing along the line of his vision, drawing to him the material to make it real.

A poor girl, the daughter of humble people in Maine who thought that to become a public singer was an unforgivable sin, could not in the beginning see any possible way to realize the dreams she held in secret, but she kept visualizing her dream, nursing her desire and doing the only thing for its realization her parents would allow—singing in a little church choir. Gradually the way opened, and one step led to another until the little Maine girl became the famous Madame Nordica, one of the world's greatest singers.

No matter, if you are a poor girl away back in the country, and see no possible way of leaving your poor old father and mother in order to prepare for your career, don't let go of your desire. Whether it be music, art, literature, business or a profession, hold to it. No matter how dark the outlook, keep on visualizing your desire and light and opportunity will come to enable you to make it a reality. Whatever the Creator has fitted you to do He will give you a chance to do, if you cling to your vision and struggle as best you can for its attainment.

Think of the Lillian Nordicas, the Lucy Stones, the Louisa Alcotts, the Mary Lyons, the Dr. Anna Howard Shaws, the thousands of women who were hedged in just as you are, by poverty or forbidding circumstances of some sort, yet succeeded in spite of everything in doing what they desired to do, in being what they longed to be. Take heart and believe that God has given you also "all implements divine to shape the way" to your soul's desire

If you are a boy on a farm and feel that you are a born engineer, yet see no possible way to get a technical education, don't lose heart or hope. Get what books you can on your specialty. Cling to your vision. Push out in every direction that is possible to you. It may take years, but if you are true to yourself your concentration on your desire, your pushing toward it, will open a door into the light and before you know it you will be on the road to your goal.

Washington, Lincoln, Faraday, Edison—the men who have done so much, had to struggle as hard as you are struggling to attain their hearts' desires. And today, the opportunities are ten to one to what they were one hundred, or fifty, or even twenty-five years ago. The great danger in our time is not lack of chance or opportunity but of losing our vision, of letting our ambition die.

Most of us instead of treating our desires seriously, trifle with them as though they were only to be played with, as though they never could be realities. We do not believe in their divinity. We regard our hearts' longings, our souls' yearnings, as fanciful vagaries, romances of the imagination. Yet we know that every invention, every discovery or achievement that has blessed the world began in a desire, in a longing to produce or to do a certain thing, and that the persistent longing was accompanied by a struggle to make the mental picture a reality.

It is difficult for us to grasp the fact that ambition, accompanied by effort, is actually a creative power which tends to realize itself. Our minds are like that of the doubting disciple, who would not believe that his Lord had risen until he had actually thrust his finger into the side which had been pierced by a cruel spear. Only the things that we see seem real to us when, as a matter of fact, the most real things in the, world are the unseen.

We never doubt the existence of the force that brings the bud out of the seed, the foliage and the flower out of the bud, the fruits, and vegetables from the flower. It is invisible. We cannot sense it, but we know that it is mightier than anything we see. No one can see or hear or feel the force of gravity, or the forces which balance the earth and whirl it with lightning speed through space, bringing it round its orbit without a variation of the tenth of a second in a century, yet who can doubt their reality? Does any one question the mighty power of electricity because it cannot be seen or heard or smelled?

The potency of our desires of our soul longings, when backed by the effort to make them realities, is just as real as is that of any of the unseen forces in Nature's great laboratory. The great cosmic ether is packed with invisible potentialities. Whatever comes out of it to you comes in response to your call. Everything you have accomplished in life has been a result of a psychic law which, consciously or unconsciously, you have obeyed.

Do not make the mistake of thinking that the way will not open because you cannot now see any possible means of achieving that for which you long. The very intensity of your longing for a certain career, to do a certain thing, is the best evidence that you have the ability to match it, and that this ability was given you for a purpose, even to play a divine, a magnificent part in the great universal plan. The longing is merely the forerunner of achievement. It is the seed that will germinate if nurtured by effort.

If, however, you stop at sowing the seed you will get just about as much harvest as a farmer would get if he should sow his seeds without preparing the soil, without fertilizing or cultivating it or keeping down the weeds. It is the blending of the practical with the ideal that brings the harvest from the seed thought. You must keep on struggling toward your ideal. No matter how dark and forbidding the way ahead of you, just imagine you are carrying a lantern which will advance with you and give light enough for the next step. It is not necessary to see to the end of the road. All the light you need is for the next step. Faith in your vision and persistent endeavor will do the rest. If you do your part, faith in having an appointed place in the plan of the universe will bring things out better than you can plan or even imagine.

Send out your wishes, cherish your desires, force out your yearnings, your heart longings with all the intensity and persistency you can muster, and you will be surprised to see how soon they will begin to attract their affinities, how they will grow and take tangible shape, and ultimately become actual things. Fling out your desires into the cosmic ether boldly with the utmost confidence. Therein you will gather the material which shall build into reality the castle of your dreams.

The trouble with us is that we are afraid to do this. We fear that fate will mock us, cast back to us our mental visions empty of fruition. We do not understand the laws governing our thought forces any more than we understand the laws governing the universe. If we had faith in their power, our earnest thoughts and efforts would germinate and bud and flower just as does the tiny seed we put into the earth.

Think how the seed must be tended and nurtured before it will give forth the new life. See how the delicate bud has to be coaxed by the sun and air for many weeks or months before it pushes its head up through the tough sod to the light. Suppose it were afraid to make the attempt and, should say: "It is impossible for me to get out of this dark earth. There is no light here. I am so tender the slightest pressure will break me and stop my growth forever. The only way out of my prison is to push up through this tough sod, and it would take a tremendous force to do that. I would be crushed, strangled, before I got half way through."

But the sun beckons, coaxes, encourages. The bud is moved into attempting the "impossible," and behold, soon it rears its tender head above what could otherwise be considered the great enemy of its progress. And then, the dark sod, the very thing which appeared to make its future impossible, becomes its support and strength. The very struggle to get up through the soil has strengthened its fiber and fitted it to cope with the elements above, with the storms it must meet.

Just like this tender plant, you may be hemmed in by seemingly insurmountable obstacles; you may not see a ray of light through the sod of hard, forbidding circumstances. Hold your vision and keep pushing. In your struggle you will develop strength, you will find sunshine and air, growth and life. You may be shut in by an uncongenial occupation and tempted to lose heart and give up your dreams because you can see no way to better yourself. This is just the time to cling to them, and to insist that they shall come true. Without knowing it you may be just in the middle of the sod, and if you keep pushing where you are, in season and out of season, you will come to the sunlight and the air, to freedom.

There is no human being who doesn't have some sort of a chance. If your present position cramps you; if it does not give you room to express yourself, you can make room by filling it to overflowing, by doing your work as well as it can be done, by keeping your mind steadfastly fixed on the ladder of your ascent. In your mind you make the stairs by which you ascend or descend. Nobody else can do it for you. The master key which will unlock that cruel door that keeps you back is not in the hand of fate. You are fashioning it by your thoughts.

Your next step is right where you are, in the thing you are doing today. The door to something better is always in the duty of the moment: The spirit in which you do your work, the energy which you throw into it, the determination with which you back up your ambition—these, no matter what opposes, are the forces that unlock the door to something better. If you hold to your vision and are honest, earnest and true, there is nothing that can stand in the way of its realization.

I have never known a person who was dead-in-earnest in his efforts to gain his or her heart's desire who has not finally reached the goal. No great, insistent, persistent, honest longing backed by downright hard, conscientious work ever comes back empty-handed.

Desire is at the bottom of every achievement. We are the product of our desires. What we long for, strive for, the vision we nurse, is our great life shaper, our character molder.

Very few can realize the close coordination which exists between their visions, their mind pictures, and the actual accomplishments of their career. If I were asked to name the principal cause of the majority of failures in life I should say it was the failure to understand this, to grasp the relation of thought to accomplishment. The gradual fading out of one's dreams, the losing of one's vision, may be traced to this cause.

When we first start out in life we are enthusiasts. Our vision is bright and alluring and we feel confident we are going to win out, that we shall do something distinctive, something individual, unusual. But after a few setbacks and failures we lose heart, and faith in our vision dies. Then we gradually awaken to the fact that our ambition is beginning to deteriorate. It is not quite as sharply defined as formerly. Our ideals are a trifle dimmed, our longings a trifle less insistent. We try to find reasons and excuses for our lagging efforts and waning enthusiasm. We think it may be due to over-work—because we are tired and need a rest, or because our health is not quite up to standard—and that, by and by our former intense desire to realize our dreams will return. But the whole process is so insidious that before we realize it our fires, for lack of fuel, are quite burned out. Our grip on our vision was not strong enough. We did not half understand its mighty power, when firmly and persistently kept in mind, to help us to our goal.

What we get out of life depends very largely on fidelity to our visions. If we believe in them, we will not let them die for lack of nursing. If we really have ability to match them, and are not self-deceived by egotism, petty vanity, and conceit, then no misfortunes, no failure of plans, no discouragements, no obstacles—nothing in the world—can separate us from them. We will cling to them to our dying day.

The world stands aside for such a one who believes in his or her vision, who consecrates himself or herself without reserve to its fulfillment. People know there is something back of the dreamers who have such faith in their life dreams that they will sacrifice everything to make them come true.

How much of a grip has your vision on you? Does it clutch you with a force that nothing but death can relax, or does it hold you so lightly that you are easily separated from it, discouraged from trying to make it real?

Constant discouragements are a great temptation to abandon one's life dreams, to drop one's standards. One's vision is apt to become blurred in passing through great crises, in periods of general depression, in times of financial stress, but this is really the test of a strong character—that obstacles are not allowed to divert one from one's aim. Those who are made of the stuff that wins, hang on to their vision, even to the point of starvation, for they know that there is only one way of bringing it down to earth, and that is by clinging to it through storm and stress, in spite of every obstacle and discouragement.

Never mind what discouragements, misfortunes or failures come to you, let nobody, no combination of unfortunate circumstances, destroy your faith in your dream of what you believe you were made to do. Never mind how the actual facts seem to contradict the results you are after. No matter who may oppose you or how much others may abuse and condemn you, cling to your vision, because it is sacred. It is the God-urge in you. You have no right to allow it to fade or to become dim. Your final success will be measured by your ability to cling to your vision through discouragement. It will depend largely upon your stick-to-it-ive-ness, your bulldog tenacity. If you shrink before criticism and opposition you will demagnetize your mind and lose all the momentum which you have gained in your previous endeavor. Keep working, keep visualizing your life dream, and some unexpected way will surely open for its fulfillment.

Put out of your mind forever any thought that you can possibly fail in reaching the goal of your longing. Set your face toward it; keep looking steadfastly in the direction of your ambition, whatever it may be. Resolve never to recognize defeat, and you will, by your mental attitude, your resolution, create a tremendous force for the drawing of your own to you. If you have the grit and stamina to stick, to persevere to the end, if you persistently maintain the victorious attitude toward your vision, victory will crown your efforts.

Twenty Nine

LOOK LIKE A SUCCESS

When Frank A. Vanderlip, former president of the National City Bank, New York, was a reporter on the Chicago *Tribune*, he asked his chief to tell him what he thought would be the greatest help to a man struggling to succeed. "*Look as if you had already succeeded,*" was the prompt reply.

This made a great impression upon young Vanderlip and completely changed some of his ideas on the subject, especially in regard to dress. From that time he began to spruce up, to be more particular about his general appearance. His chief had opened his eyes to the great value of appearances, especially in making a first impression. He became convinced that if a man did not look prosperous, people would think he did not have the right ambition or the ability to succeed; that there must be something the matter with him, or else he would dress better and make a better appearance.

Charles W. Eliot, President-emeritus of Harvard, said that much of one's success would depend on the opinions of those to whom one had never spoken a word, had never even seen. One's reputation travels by various routes in every direction and, according to its nature, will have a big influence on one's career.

It is a great thing to form a habit of going through the world giving the impression to everybody that you are a winner, that you are bound to be somebody—to stand for something worth while in the world. Let this idea stand out in everything you do, in your conversation, your appearance. Let everything about you make the world say, "He (or she) is a winner; keep your eye on him (or her)."

If you are eager to win out in a large way, cultivate the bearing of success, the appearance of a successful person. If you go about with a defeated, poorhouse atmosphere; if your appearance is slovenly, slipshod, and suggests a lack of orderliness, the lack of energy, of push, of the progressive spirit, you can't expect others to think that you are an efficient person, pushing to the front.

Of course every employer knows that it sometimes happens that a shabbily dressed applicant may nevertheless possess a lot of the good stuff—but they don't expect it. The chances of finding a very valuable employee with such an advertisement of himself or herself is so small that most employers won't take the risk.

Your dress, your bearing, your conversation, your conduct, should all square with your ambition. All of these things are aids to your achievement, and you cannot afford to ignore any one of them. The world takes you at your own valuation.

If you assume the victorious attitude toward it, it will give you the right of way.

One reason why it is so difficult for many to either get the right start or to get on comes from the fact that they do not realize how much their reputation has to do with their getting on in the world. They do not realize that other people's confidence is a tremendous force. They do not, from the outset, create in others the impression of power, of the force that achieves, that does things.

A physician or lawyer gets his reputation largely from the impression which he makes upon people, not only in the way he performs the duties of his profession, but also in his general attitude.

Walk, talk, and act as though you were already the person you long to be, and you are unconsciously putting into operation unseen forces that bend circumstances to the accomplishment of your will.

Let your air be that of a winner, of one who is resolved to make his or her way in the world—to make oneself stand for something. Put energy and life into your step; vim, force, vitality, pep into every movement of your body. Look straight forward; never wince. Don't apologize for taking up room on the earth which might be filled to better advantage by another. You have just as much right here as any other human being, if you are making good. And if you are not making good, you should be.

No matter what defeat comes to you, never lose your victorious consciousness. Let people read this declaration in your bearing, in your life generally: "I am a winner; I have not shown the white flag!"

The more trying your situation, the harder the way looks to you, the darker the outlook, the more necessary it is to carry that victorious consciousness. If you carry the down-and-out expression, if you confess by your very face that you are beaten—or that you expect to be—you are a goner. The victorious idea of life not the failure idea, the triumphant not the thwarted, is the thing to keep ever uppermost in demeanor—for it is this attitude that will lead you to the goal you aspire to reach.

The conviction that you are born to win is a tremendous creative force in your life, just as the conviction that you are a failure will keep you down.

The great trouble with all failures is that they were not started right. It was not drilled into the very texture of their being in youth that what they would get out of life must be created mentally first, and that inside the man, inside the woman, is where the great creative processes of all that we realize in our careers are carried on. Most of us depend too much upon the things outside of us, upon other people, when the mainspring of life, the power that moves the world of men and things, is within us.

Think what it would mean to the world today if all the people who look upon themselves as nobodies and failures, dwarfs of what they might have been and ought to be, would get this triumphant idea of life into themselves; if they would glimpse and hold onto their own possibilities, and would assume the victorious, the triumphant, attitude; if every little setback, every little difficulty, did not result in their saying "What's the use!" and feeling that their work is ineffective, and they do not, *cannot*, attract the things they desire. What a revolution of progress would enter into the world.

Set your character and your whole life towards triumph, towards victory. Hold the victorious thought towards yourself, towards your future, towards your career; it will tend to create the conditions favorable to the carrying out of your ambition, the fulfilling of your desires.

> "Go boldly, go serenely, go augustly;
> Who can withstand thee then!"

One of the most obstinate habits to overcome, and one that is fatal to efficiency and prosperity, is the habit of thinking and feeling defeated. Never allow yourself to fall into it. You may experience defeats—indeed, you most surely will—but look in every defeat for a lesson that will become a stepping-stone to your ambition. Think of wrestling with difficulties as like practicing in a gymnasium, where every victory over your muscles makes you so much stronger, and makes the next attempt so much surer and easier.

Success is every human being's normal condition; he was made for success; he is a success machine, and to be a failure is to pervert the intention of his Creator. Every youth should be taught to assume a triumphant attitude towards life, to carry himself like a winner, because he was made to win.

No one is really educated until he or she has learned to live a victorious life.

Hold the triumphant thought towards your future, towards your ideal, your dream. Carry the atmosphere of the victor. Radiate power. Let everything about you bespeak confidence, strength, masterfulness, victory. Let everybody who has anything to do with you see that you are a born winner.

Let the world see, as you walk about, that you think well of yourself, that you believe that you came to the earth with a message for others, and that you will be delivering it like an ambassador. Let people see that you are conscious you are on a superb mission, playing a superb part in the great life game. You will soon begin to see the thing you are looking for instead of the thing you are afraid of, and will find your dreams coming true.

Thirty

SELF-HELP & PERSEVERANCE

*T*hey are strongest who owe the most to themselves.

It is not those who have inherited most, except be it in nobility of soul and purpose, who have risen highest; but rather it is those with no "start" who have won fortunes and have risen up the steep mount, where "Fame's proud temple shines afar."

You may leave your millions to your children, but have you really given them anything? You cannot transfer the discipline, the experience, the power which the acquisition has given you. You cannot transfer the delight of achieving, the joy felt only in growth, the pride of acquisition, the character which trained habits of accuracy, method, promptness, patience, dispatch, honesty of dealing, politeness of manner have developed. You cannot transfer the skill, sagacity, prudence, foresight, which lie concealed in your wealth. It meant a great deal for you, but means nothing to your heirs. In climbing to your fortune, you developed the muscle, stamina, and strength which enabled you to maintain your lofty position, to keep your millions intact. You had the power which comes only from experience, and which alone enables you to stand firm on your dizzy height. Your fortune was experience to you, joy, growth, discipline, and character; to your heirs it will be a temptation, an anxiety, which will probably dwarf them. It was wings to you, it will be a dead weight to them. It was education to you and expansion of your highest powers; to them it may mean inaction, lethargy, indolence, weakness, ignorance. Yon have taken the priceless spur—necessity—away from your heirs . . . the spur which has goaded nearly all the great achievements in the history of the world.

You thought it a kindness to deprive yourself in order that your children might begin where you left off. You thought to spare them the drudgery, the hardships, the deprivations, the lack of opportunities. But you have put a crutch into their hands instead of a staff. You have taken away from them the incentive to self-development, to self-elevation, to self-discipline and self-help, without which no real success, no real happiness, no great character is ever possible. Their enthusiasm will evaporate; their energy will be dissipated. Their ambition, not being stimulated by the struggle for self-elevation, will gradually die away. If you do everything for your children and fight their battles for them, you will quite likely have weaklings on your hands at twenty-one.

"If I had only had firmness enough to compel my boys to earn their living," said the dying Cyrus Field, "then they would have known the meaning of money."

When Beethoven was examining the work of Moscheles, he found written at the end "Finis, with God's help." He wrote under it, "Man, help yourself."

A young man stood listlessly watching some anglers on a bridge. He was poor and dejected. At length, approaching a basket filled with fish, he sighed, "If now I had these I would be happy. I could sell them and buy food and lodgings." "I will give you just as many and just as good," said the owner, who chanced to overhear his words, "if you will do me a trifling favor." "And what is that?" asked the other. "Only to tend this line till I come back; I wish to go on a short errand." The proposal was gladly accepted. The old man was gone so long that the young man began to get impatient. Meanwhile the fish snapped greedily at the hook, and he lost all his depression in the excitement of pulling them in. When the owner returned he had caught a large number. Counting out from them as many as were in the basket, and presenting them to the youth, the old fisherman said, "I fulfill my promise from the fish you have caught, to teach you whenever you see others earning what you need, to waste no time in foolish wishing, but cast a line for yourself."

A white squall caught a party of tourists on a lake in Scotland, and threatened to capsize the boat. When it seemed that a crisis had really come, the largest and strongest man in the party, in a state of intense fear, said, "Let us pray." "No, no, my man," shouted the bluff old boatman; "*let the little man pray. You take an oar.*"

From Crœsus down to Rockefeller the story is the same, not only in the getting of wealth, but also in the acquirement of eminence; those have won most who relied most upon themselves.

"The male inhabitants in the Township of Loaferdom, in the County of Hatework," says a printer's squib, "found themselves laboring under great inconvenience for want of an easily traveled road between Poverty and Independence. They therefore petitioned the Powers that be to levy a tax upon the property of the entire county for the purpose of laying out a macadamized highway, broad and smooth, and all the way downhill to the later place."

"Man exists for culture," says Goethe, "not for what he can accomplish, but for what can be accomplished in him."

Labor is the only legal tender in the world to true success and prosperity. The gods sell everything for that, nothing without it. You will never find success "marked down."

Circumstances have rarely favored greatness. It finds its own way, makes its own circumstances through all sorts of opposition.

The founder of Boston University left Cape Cod for Boston to make his way with a capital of only four dollars. Like Horace Greeley, he could find no opening for a boy; but what of that? He made an opening. He found a board, and made it into an oyster stand on the street corner. He borrowed a wheelbarrow, and went three miles to an oyster shack, bought three bushels of oysters, and wheeled them to his stand. Soon his little savings amounted to $130. Then, he bought a horse and cart. This poor boy with no chance kept right on till he became the millionaire Isaac Rich.

Self-help has accomplished about all the great things of the world. Yet how many falter, faint, and dally with their purpose because they have no capital to start with—and wait and wait for some good luck to give them a lift. Prosperity is the child of drudgery and perseverance. It cannot be coaxed or bribed. Pay the price and it is yours.

"Success, honor, fame—magic words these, that make the fiery blood of ambition surge to your brain," said Kuhn. "But forget not, they are effects, not causes—the reward for initiative, patience, industry. It is the inexorable law of compensation: they win the prize who pay the price."

Are you paying the price for the prize you seek?

A will finds a way.

Where is the person today who has less chance to rise in the world than Elihu Burritt, apprenticed to a blacksmith, in whose shop he had to work at the forge all the daylight, and often by candlelight? Yet, he managed, by studying with a book before him at his meals, carrying it in his pocket that he might utilize every spare moment, and studying nights and holidays, to pick up an excellent education in the odds and ends of time which most boys throw away. Think of a boy working nearly all the daylight in a blacksmith's shop, and yet finding the time to study seven languages in a single year! By thirty years of age, he was master of every important language in Europe and was studying those of Asia.

Ninety percent of what is called prosperity is merely the result of persistent, determined industry—in most cases, downright hard work. It is the slavery to a single idea which has given to many a mediocre talent the reputation of being a success.

It is interesting to note that those who talk most about success and prosperity are those who like to work the least. The less self-driven the person, the less relentless in pursuit of a driving ambition, the more he or she will have to say wistfully about great things being done by others.

The greatest successes have been the greatest workers.

Richard Sheridan was considered a genius, but it was found that the "off-hand sayings" with which he used to dazzle the House of Commons were elaborated, polished, and repolished, and put down in his memorandum book ready for any emergency.

What we refer to as "genius," has been well defined as the infinite capacity for taking pains. If men and women who have done great things could only reveal how much of their reputations was due to downright hard digging and plodding, what an uplift of inspiration and encouragement they would give. How often I have wished that the discouraged and struggling could know of the heart-aches, the head-aches, the nerve-aches, the disheartening trials, the discouraged hours, the fears and despair involved in achievements which have gained the admiration of the world, but which have taxed the utmost powers of their authors. You can, for example, read in a few minutes or a few hours a poem or a book with pleasure and delight—but the days and months of weary plodding over details and dreary drudgery often required to produce it would stagger belief.

The greatest works in literature have been elaborated and elaborated, line by line, paragraph by paragraph, often rewritten a dozen times. The drudgery which literary successes have put into the productions which have stood the test of time is almost incredible. Lucretius worked nearly a lifetime on one poem. It completely absorbed his life. It is said that Bryant rewrote "Thanatopsis" a hundred times, and even then was not satisfied with it. John Foster would sometimes linger a week over a single sentence. He would hack, split, prune, pull up by the roots, or practice any other severity on whatever he wrote, till it gained his consent to exist. Chalmers was once asked what Foster was about in London. "Hard at it," he replied, "at the rate of a line a week." Dickens, one of the greatest writers of modern fiction, was so worn down by hard work that he looked as "haggard as a murderer." Hume toiled thirteen hours a day on his *History of England.* Lord Eldon astonished the world with his great legal learning, but when he was a student too poor to buy books, he had borrowed and copied many hundreds of pages of large law books, such as Coke upon Littleton, thus saturating his mind with legal principles which afterward blossomed out into what the world called remarkable genius. Matthew Hale for years studied law sixteen hours a day. Rousseau said of the labor involved in his smooth and lively style: "My manuscripts, blotted, scratched, interlined, and scarcely legible, attest the trouble they cost me. There is not one of them which I have not been obliged to transcribe four or five times before it went to press. . . . Some of my periods I have turned or returned in my head for five or six nights before they were fit to be put to paper."

Beethoven probably surpassed all other musicians in his painstaking fidelity and persistent application. There is scarcely a bar in his music that was not written and rewritten at least a dozen times. His favorite maxim was, "The barriers are not yet erected which can say to aspiring talent and industry 'thus far and no further.'"

Those who waste their evenings, wonder at the genius which can produce *The Decline and Fall of the Roman Empire,* upon which Gibbon worked twenty years. Even Plato, one of the greatest writers that ever lived, wrote the first sentence in his *Republic* nine different ways before he was satisfied with it. Burke's famous "Letter to a Noble Lord," one of the finest things in the English language, was so completely blotted over with alterations when the proof was returned to the printing-office that the compositors refused to correct it as it was, and entirely reset it. He wrote the conclusion of his speech at the trial of Hastings sixteen times. It took Virgil seven years to write his *Georgics*, and twelve years to write the *Æneid*. He was so displeased with the latter that he attempted to rise from his deathbed to commit it to the flames.

When a man like Lord Cavanagh, without arms or legs, manages to put himself into Parliament, when a man like Francis Joseph Campbell, a blind man, becomes a distinguished mathematician, a musician, and a great philanthropist, we get a hint as to what it means to make the most possible out of ourselves and opportunities. Perhaps ninety-nine out of a hundred under such unfortunate circumstances would be content to remain helpless objects of charity for life.

A French doctor once taunted the Bishop of Nismes, who had been a tallow-chandler in his youth, regarding the meanness of his origin. The Bishop, "If you had been born in the same condition that I was, you would still have been but a maker of candles."

The Duke of Argyle, walking in his garden, saw a Latin copy of Newton's *Principia* on the grass, and supposing that it had been taken from his library, called for some one to carry it back. Edmund Stone, however, the son of the duke's gardener, claimed it. "Yours?" asked the surprised nobleman. "Do you understand geometry, Latin, and Newton?" "I know a little of them," replied Edmund. "But how," asked the duke, "came you by the knowledge of all these things?"

"A servant taught me to read ten years since," answered Stone. "Does one need to know anything more than the twenty-four letters, in order to learn everything else that one wishes?" The duke was astonished. "I first learned to read," said the lad. "The masons were then at work upon your house. I approached them one day and observed that the architect used a rule and compasses, and that he made calculations. I inquired what might be the meaning and use of these things, and I was informed that there was a science called arithmetic. I purchased a book of arithmetic and learned it. I was told that there was another science called geometry; I bought the necessary books and learned geometry. By reading I found that there were good books on these sciences in Latin, so I bought a dictionary and learned Latin. I understood, also, that there were good books of the same kind in French; I bought a dictionary, and learned French. This, my lord, is what I have done; it seems to me that we may learn everything when we know the twenty-four letters of the alphabet."

A learned scientist gave a friend, who was interested in his collection of butterflies, a chrysalis, telling him that it would develop into a rare and beautiful butterfly, but that he must leave it undisturbed, watch it carefully, and note the many stages of its development.

The friend watched the chrysalis, and after a while noticed that the shell of the cocoon was gradually getting thinner and more transparent—until he could see the little grub inside. Before long he saw that the grub began to move, and continued moving a little more and more each day until he thought that it was trying to get out of the cocoon. For some time he resisted the temptation to break the shell, but at last his curiosity got the better of him, and he began to make tiny punctures in it with a needle. Soon after, the gorgeous butterfly which had been described to him by his friend, emerged, fluttered into the air, and then dropped, never to fly again. Several times it tried to rise on its wings, but all it could do was to crawl about on the earth.

The scientist told his friend that by assisting it to get out of the cocoon, he had deprived the butterfly of the very struggle which it needed to gain the strength in its wings necessary to support it in flying. The result of helping the beautiful creature spelled its ruin.

The ancients said, "Know thyself." The present century says, "Help thyself."

Self-culture gives a second birth to the soul.

If you don't believe in your power to get what you want you won't get it. Until you encourage your longings and believe in your power to realize them, they will never be satisfied. You cannot rise out of your present condition until you believe you can. The limit of your thought will be the boundary of your possibilities. Your limited ideal of yourself will limit your execution.

On the other hand, if you have the faith that creates, the faith that believes the best is coming to you, you can reach out mentally into the great stream of universal supply and get material aid to build what you will. The supply is there. It rests with you to make the connection that will draw it to you.

Self-help which is as necessary to the development of each of us as to a butterfly, is one of the supreme blessings of humanity. It is the great unfolder of ability, of character, the only thing that continually calls into play the best qualities of each of us—those qualities that make us human giants.

We do our most effective work in our struggle to get what we are after, to arrive at the goal of our ambition. We make our greatest effort, our most strenuous endeavor, while we are climbing, not after we have arrived at our goal.

Before me is a letter from an employee in a large business concern, who complains that he has remained in the same position for a number of years with practically no advancement in salary or prospects. "I do just as well as the other fellows in my department," he says, "but every one else gets along while I remain at the same old stand. The trouble is they have an inside 'pull,' and I have none. What can I do to get ahead?" Now I am convinced that the trouble with this young man, the thing that is holding him back, as I have found in almost every case like his, is inside, not outside of him.

Many idle away their lives, waiting for something to turn up, for somebody to boost them; while others, with half their chance, educate and lift themselves. The great trouble with the majority of people is their belief that the door to their ambition, the door just ahead of them, is closed by some mysterious fate or destiny; and that unless they have some influence, some pull, some one to help them get a "start" in the world, they can never open it. They don't realize that no one closes that door or keeps it closed but themselves.

Starting right where you are, without a bit of outside help, with what tools you have, working with the law of opulence, of divine supply, you could absolutely revolutionize your situation in one year. You could be on the other side of the door which you think is barred against you. It will open wide when you are ready to enter—that is, when you have paid the price of admission. No one can give you a free pass, and admission tickets are not transferable. You must pay the price yourself or stay outside. The price is self-effort.

No matter what you attempt to do, you will always find plenty of pessimists who will predict your failure. They will tell you that you never can build up a business without a lot of capital and outside help in these times of terrific competition; that you can never be whatever you are dreaming of and longing to be. You will have plenty of obstacles to overcome; you will, perhaps, meet much opposition, and it will take a very stiff backbone, a lot of sand and grit to keep pushing on towards your goal against great odds.

But your real competitor is your higher, possible self—the person you are capable of measuring up to.

If you do not respond to the urge of this invisible competitor, all of your success qualities will be of no avail. You will fall away below the level of your ability. The great thing is to keep your highest possibilities—the utmost which you are capable of achieving—always in view.

You cannot climb higher than your own capabilities, the mountain top of your possible achievement—but if you stay down in the valley, you will never know the view from the mountain top.

You were made to reach the mountain top, to make success of your life. To do this, nothing will help you more than to keep in mind a vision of your imaginary competitor, your higher self, standing in your shadow all the time.

The divine, invincible power inside of you, flows through your higher self. If you have the will to succeed and work in harmony with this power, you will batter down any barricade between you and the door of your desire.

The microscope does not create anything new, but it reveals marvels. To educate the eye adds to its magnifying power until it sees beauty where before it might have seen nothing—no opportunity.

But be careful to avoid that over-intellectual culture which is purchased at the expense of effort. An observant professor of one of our colleges has remarked that too many are "apt to forget the great end of life which is to be and do, not to read and brood over what other men have been and done."

All learning is ultimately self-teaching, self-help.

It is upon your truly committing to your own self-help that your progress depends.

Thirty One

THE SECRET KEY TO PROSPERITY

Grit is the master key which unlocks all difficulties. What has it not accomplished?

It has paid the mortgage on the farm in innumerable cases. It has enabled delicate women to save the home for the family. It has stood in the gap and saved thousands of men from destruction in disastrous and great emergencies, in hard times and business panics. It has enabled poor boys and girls to pay their way through college and to make places for themselves in the world. It has given cripples strength to support aged and invalid parents. It has tunneled mountains, bridged rivers, joined continents with cables and spanned them with railroads. It has discovered continents and won the greatest battles in history.

No substitute has ever been discovered for tenacity of purpose. Nothing can take the place of clear grit. An education cannot, rich parents cannot, influential "pulls" cannot, nor can any advantage of birth or fortune.

Tenacity of purpose is characteristic of all those who have accomplished great things. They may lack other desirable traits, may have all sorts of peculiarities, weaknesses, but the quality of persistence, clear grit, is never absent from those who do things. Drudgery cannot disgust them, labor cannot weary them, hardships cannot discourage them. They will persist no matter what comes or goes, because persistence is part of his nature.

More have achieved success in life with grit as capital, than with money capital to start with.

The whole history of achievement shows that grit has overcome the direst poverty; it has been more than a match for lifelong invalidism.

The late Mrs. Craigie (John Oliver Hobbes) said that one secret of the American's success is that they are not afraid of failure, that they plunge into the thing they have set their heart on with all their might and enthusiasm, without even a thought of the possibility of failing, and that if they do fail, they get up with more determination than before and fight until they wins.

For some, every defeat is a Waterloo, but there is no Waterloo for those who have grit, who persist, who never know when they are beaten. Those who are bound to win never think of defeat as final. They get up after each failure with new resolution, more determination than ever to go on until they win.

Have you ever seen those who have no give-up in them, who whatever happened would never let go their grip, who every time he failed would come up smiling and with greater determination than ever to push ahead?

Have you ever seen those who did not know the meaning of the word failure, who, like Grant, never knew when they were beaten, who had cut the words "can't" and "impossible" from their vocabulary—those whom no obstacles could down, no difficulty phase, who were not disheartened by any misfortune, any calamity?

If you have, then you have seen a conqueror—a person prosperity cannot elude.

Resilience has ever been characteristic of great achievers. Those who shrink from hardships, who cannot forego their ease or postpone their desires, on the other hand, must be content with small achievement.

Look out for the period in your life when you are tempted to turn back! That may well be the decisive period.

All the great things of history have been accomplished after the great majority would have turned back.

Many lives are filled with half-finished tasks which were begun with enthusiasm, but which were later dropped because the enthusiasm did not have enough grit to carry it to a conclusion.

How easy it is to start a thing when the mind is aglow with zeal, before disappointment has dulled ambition!

The test of your character, your opportunity for prosperity, is your ability to persist in what you undertake until you add the finishing stroke. We cannot judge success by one's speed at the beginning of the race, it is the homestretch that counts. You must have persistence and grit enough to carry you across the line in the last heat.

But the ability to hold on is one of the rarest of human virtues. There are plenty who will go with the crowd, and who will work hard as long as they can hear the music, but when the majority have dropped out, when others have turned back and one feels oneself alone fighting for a principle, it takes a very different order of ability to persist. This requires grit and stamina.

After a friend of a New York merchant had named a number of good qualities in recommending a boy for a position, the merchant said, "Does he keep at it? That is the principal thing. Does he have staying qualities?"

Yes, that is your life-interrogation. "Do you keep at it?" "Have you staying qualities?" "Can you stick by your proposition?" "Can you persevere after failure?" "Have you grit—grit enough to hold-on, to stick and hang, in spite of the most disheartening obstacles?"

If you have, and if you are pursuing what you truly wish and paying attention to every step along the way, then prosperity will be yours.

Thirty Two

MAKING ROOM IN YOUR LIFE FOR PROSPERITY

It is a law working in all nature—through plant, insect, animal, and man—that in order to have and enjoy the new, we must first rid ourselves of the old.

If the tree held stingily on to last year's fruit and leaves and refused to drop them, would not the branches for next year's fruit and leaves be choked up? If the bird, from dislike of parting with old possessions, could at its molting season hold on to its old plumage, would not the growth of the newer and fresher plumage be stunted.

It's a physical and spiritual law that the old *must* be cast off before the new can come.

The same law that governs the growth and fruitage of a tree, the growth and plumage of a bird—the growth of *all* life—governs the growth of your spirit. Only as regards your spirit, it is infinitely more varied and complicated in its workings.

If you wish to enjoy the new clothes, the new house—the newer and better surroundings of every sort—that you long for, cease in mind to cling and hang on to *all* things you have no use for in the present or soon-to-come future. If you hold on to the little or never-used item of any sort, through the mere love of keeping it, you are barring out the better thing coming to you. If you hold on to the inferior, you keep from you the superior.

You know these truths in the personal relationships of your life. If you retain the company of people who only tire you and bore you, who ridicule your ideas if you express them, and are utterly profitless to you, you keep the better people from you.

In like manner, if you cling to the old worn-out suit of clothes and out of stinginess hate to give it away, if you expend any amount of your force in haggling and dickering to sell it for a dime, you will not nearly as soon have the better clothing—for every thought put into the old represents just so much force, which could have better been put into a plan to bring you hundreds of dollars instead of dimes.

Keeping of things, possessions, which you own and have used but which you cannot, or do not, now use, diverts your spiritual or thought-power from gaining the fresher and better. It uses up that power on the care and keeping of things now of no use to you, and therefore in actuality a liability to you.

You do not keep the top, the pens and pencils, the clothing of your childhood. Why? Because you know you have outgrown them, that they are now of no use to you, that you want your strength and time and thought focused on those things more suited to your present interests and aspirations.

If you have more things about you than you need for immediate use and enjoyment, they prove not only an annoyance, but that annoyance prevents you from gaining the newer and better.

It is like filling yourself at a restaurant on the bread and hors d'oeuvres, leaving no room for the desired main course—the meal for which you looked forward to going to that restaurant to in the first place.

If you have a room, attic, basement, or garret full of old chests and chairs and furniture, or drawers full of half-worn clothing, all of which you keep simply from love of keeping them, or from the idea that you may need these things some time or other, it is far more profitable to sell them or give them away. These old and unused things not only keep newer and better things from you, but more critically, by being a care, they are a load on your mind.

It is not so much the possession of the seldom used or unused that is so injurious to your attainment of prosperity, but the care—the effort of thought and time that you must give to these things that thwarts your prosperity.

Thousands of people go through life with old pots, pans, and kettles they have no use for. What would you think of a man, who, for the sake of keeping a crowbar, should chain it to his ankle and drag it along with him. You can so chain crowbars to your mind.

One secret of the successes of prosperity is that they know when to rid themselves of possessions upon seeing that those possessions can be of no further use to them. Far-sighted corporations and businesses are, at this moment, "unloading" themselves of properties which they see have no immediate money in, while near-sighted businesses are at this moment buying those properties, which will for years lay on their hands as a care without recompense, and an encumbrance and obstacle to more immediate gain.

The real cost of keeping things is the amount of thought you put into their keeping. If you will keep an old bedstead or bureau, or anything else you never have any use for, and take it about with you at every house-moving, studying and calculating as to the place it shall occupy in your new home, and then worry because it takes room which you need for everyday purposes, you are putting the mental energy into a (to you) useless article—energy that could, if more wisely directed, buy a hundred new beds or bureaus.

The desire of simply keeping and hoarding, keep many people poor, and even make paupers.

Nor is hoarding good business. If everyone put away money as they gained it, hoarding what they have, and lived on as little as possible and continually decreased their expenses, the world's business would soon stop—not so much from lack of money lying useless in chests and old stockings, but because there would soon be little left for people to do to gain money.

It is aspiring, in the reaching out for new growth, in the erection of magnificent buildings and not hovels, that keeps the laborer, the mechanic, the artist in any department, at work, and keeps the stream of money flowing.

Mere hoarding brings nothing in the end to those who hoard but pain and trouble.

Misers are but a one-sided successes. They gain money only to pile it away in vaults—money that brings them only the gratification of owning it and of adding to the pile. That is but a mania. The miserly get from their money little pleasure for their bodies, little pleasure coming from the gratification of intellectual or artistic tastes. They own only a pile of stamped metal or paper, and thus, no matter the wealth of their houses, they are poor men and women.

"It is easier for the camel to pass through the needle's eye than for a rich man to enter the kingdom of heaven," we have been told. The "kingdom of heaven" is located in no particular place in space, but can be and will be wherever the mind grows wise enough and strong enough to make it. The "rich man" who cannot enter the kingdom of heaven is in reality the person who is loaded down with things he or she cannot use, and by holding onto is not allowing others to use—and so cannot enter the kingdom of heaven because by such hoarding is thwarting his or her own ability to make his or her life a kingdom of heaven.

On the other hand, the rich person who knows the secret and power of attracting the world's best of everything by making room for it in his or her life, not only that he or she may use and enjoy what life offers but use it to contribute to the good and happiness of all, lives, in so doing, in the kingdom of heaven.

The plant appropriates and uses only what it needs for the hour—of air, water, sunshine, and the earth's elements. If more is supplied to the plant than is necessary for its present needs, thereby is caused blight and disease. The elements of life must be used, not hoarded, if real profit and benefit is desired from them.

Rust is often considered destructive, but in fact it is a means of the Source of Infinite Good to prevent hoarding. It does not really destroy. It consumes the elements of materials that have laid in disuse or neglect and scatters and distributes them, that they may enter into new forms of combination and serve new uses.

If you owned this whole earth, you could only use and enjoy such portion of its air, sunshine, water, foods, and forces, as would satisfy your needs for the hour, the day, the month, the year, and so on. The keeping of the rest would ultimately destroy the planet. Your ownership would be a farce. You would have "gained the whole world and lost your own soul." To truly own "your own soul"—the power latent in you—you must ever increase your thought-force so as to draw all things to you to use and enjoy, and then rid yourself of them, so as to gain the newer and better.

Following the law common to all life, that of throwing off the old in order to receive the new, exactly as your body throws off what it cannot assimilate and convert into bone, muscle, and blood; will give your spirit more and more power. You are then going forward on the road to complete command over all material things.

Live in your mind in a palace, and palatial surroundings will gravitate to you. But when you have no further use for your palace, give others the use of it, or it will become your poorhouse. If you store it away, you store with it so much weight on your mind—so much thought to be expended in storage; so much spiritual force which might otherwise have been put in the cultivation of a talent.

And whether you have five talents or ten, it is your necessity to cultivate them all at times, and for that you want all your powers unshackled. In the full use of your talents is your prosperity. To fully use and cultivate your talents toward your prosperity, continually examine your life. Remove from your talents the weight of outmoded, outdated habits and encumbrances that in the demands of time needed for their care are drawing into dead-ends the focus of your spirit.

Remove from your life that which, by virtue of its presence in your life, is restricting your talents, your aspirations, your abilities to move toward prosperity in your life—to make room for in your life for prosperity.

Thirty Three

THE MASTER KEY: TO BE GREAT, CONCENTRATE

There is no more powerful magnet in the world for attracting the thing we desire, no force more effective in realizing the ambition we long to attain than concentration. It has been the chief factor in all the great achievements of history. It is the cornerstone of success in every line; the principle upon which all progress is based. All the inventions, all the discoveries, all the modern facilities which the world enjoys are the children of focused minds. Whatever you long to be, or to have, you can be, you can have, by focusing your mind and concentrating your efforts on that one thing.

When Franz Liszt, the great composer, was a mere youth, his elder brother chided him for spending his time on music and told him that he himself was going to be a great landowner. The would-be landowner scorned his young brother's musical bent, holding that a talent for music would only ruin a man. Franz, however, stuck to his bent, and even ran away several times in order to gratify his ambition for a musical career, which was discouraged at home.

Years later when the elder brother had become a wealthy landowner he called on Franz, who was still a struggling musician. Not finding him at home he left his card, which bore the inscription, "Herr Liszt, Landowner." When more years had passed and the young composer had finally won out, he returned the call of his landowner brother and presented his card, which read, "Herr Liszt, Brain-owner."

Aside from the humor of this little story, the point is, that each of the brothers got what he concentrated on: the one became a wealthy landowner, the other a world-famed musician and composer.

If your ambition is like that of the elder brother, to become a wealthy landowner, a prosperous man of affairs, then you must concentrate on prosperity, on the acquisition of wealth in some form. We all know people who seem to attract money from every direction. Everything they touch turns to money, as we say, while others who work just as hard for the same end have no success at all. The different results are due to the difference in intensity and persistence of concentration. The natural, the born money-maker, thinks in terms of money. He or she is making money mentally all the time, so to speak, because of a mind focused on money. Money-makers are always nursing their money vision. They are positive in their conviction that they will make money, will be wealthy, and they concentrate on this objective with such intensity and singleness of aim that they literally create money.

On the other hand, those who want money but who don't concentrate intensely on getting it; who don't believe very much in their ability to get it, who fear they will never be even what we call well-to-do, are like those who want to be successful but are always thinking about failure—worrying about it, fearing, believing that they never will become a success. They are the ones who scatter their forces in a dozen different directions, hoping that by chance they might manage to succeed in some one of them.

There is no such thing as succeeding in anything by chance. The greatest genius in the world never created a masterpiece in any line by chance. Concentration is the master key to all success. It is the fundamental law of achievement. Those who do not concentrate will be either a half success, a mediocrity, or a complete failure.

The French have a proverb, "He who does one thing is terrible." In other words, the person who sticks to one thing is irresistible. No matter if the world opposes that person's progress, he or she would forge a way through to the goal.

"To make a success of the shoe business is my one great ambition," said the head of one of the largest shoe companies in the world. "I am not a director or trustee of any bank. I do not scatter my energies. I don't pretend to know many things, but I do know something about the shoe business. *I have put my ability, my energy, my life into the work of making good shoes.*"

This man, who began life on the lowest round of the ladder, without capital or influence, built up a business which keeps a force of two hundred traveling salesmen and saleswomen on the road today and is turning over some $25,000,000 a year.

Emerson said, "The one prudence in life is concentration; the one evil is dissipation." Scattering our energies, dissipating our creative force, failing to bring our mind to a focus and to hold it there, is responsible for nine-tenths of the failures in life and most of the poverty of the world.

I know one of those dissipators who generates more new ideas and outlines more new schemes than anyone else I have ever met. Yet he has never accomplished anything more than the making of a meager living, because he never sticks long enough to any one thing to make it go. His brain power and all of his energy are scattered in following one new thing after another without ever carrying any of them forward to completion. Every time I talk with him he amazes me with the fertility of his mind, his resourcefulness in developing original ideas, many of which would prove valuable if they were only put into execution, but they never get beyond the mental stage. The concentration necessary to bring them down to earth, to put them to work, is lacking. There are thousands like this man, getting small salaries in very ordinary positions, whose knowledge of a dozen different occupations, concentrated in one line, would have made them efficient specialists. No matter how brilliant or versatile you may be you cannot afford to divide your ability, to throw away valuable experience in jumping from one vocation to another. If you would succeed in a worth-while way, you must be a person with undivided interests, able to fling the weight of your entire being into one calling. No one is large enough to be split up into many parts; and the sooner you can stamp this truth upon your mind, the better your chances for becoming a prosperous member of society.

Coleman Dupont furnished a good example of the masterperson. When he was called to the head of Dupont Powder Company, the business it was losing ground rapidly, but he very soon turned the tide and headed the company toward success. When an interviewer asked Mr. Dupont how he did this, he said: "I talked powder, I ate powder, I dreamed powder. I thought of little else but powder."

No matter what your business, trade, or profession, you cannot make a mistake in following Colman Dupont's procedure for success and prosperity. Think the thing you want; talk it; live it; breathe it; dream it; act it; radiate it from every pore of your body; saturate your life with it; visualize it; believe that it is already yours. That's the only way to get any thing of value in this world.

If we could only realize the marvelous power of thought, the creative force in concentration, the drawing power of intense visualizing, how much more we could accomplish! It is this which really makes the mind a powerful magnet to attract what it desires, what it longs for most. Everywhere we see illustrations of the attractive force of positive, definite thought concentrated on one point.

To demonstrate prosperity, you must concentrate on prosperity; you must hold the prosperity attitude. It is not enough to long for abundance, you must believe that you will be, *that you already are*, prosperous. You must expect it.

"According to your faith be it unto you" (Mat. 9:29).

You must hold in mind that thing, whatever it is that you wish to express in your life, and you must believe it will come.

You can't expect to become prosperous if you don't hold fast to the prosperity vision. If your mind is occupied with something else most of the time; if it is filled with doubts about ever accumulating property or becoming prosperous in any line of business, don't deceive yourself with the idea that prosperity will come to you if you only work hard. It won't. Nothing will come into your life except by the doorway of your concentrated thought, expectation, and faith.

Concentration is indispensable to success in anything. As Dr. Julia Seaton says: "Concentration is the vital essence of all life, and without it there is no real purpose, no real control. Upon the power of concentration more than upon any other one thing, depends our law of attracting, controlling and mastering life's conditions."

If you feel discouraged because you are not getting on as you hoped you would, something is wrong. Your mind is not pulling in harmony with your effort on the physical plane. Something has arrested your progress, and that something is a mental stumbling-block which you yourself put in your path. You are not thinking yourself on, you are not putting yourself in the getting-on current by concentrating with confidence, with faith, along the line of your ambition. Whether it is discouragement, doubt, a wavering, divided mind; the scattering of your efforts by frittering away your energies through giving your spare time to sidelines—trying to make a little success here, a little there; by not giving the whole of yourself to your life work—something or other is neutralizing the force which would naturally take you to your goal.

In Maine, the farmers say that it makes a horse a gawk to drive it without blinders, because its attention is drawn this way and that, which ruins the animal's gait and speed. Many a person has similarly been ruined by not confining himself or herself within sufficiently narrow limits to give concentration and direction to his or her energies.

"When I have a subject in hand I study it profoundly," said Alexander Hamilton. "Day and night it is before me. My mind becomes pervaded with it. Then the success I make, the people are pleased to call genius. It is the fruit of thought and labor."

Don't be afraid of being known as a person of one idea. Those who have moved the world have been those of this kind.

Genius without concentration never accomplishes as much as concentration without genius.

It is those who have their purpose burned into every fiber of their being, who have the faculty of focusing their energies on one point—as a burning glass focuses the scattered rays of the sun—who succeed on the path to prosperity.

Thirty Four

SEIZE YOUR OPPORTUNITY

"There is nobody," said a Roman Cardinal, "whom Fortune does not visit once in this life; but when she finds the individual is not ready to receive her, she goes in at the door, and out through the window."

Opportunity is coy. The careless, the slow, the unobservant, the lazy fail to see it, or clutch at it when it has gone. The sharp detect it instantly, and catch it when on the wing.

Zion's Herald reported that Isaac Rich, who gave one million and three quarters to found Boston University of the Methodist Episcopal Church, began business thus: At eighteen he went from Cape Cod to Boston with three or four dollars in his possession, looking about for something to do, rising early, walking far, observing closely, reflecting much. Soon he had an idea: he bought three bushels of oysters, hired a wheelbarrow, found a piece of board, bought six small plates, six iron forks, a three-cent pepper-box, and one or two other things. He went to the oyster boats buying his oysters at three o'clock in the morning, wheeled them three miles, set up his board near a market, and began business. He sold out his oysters as fast as he could get them, at a good profit. He continued to deal in oysters and fish at that same market for forty years—becoming king of the business and founding a college. His success was won by industry and honesty.

Many of us who think we are poor are rich in opportunities if we could only see them—in possibilities all about us, in faculties worth more than diamond bracelets, in power to do good.

In our large eastern cities it was been found that at least ninety-four out of every hundred found their first fortune at home, or near at hand, and in meeting common, everyday wants. But many cannot see cannot see any opportunities where they are, and think instead that they can do better somewhere else.

Several Brazilian shepherds organized a party to go to California to dig gold, and took along a handful of clear pebbles to play checkers with on the voyage. They discovered after arriving at Sacramento, after they had thrown most of the pebbles away, that they were all diamonds. They returned to Brazil only to find that the mines had been taken up by others and sold to the government.

The richest gold and silver mine in Nevada was sold for forty-two dollars by the owner, to get money to pay his passage to other mines where he thought he could get rich.

Professor Agassiz told the Harvard students of a farmer who owned a farm of hundreds of acres of unprofitable woods and rocks, and concluded to sell out and try some more remunerative business. He studied coal measures and coal oil deposits, and experimented for a long time. He sold his farm for two hundred dollars and went into the oil business two hundred miles away. Only a short time afterward the man who bought the farm discovered a great flood of coal oil, which the farmer had ignorantly tried to drain off.

A man was once sitting in an uncomfortable chair in Boston talking with a friend as to what he could do to help mankind. "I should think it would be a good thing," said the friend, "to begin by getting up an easier and cheaper chair." "I will do it," he exclaimed, leaping up and examining the chair. He found a great deal of rattan thrown away by the East India merchant ships, whose cargoes were wrapped in it. He began the manufacture of rattan chairs and other furniture—astonishing the world with what he has done with what others threw away.

If you want to get rich, study yourself and your own wants. You will find millions of others have the same wants, the same demands. The safest business is always connected with humanity's prime necessities. We must have clothing, a dwellings, and we must eat. We want comforts, facilities of all kinds, for use and pleasure, luxury, education, culture.

Those who can supply any of the great wants of humanity, improve any methods which have already been in use, supply any demand or contribute in any way to our well-being, can make a fortune.

But it is detrimental to the highest success to undertake anything merely because it is profitable. If the vocation does not supply a human want, if it is not healthful, if it is degrading, if it is narrowing, don't touch it.

A selfish vocation never pays. If it belittles one's self-hood, blights the affections, dwarfs the mental life, chills the charities and shrivels the soul, don't touch it.

Choose that occupation, if possible, which will be the most helpful to the largest number.

It is estimated that five out of every seven of the millionaire manufacturers began by making with their own hands the articles on which they made their fortune.

A keen, cultivated observation will see a fortune where others see only poverty.

An observing man, the eyelets of whose shoes pulled out, but who could ill afford to get another pair, said to himself, "I will make a metallic lacing hook, which can be riveted into the leather." He succeeded in doing so and became a very rich man.

An observing barber in Newark, N.J., thought he could make an improvement on shears for cutting hair. He invented "clippers" and became very rich.

A Maine man was called from the hayfield to wash out the clothes for his invalid wife. He had never realized what it was to wash before. He invented the washing-machine and made a fortune.

A man who was suffering terribly with toothache, said to himself, "There must be some way of filling teeth to prevent them aching." He invented gold filling for teeth.

The great things of the world have not been done by those of large means. Want has been the great schoolmaster of the race; necessity the mother of all great inventions.

Ericsson began the construction of a screw-propeller in a bath-room.

John Harrison, the great inventor of the marine chronometer, began his career in the loft of an old barn.

Parts of the first steamboat ever run in America were set up in the vestry of an old church in Philadelphia by Fitch.

McCormick began to make his famous reaper in an old grist-mill.

The first model dry-dock was made in an attic.

Clark, the founder of Clark University of Worcester, Mass., began his great fortune by making toy wagons in a horse shed.

Opportunities? They crowd around us. There is power lying latent everywhere, waiting for the observant eye to discover it.

First find out what the people need and then supply that want. An invention to make the smoke go the wrong way in a chimney might be a very ingenious thing, but it would be of no use to humanity. The patent office at Washington is full of wonderful devices, ingenious mechanism—but not one in hundreds is of earthly use to the inventor or to the world. Yet how many families have been impoverished and have struggled for years mid want and woe, while the someone was working on one of these useless inventions.

Don't think you have no chance in life because you have no capital to begin with. Most of those who have become rich began poor.

You are as rich as you need be if you have good health. You are rich as you need be if you have good head, a good disposition, and a good heart. You are as rich as you need be if you have two good hands, with five chances on each.

Equipped?

We all are equipped by life.

It is not the equipment, but what one does with it—the individual effort—that has accomplished everything worth accomplishing in this world.

Money to start with is only a crutch, which, if any misfortune knocks it from under you, would only make your fall all the more certain.

If you are determined to make the most of your eyes and let nothing escape them which you can possibly use for your own advancement, if you keep yours ears open for every sound that can help you on your way, if you keep your hands open that they may clutch every opportunity, if you are ever on the alert for everything which can help you to get on in the world, if you seize every experience in life and grind it up into paint for your life's great picture, if you keep your heart open that it may catch every noble impulse and everything which may inspire you, you will be sure to live a successful and prosperous life.

There are no ifs or ands about it.

Thirty Five

HOW TO INCREASE YOUR ABILITY

A prominent business man once told me that the best contract he ever got was one he lost. Why? Because it set him to investigating the cause of the loss, to investigating himself, to finding the weak places in himself and in his business methods. It was the lost contract that led him to the discovery that he was not using more than half the ability he actually possessed.

Many of us rob ourselves of success and fortune by mistaken ideas about our ability. We are like a young legal secretary who told me that if she had the ability to become an expert in her line, she would go to evening school, study nights, and do everything she could to improve her education and to develop herself in all possible ways. But, as she was sure that she had only a very moderate share of ability, she was convinced that there was no use in trying, and that she must be satisfied with an ordinary position. She believed that her ability was a fixed quantity; something which could not be enlarged or diminished, which she could not change in any respect any more than she could change the color of her hair or of her eyes.

The idea that our ability is an invariable quantity, fixed by heredity, or some immutable law which we can neither understand nor control, is one of the most unfortunate that could take possession of anyone's mind. And nothing could be farther from the truth, for, as a matter of fact, human ability is a very variable and a very elastic quantity. It can be expanded almost indefinitely, or contracted, in a great many ways. It is like an accordion, which the player sometimes draws out to its full extent, and again closes completely. You can close up your ambition accordion by wrong thinking until but a mere fraction of your possible ability is available, or you can open it up by right thinking and make every bit of it count in making your work, your life, a grand success.

Multitudes of people go through life with their actual ability so cramped, so muzzled and suffocated by their negative, destructive mental attitude, their doubts, fears, worries, superstitions and preconceived ideas, their lack of courage, their lack of faith in themselves and in their mission, that they make but a very small percentage of themselves count in their life's work.

Everywhere we see men and women, hard workers, who do not accomplish a tithe of what they could accomplish, because what natural abilities they do have are unavailable—bottled up by their pessimism, doubts, fears, and lack of faith.

If you had a valuable gold mine on your property, and, instead of ridding yourself of all obstructions to get at the ore you should add a lot more, your gold mine wouldn't add one particle to your available wealth. Potentially you have an immense fortune, but it might just as well not be there, for you derive no benefit from gold you cannot get at and exchange for the good things of life that you desire.

Likewise, if you cover over your abilities with all sorts of mental obstructions, they will never expand, will never yield you anything.

Many of us think if we only had some other person's talent or opportunities; if we only had the advantages of some other person; if only we were superbly equipped with facilities for some particular work, that we would do wonderful things. But in truth we have all come into this world with just the tools required for a job which we are qualified in every respect to do. The Creator didn't sharpen those tools for us, because if He had done, He would have deprived us of the very thing that is designed for our expansion and growth. It is by overcoming obstacles day by day, by clearing away the rubbish and mental debris that choke our growth and by always reaching up to the attainment of our highest ideal, that we unfold, layer after layer, the wealth of ability that is enfolded in ourselves, no matter what our seeming disabilities or handicaps.

Helen Keller is, perhaps, one of the most remarkable examples the world has ever seen of the power of the determined soul to overcome everything that stands in the way of its complete development. Deaf, mute, and blind at the age of eighteen months, what opportunity was there for a human being so handicapped to do anything of value in the world; to become anything other than a despair to herself, a hopeless, helpless burden on her relatives? Yet out of her world of darkness the indomitable spirit within evolved a being of such remarkable ability and power that there are few who have rendered greater service and inspiration to humanity than this woman who, apparently, at the outset of life was hopelessly handicapped. She is a wonderful illustration of the truth that there is no limit to one's development, and no insuperable obstacles, except those we ourselves put in our way.

Avoid as you would poison everything that tends to make you negative: worry, anxiety, jealousy, envy, fear, cowardice, the whole family of depressing, despondent thoughts. These are all power destroyers. Every feeling of discouragement, of despondency, every doubt, every fear, is a crippler of ability.

A great artist who put his whole soul in his work once said that he would never look at inferior pictures, because if he did, he would become familiar with false artistic ideals, and his own pencil would soon catch the taint of inferiority.

Our ability, in other words, is extremely sensitive to our moods, to our mental condition generally. When we don't feel like it, when we are out of sorts, when for one reason or another we feel blue, discouraged, despondent, full of doubt and anxiety, our ability is very much contracted. On the other hand, when we are in good trim, when our minds are harmonious, not anxious or worried about anything, it is enormously expanded. That is, all the positive, uplifting, encouraging, cheerful emotions and feelings expand or increase our ability, while gloomy ones contract or lessen it.

We all know how much more capable of planning and doing things we are when our courage is up and we believe in ourselves. We know from experience that our consciousness of our ability expands when we feel as though we could tackle almost anything. The abilities within us are greatly enlarged by a sublime self-confidence, an unwavering faith.

Make this your habitual state of mind and your ability will always be available, always be at its maximum.

On the other hand, we also are conscious of how whatever ability we have is contracted by the lack of faith in ourselves, by self-depreciation, by timidity, by lack of courage. Hold a poor opinion of yourself, refuse to assume responsibility for our destiny, always berate yourself and belittle your powers, and you could have the ability of a Michelangelo, a Carnegie, a Shakespeare, a Beethoven, a Marie Curie, a Louisa May Alcott, and yet you would never amount to anything.

The self-limiting mental attitude holds down more real ability, keeps more deserving merit in mediocre positions, than perhaps any other handicap in the gamut of human disabilities. Multitudes who have excellent mental endowments and splendid traits of character remain practically nobodies all their lives because of timidity, a sense of inferiority—a doubting, self-depreciating attitude toward themselves, while others with half their natural ability forge ahead, make fortunes, attain places of power and influence.

Every one of us has more ability than we think we have, more than we ever use ordinarily. But, under the impulse of a strong motive, such as having a great responsibility thrust upon us or being put in a situation where we must either sink or swim, there isn't one among us that wouldn't respond to the demand and unfold an amount of ability which we never before dreamed we possessed. If a scientist should invent an instrument by means of which it would be possible for men and women to increase their natural ability fifty per cent, there is no price we would not be willing to pay for such an instrument. Yet there isn't a man or woman living today who doesn't already possess this instrument in the exercise of right thinking—by facing life the right way and by using the opportunities that are at hand.

Right where you are, no matter what your environment, what your disadvantages or handicaps, you have enough ability to make you a success in whatever you desire to do; to lift you out of lack and poverty and make you a millionaire. Do everything that will enable you to stretch your ambition accordion to its limit, and you will be amazed at what you can accomplish.

Thirty Six

BRING OUT THE PERSON YOU CAN BE

Said the great psychologist, William James, "The average individual develops less than ten per cent of his brain cells and less than thirty per cent of his possible physical efficiency. We all live below our maximum of accomplishment."

Suppose a human being, because of lack of proper nourishment, or of some accident in childhood, should attain only ten per cent of his or her possible physical height and only thirty per cent of his or her normal weight! We would all think, What a tragic circumstance.

Yet most of us are self-made dwarfs—self-made—falling short ten, twenty, thirty, and even at times one hundred per cent of our possible development. Even those who climbed to the mountain peaks of human achievement—the Michelangelos, the Beethovens, the Shakespeares, the Miltons, the Dantes, the Brontes: the great men and women in every field of creative work—never reached the maximum of their possible accomplishment.

Just as unfavorable conditions in the vegetable kingdom dwarf a possible giant tree and make it a pigmy, so too do unfavorable conditions in the animal kingdom dwarf a possible giant in a person and make him or her a pigmy. But while the tree has no power of itself to change conditions, to alter or improve its environment, we can bend conditions to our wills, overcome all obstacles that may hinder or delay our highest possible development. In other words, every acorn, if conditions are just right, may become a grand oak, but every human acorn, *in spite of conditions*, no matter how bad they may be, can become, if he or she will, a grand individual.

"We actually have powers of many kinds which we habitually fail to use," says Dr. James J. Walsh. "*We have acquired the habit of not being equal to ourselves.*" This habit of not being equal to ourselves is what causes a great majority of human beings to underestimate what they are capable of doing. They measure their capacity by what they have done in the past or, by what others think they can do, and so they plod along in a narrow groove of inferiority, in which their real power is never exercised. Unless some fortunate accident intervenes, the larger person within them remains undiscovered, and they go to their graves without ever having gone below the surface to their almost limitless hidden powers.

Not what you have done or have failed to do, but what you are capable of doing now; not what you are, but what you are capable of becoming—these are the important facts in your life. It doesn't matter so much what others think of you, what they believe is possible for you, it is what you think of yourself—what you believe you have the ability to do—that counts. This is of immense importance to you, because you will not begin to touch your possibilities until you make the acquaintance of your real self, the bigger possible "me" in you.

Many of the richest mines in the world were abandoned time and again before their hidden wealth was discovered by the more persevering prospectors. These men were not satisfied with superficial digging, but went down into the very bowels of the earth until they found the treasure they were after. They became fabulously rich, while those who quit or wandered from claim to claim, never giving time or energy enough to one, never having enough faith in its possibilities to dig deeper, died in poverty.

I know of a man, for example, who mortgaged everything he had in the world, borrowed all he could—even sold his clothing—to raise enough money to enable him to sink a shaft below the point at which a former prospector had quit. Going only a few yards deeper than his predecessor, he struck one of the richest silver mines on this continent.

Many of us are like the prospectors who dug only a little way down into their claims and then quit, dying in poverty and wretchedness when they might have been rich beyond their wildest dreams. There are thousands who have possibilities that would make them leaders in different vocations; there are multitudes of employees, much abler men and women than their employers, plodding hopelessly in inferior positions, who have enough undiscovered ability hidden away in them to make them supreme in their line—but they have never had the perseverance to dig down to the treasure house of their hidden wealth. They prospected a little along the surface of their being and then quit.

Don't be willing to go through life as a pigmy when there is something in you which even now is telling you that you can be a giant. Don't sit around waiting for luck or something outside of yourself to come to your assistance—to give you a lift.

You will never unfold the bigger person that is wrapped up within you that way. There is just as much success material, success potential, in you who have not achieved the prosperity you rightly feel you deserve as there is in those around you who *have* obtained it. But the only power that will develop the giant in you is inside of you.

The seed must reach deep into the soil, it must never withdraw before obstacles or weaken under adversity, if the grand tree lying within it is to grow and prosper.

Thirty Seven

WHY DON'T YOU BEGIN?

When do you expect to do the wonderful things you have been dreaming about? Why don't you begin? What are you waiting for? Why don't you start? Are you waiting for a "good thing" to come to you, waiting for influence, for pull, for some one to help you?

Do you know that nothing is more demoralizing to the life, weakening to the character, than to be constantly wishing and dreaming of the great things we are going to do without a corresponding effort to actualize our dreams? Wishing without a corresponding effort to realize degenerates the mind, destroys initiative.

Our visions are the plans of our lives, but they will end as merely plans if we do not persistently follow them up with a vigorous effort to make them real—just as an architect's plans will end up as simply drawings if they are not followed up and made real by the builder.

As mentioned earlier, three things we must do to make our dreams come true:
* Visualize our desire
* Concentrate on our vision
* Work to bring it into the actual

The implements necessary for this are inside of us, not outside. No matter what the accidents of birth or fortune, there is only one force by which we can fashion our life material—mind.

Those who have achieved great things have been dreamers, and what they have accomplished has been in proportion to the vividness, the energy and persistency with which they visualized their ideals; held to their dreams and struggled to make them come true.

It is a good thing to ask ourselves every now and then whether we are making good; whether we are making the most of our opportunities; whether we are going up or down.

U.S. Supreme Court justice Oliver Wendell Holmes said it does not matter so much where we stand, as the direction in which we are moving.

In what direction are you moving?

There are thousands of people today who aren't moving but waiting. They have splendid ambitions, have made resolutions to carry out those ambitions, but are victims of doubt which keeps them from making a start. They are unable to make a beginning while this monster stands at the door of their resolution. They are afraid to burn their bridges behind them, to commit themselves to their purpose.

Make up your mind that you are going to be a conqueror in life; that you are going to be the master of your mental realm and not a slave to any treacherous enemy; that you will choose the wisest course, and, no matter how forbidding or formidable the difficulties in the way, that you will take the turn which points toward the goal of your ambition, no matter who or what may bar your onward path.

Don't let doubt balk your efforts. Don't let it paralyze you and make you a pigmy, so that you will not half try to make good when you have a waiting giant in you.

Confidence, self-assurance, self-faith—these are the great friends which will kill the traitor doubt.

The fact that you have an almost uncontrollable impulse, a great absorbing ambition to do a thing which meets with the approval of your judgment and your better self, is a notice served upon you that you can do the thing, and should do it at once.

Do not be afraid of taking responsibilities. Make up your mind that you will assume any responsibility which comes to you along the line of your legitimate career and that you will bear it a little better than anybody else ever before has. There is no greater mistake in the world than that of postponing responsibility, thinking that you will be better prepared to assume it later. It is accepting responsibilities as they come, that gives us the preparation.

No matter how much you may suffer from a feeling of unpreparedness, in the resolution to do the thing which you know would be best for you, which you know well would move you closer to your goal may, lies the development of your manhood or womanhood.

Do not be afraid to demand great things of yourself. Affirm your ability to do and be—and powers which you never dreamed you possessed will leap to your assistance.

There is no one that can shut the door which leads to any legitimate ambition, to a larger, fuller life, but yourself. There are no obstacles, no difficulties, no power on earth, nothing but yourself that can cancel the Great Promise given to you: "Behold, I have set before you an open door which no man can shut."

We are all reservoirs of power, and what we make of ourselves, what we achieve in life, is not dependent on the outward things, but on the extent to which we draw on our hidden forces—our latent talents and resources. Our heart longings, our soul aspirations, are something more than mere vaporings of imagination. These latent potencies were not given to mock us. They are prophecies, predictions, couriers, forerunners of things that can become realities.

There are no sealed orders wrapped within the brain without the accompanying ability to execute them.

Hold the picture—the plan of the man or woman you long to be and that you are resolved to be—and stick to it. With your eyes ever fixed on your ideal, work with heart and hand and brain; with a faith that never grows dim; with a resolution that never wavers; with a patience that is akin to genius. Persevere unto the end, for as you advance, your ideal as steadily moves toward you.

Do not give up in your discouraged moments or allow any obstacle to blur your ideals. Persist in visualizing the ideal you are determined to be, and always think of yourself as you desire to become. This mental attitude will help you to match your dream with its reality. It will establish your relationship between yourself and the thing you are seeking.

There is a magnetic, attractive power in holding to mighty thoughts. Begin now.

PART IV
Another Look at Prosperity

Thirty Eight

RICH WITHOUT MONEY

Many a person is rich without money. Thousands with nothing in their pockets, and thousands without even a pocket, are rich.

A collector bought at public auction in London, for one hundred and fifty-seven guineas, an autograph of Shakespeare—but with a library card, everyone can absorb the riches of *Hamlet*.

In the Middle Ages wealth was looked upon as criminal and even contemptible.

The North American Indians considered it unbecoming for a chief to be rich, and he was often one of the poorest in the tribe.

In Thomas Moore's *Utopia*, gold was despised. Criminals were forced to wear heavy chains of it and to have rings of it in their ears; it was put to the vilest uses to keep up the scorn of it. Bad characters were compelled to wear gold headbands.

Diamonds and pearls were used to decorate infants, so the youth would discard and despise it.

Benjamin Franklin said that mere money never made a person happy yet—there is nothing in its nature to produce happiness. Indeed, the more one has, the more one wants. Instead of filling a vacuum, it makes one.

In excavating Pompeii, a skeleton was found with the fingers clenched round a quantity of gold.

A poor man, while scoffing at the wealthy for not enjoying themselves, was met by a stranger. The stranger gave him a purse, in which the poor man was always to find a ducat—as fast as he took one out, another would drop in. But he was told that he could not to begin to spend his fortune until he had thrown away the purse. He took out ducat after ducat out, continually putting off the hour of enjoyment until he had gotten "a little more" and died counting his millions.

A beggar was once met by Fortune, who promised to fill his satchel with gold, as much as he might please, on the condition that whatever touched the ground would turn at once to dust. The beggar opens his satchel, asking for more and yet more, until the bag burst. The gold fell to the ground, and all was lost.

When the steamer *Central America* was about to sink, the stewardess, having collected all the gold she could from the staterooms, and tied it in her apron, jumped for the last boat leaving the steamer. She missed her aim and fell into the water, the gold carrying her down head first.

In the year 1843, a rich miser who lived in Padua, Italy, was so mean and sordid that he would never give a cent to any person or charity—and he was so afraid of the banks that he would not deposit with them, but would sit up nights with sword and pistol by him to guard his idol hoard. When his health gave way from anxiety and watching he built an underground treasure-chamber, so arranged that if anyone ever entered, they would step upon a spring which would precipitate them into a subterranean river, from which they could neither escape nor be heard. One night, the miser went to his treasure-chamber to see that all was right. His foot touched the spring of the trap, and he was hurled into the deep, hidden stream.

An Asiatic traveler tells us that one day he found the bodies of two men laid upon the desert sand beside the carcass of a camel. They had evidently died from thirst, and yet around the waist of each was a large store of jewels of different kinds, which they had doubtless been crossing the desert to sell in the markets of Persia.

One of the great lessons of life is to learn the true estimate of values. During our lives, all sorts of wares will are imposed upon us, and all kinds of temptations will be used to induce us to buy. Vulgar Wealth will flaunt her banner before our eyes, and claim supremacy over everything else. A thousand different schemes will be thrust into our face with their claims for superiority. Every occupation and vocation will present its charms in turn, and offer its inducements. Those who would succeed must not allow themselves to be deceived by appearances, but must place the emphasis of life where it belongs. Our success in life will depend very largely upon our ability to estimate properly—not the apparent, but the real value of everything presented to us.

The Greek philosopher Diogenes condemned the corruption of those about him and went through the streets looking for "an honest man." Teaching that the simple life is the virtuous life, he despised wealth and affectation. "Lord, how many things are in the world of which Diogenes hath no need!" he said, as he wandered among the miscellaneous articles at a country fair. He exemplified his teaching by living in a tub. "Do you want anything?" asked Alexander the Great, impressed by the abounding cheerfulness of the philosopher under such circumstances. "Yes," replied Diogenes, "I want you to stand out of my sunshine and not to take from me what you cannot give me." "Were I not Alexander," exclaimed the great conqueror, "I would be Diogenes."

The truly prosperous do not work for gold. They work for love, for honor, for character. A friend of Louis Agassiz, the Swiss-American zoologist and geologist, once expressed his wonder that a man of such abilities should remain contented with such a moderate income as he received. "I have enough," was Agassiz's reply. "I have no time to waste in making money. Life is not sufficiently long to enable a man to get rich and do his duty to his fellow-men at the same time."

How were the thousands of business men who lost every dollar they had in the Chicago fire enabled to go into business at once, some into wholesale business, without money? *They drew on their character.* The banks said they were square men; that they had always paid one hundred cents on a dollar; that they had paid promptly, and that they were industrious and dealt honorably with all men. This record was as good as a bank account. Character was the coin which enabled these penniless men to buy thousands of dollars' worth of goods. Their integrity did not burn up with their stores. The best part of them was beyond the reach of fire and could not be burned.

A great bank account does not assure one of prosperity; nor does the possession of great lands. We are rich or poor according to what we are, not according to what we have.

A bankrupt merchant, returning home one night, said to his noble wife, "My dear, I am ruined; everything we have is in the hands of the sheriff." After a few moments of silence, his wife looked into his face and asked, "Will the sheriff sell you?" "Oh, no!" he exclaimed. "Will the sheriff sell me?" "Oh, no." "Then do not say we have lost everything. All that is most valuable remains to us—manhood, womanhood, childhood. We have lost but the results of our skill and industry. We can make another fortune if our hearts and hands are left us."

It is all very well to urge youth on to success, but the great majority can never reach or even approximate the goal of fame and fortune constantly preached to them. And nor would civilization profit if they could. There will always be need for those who turn the wheels, pull the levers, tighten the nuts and bolts, and pick up the leaves. One of the great lessons to learn is how to be rich without money, and how to achieve success that is not always in accordance with the popular standard.

We should be judged by the happiness we create in those around us. Great prosperity is in the soul which thirsts not for fortune, but for truth, beauty, and the good. A noble spirit will cast a radiance of beauty over the humblest home, which the upholsterer and decorator can never approach.

Are you an animal loaded with ingots, or a human being filled with a purpose? The object for which we strive tells the story of our lives: Noble deeds always enrich, while millions in money may impoverish.

Thirty Nine

RICHES WITHOUT WINGS

"I don't want such things," said Epictetus to the rich Roman orator who was making light of his contempt for money-wealth. "And besides," said the stoic, "you are poorer than I am, after all. You have silver vessels, but earthenware reasons, principles, appetites. My mind to me a kingdom is, and it furnishes me with abundant and happy occupation in lieu of your restless idleness. All your possessions seem small to you; mine seem great to me. Your desire is insatiate, mine is satisfied."

"Lord, how many things are in the world of which Diogenes hath no need!" exclaimed the stoic, as he wandered among the miscellaneous articles at a country fair.

"One would think," said Boswell, "that the proprietor of all this (Keddlestone, the seat of Lord Scarsfield) must be happy:" "Nay, sir," said Johnson, "all this excludes but one evil, poverty."

RICHES WITHOUT WINGS

"What property has he left behind him?" people ask when a man dies; but the angel who receives him asks, "What good deeds hast thou sent before thee?"

"What is the best thing to possess?" asked an ancient philosopher of his pupils. One answered, "Nothing is better than a good eye"—a figurative expression for a liberal and contented disposition. Another said, "A good companion is the best thing in the world;" a third chose a good neighbor; and a fourth, a wise friend. But Eleazar said: "A good heart is better than them all." "True," said the master. "Thou hast comprehended in two words all that the rest have said."

"My kingdom for a horse," said Richard III of England amid the press of Bosworth Field. But, "My kingdom for a moment," said Queen Elizabeth on her deathbed. And millions echo her sentiment. For when we feel the earth, its riches and power slipping from our grasp, that which we show in our hearts that we value most is another moment of the blessed light of life—the stars and flowers and the companionship of friends.

"These are my jewels," said Cornelia to the Campanian lady who asked to see her gems; and she pointed with pride to her boys returning from school.

Accumulation is not the highest success.

There is an Eastern legend of a powerful genius, who promised a beautiful maiden a gift of rare value if she would pass through a field of corn and, without pausing, going backward, or wandering hither and thither, select the largest and ripest ear—the value of the gift to be in proportion to the size and perfection of the ear she should choose. She passed through the field, seeing a great many well worth gathering, but, always hoping to find a larger and more perfect one, she passed them all by. When, coming to a part of the field where the stalks grew more stunted, she disdained to take one from these, and so came through to the other side without having selected any.

Lincoln always yearned for a rounded wholeness of character; and his fellow lawyers called him "perversely honest." Nothing could induce him to take the wrong side of a case, or to continue on that side after learning that it was unjust or hopeless. After giving considerable time to a case in which he had received from a lady a retainer of two hundred dollars, he returned the money, saying: "Madam, you have not a peg to hang your case on." "But you have earned that money," said the lady. "No, no," replied Lincoln, "that would not be right. I can't take pay for doing my duty."

Charles Sumner, when a senator, declined to lecture at any price, saying that his time belonged to Massachusetts and the nation. Spurgeon would not speak for fifty nights in America at one thousand dollars a night, because he said he could do better: he could stay in London and try to save fifty souls.

King Midas, in the ancient myth, asked that everything he touched might be turned to gold, for then, he thought, he would be perfectly happy. His request was granted, but when his clothes, his food, his drink, the flowers he plucked, and even his little daughter, whom he kissed, were all changed into yellow metal, he begged that the Golden Touch might be taken from him. He had learned that many other things are intrinsically far more valuable than all the gold that was ever dug from the earth.

An Arab without provisions, who nevertheless was fortunate to escape death after losing his way in the desert, told of his feelings when he found a bag full of pearls, just as he was about to abandon all hope. "I shall never forget," said he, "the relish and delight that I felt on supposing it to be dried wheat, nor the bitterness and despair I suffered on discovering that the bag contained pearls."

Who would not choose to be a millionaire of deeds with a Lincoln, a Grant, a Florence Nightingale; a millionaire of ideas with Emerson, Lowell, Shakespeare, Wordsworth?

"Who is the richest of men?" asked Socrates. "He who is content with the least, for contentment is nature's riches."

"Do you know, sir," said a devotee of Mammon to John Bright, "that I am worth a million sterling?" "Yes," said the irritated but calm-spirited respondent, "I do; and I know that it is all you are worth."

"We say of someone that he or she is 'made'," said Beecher. "What do we mean? That their affections are like vines, sending out on all sides blossoms and clustering fruits? That their tastes are so cultivated that all beautiful things speak to them and bring them their delights? That their understanding is opened, so that they walk through every hall of knowledge and gather its treasures? That their moral feelings are so developed and quickened that they hold sweet commerce with Heaven? O, no—none of these things. Only that he or she is worth hundreds of thousands of dollars!

"And we say that someone is 'ruined.' Are their spouse and children dead? O, no. Have they had a quarrel with their loved one and are separated from them? O, no. Have they lost their reputation through crime? No. Is their reason gone? O, no—it is as sound as ever. Are they struck with disease? No. It's just that they have lost their property—and we say that they are ruined. We say that *the person* ruined! When shall we learn that a person's life consisteth not in the abundance of the things which he or she possesseth?'"

"You are a plebeian," said a patrician to Cicero. "I am a plebeian," replied the great Roman orator. "The nobility of my family begins with me, that of yours will end with you."

No one deserves to be crowned with honor whose life is a failure, and those who live only to eat and drink and accumulate money are surely not successful. The world is no better for their living in it.

There is scarcely an idea more infectious or potent than the love of money. It is a yellow fever, decimating its votaries and ruining more families in the land than all the plagues or diseases put together. Instances of its malevolent power occur to everywhere. Almost every square foot of land of our continent has been ensanguined through the madness for treasure.

It is, when all is said and done, not our surroundings that make us rich or prosperous, it is the mind that makes the person rich.

We are endowed with the faculty of creating, and we honor that endowment by filling our lives with the true, the beautiful, and the good. Like the bees, we should devote our lives to extracting honey from every flower.

Forty

THE GREATEST PROSPERITY

The story is told of a great king who had one little son whom he worshiped. The boy had everything he desired, all that wealth and love could give; no wish was ungratified, but he was not happy. His face was always disfigured by a scowl of discontent. One day a great magician came to the palace of the king, and told him that he could make his son happy and turn his scowls into smiles. "If you can do this," said the king, "I will give you whatever you ask." The magician took the boy into a private chamber and wrote something with a white substance on a piece of paper. He gave the paper to the boy and told him to go into a darkened room and hold a lighted candle under it and see what would happen. Then the magician went away. The young prince did as he was instructed, and the white letters, illuminated by the light from beneath, turned into a beautiful blue, and formed the words: "Do a kindness to some one every day." The prince followed the magician's advice and soon became the happiest boy in his father's kingdom.

During an epidemic of yellow fever at Memphis it was almost impossible to get enough watchers and nurses to attend the stricken. One day a man with coarse features, closely cropped hair, and shuffling gait, went to one of the attending physicians, and said, "I want to nurse." The doctor, looking him over critically, said, curtly, "You are not needed." "But I wish to nurse," persisted the man. "Try me for a week. If you don't like me then, dismiss me; if you do, pay me my wages." "Very well," said the doctor, "I'll take you," adding, mentally, "I'll keep my eye on you."

The uncouth volunteer became one of the most valuable nurses on the staff. He was tireless and self-denying. Wherever the pestilence raged most fiercely, he was also—and worked the hardest. The sufferers adored him. To them his rough face was as the face of an angel. Not only did he nurse them with the care and devotion that a mother gives to her children, but it was found afterward he also put every cent of his earnings into a relief box for the benefit of the plague-stricken.

When "John the nurse," the name he was known by, later sickened and died of the fever, those who prepared him for burial found on his body a livid mark—the brand of a convicted felon!

Forget yourself. You will never find true prosperity until you do. The mind that accomplishes things worthwhile looks out, not in; it is focused upon its object, not itself.

The real test of prosperity is in your daily life. Do you really live? Are you alive in every part of your being? Do you bring up your children to respect themselves;, to love the right and hate the wrong, to be self-reliant, strong, vigorous, and independent; to do their own thinking so they may become leaders instead of trailers? *That* is is to leave them something worthwhile.

If you have learned to be rich without money; if like the bee, you have learned the secret of extracting honey from the thistle as well as from the rose; if you can look upon your financial losses as mere incidents, not so very important to the larger and fuller life, then you have attained true wealth.

True wealth does not make others poorer . . .

It does not believe that the best part of the farm is conveyed in the title deed . . .

It can enjoy a landscape without owning the land . . .

It sees "books in the running brooks, sermons in stones, and good in everything."

Prosperity in the largest sense, then, is the attainment of the dreams that are good for us—an abundance of all that is beautiful in life, uplifting and inspiring; an abundance of all that is sublime and magnificent.

Prosperity is that which enriches the personality, the life experience.

True prosperity is the inward consciousness of spiritual opulence, wholeness, completeness.

PART V
Appendices

Appendix A

A LESSON IN PROSPERITY THINKING

In 1928, a several of the world's greatest financiers met at the Edgewater Beach Hotel in Chicago:

- the president of the largest utility company
- the greatest wheat speculator
- the president of the New York Stock Exchange
- a presidential Cabinet member
- the greatest "bear" in Wall Street
- the president of the Bank of International Settlements
- the head of the world's greatest monopoly.

These men controlled more wealth than there was in the United States Treasury; their life-stories were held up as exemplary models for the next generation to follow. But twenty-five years after their Chicago meeting, here were their stories:

- Charles Schwab, the president of the largest independent steel company, died broke, living the last five years of his life on borrowed money
- Wheat speculator Arthur Cutten died overseas, insolvent.
- Richard Whitney, the president of the New York Stock Exchange, had served a term in Sing Sing Prison.
- Albert Fall, the member of the President's Cabinet, was pardoned from prison so he could die at home.
- Jesse Livermore, Wall Street's greatest "bear," committed suicide.
- Leon Fraser, president of the Bank of International Settlements, committed suicide.
- Ivan Drueger, head of the world's greatest monopoly, committed suicide.

They had each learned how to acquire the prosperity of money, but not the prosperity of life.

Appendix B

THOUGHTS ON PROSPERITY

Economy is half the battle of life. —SPURGEON

Can anything be so elegant as to have few wants and to serve them one's self? —EMERSON

As much wisdom can be expended on a private economy as on an empire. —EMERSON

No gain is so certain as that which proceeds from the economical use of what you have. —LATIN PROVERB

Beware of little extravagances: a small leak will sink a big ship. —FRANKLIN

Better go to bed supperless, than rise with debts. —GERMAN PROVERB

Debt is like any other trap, easy enough to get into, but hard enough to get out of. —H. W. SHAW

Whatever be your talents, whatever be your prospects, never speculate away on the chance of a palace that which you may need as a provision against the workhouse.
—BULWER

Pennilessness is not poverty, and ownership is not possession; to be without is not always to lack, and to reach is not to attain; sunlight is for all eyes that look up, and color for those who choose.
—HELEN HUNT

I ought not to allow any man, because he has broad lands, to feel that he is rich in my presence. I ought to make him feel that I can do without his riches, that I cannot be bought—neither by comfort, neither by pride—and although I be utterly penniless, and receiving bread from him, that he is the poor man beside me. —EMERSON

To be content with what we possess is the greatest and most secure of riches. —CICERO

He is richest who is content with the least, for content is the wealth of nature. —SOCRATES

A great heart in a little house is of all things here below that which has ever touched me most. —LACORDAIRE

My crown is in my heart, not on my head,
Nor decked with diamonds and Indian stones,
Nor to be seen: my crown is called content;
A crown it is, that seldom kings enjoy. —SHAKESPEARE

This idol gold can boast of two peculiarities; it is worshiped in all climates without a single temple, and by all classes without a single hypocrite. —COLTON

Nor is there on earth a more powerful advocate for vice than poverty. —GOLDSMITH

Poverty wants much; but avarice, everything. —SYRUS

To have what we want is riches; but to be able to do without it is power. —GEORGE MACDONALD

Without a rich heart, wealth is an ugly beggar.
—EMERSON

Wealth is the least trustworthy of anchors.
—J. G. HOLLAND

When you are young, how well you know
A little money makes great show,
Just fifty cents will cause you bliss,
'Tis then a dollar looks like this:

$

But when you're old and bills come due,
And creditors are dunning you,
And every cent you spend you miss,
'Tis then a dollar looks like this:

$

―――

It is no sin to be rich, nor to wish to be rich:
the mistake is in being too eager after riches.

―――

Get all you can without hurting your soul,
your body, or your neighbor. Save all you can,
cutting off every needless expense. Give all you can.
—JOHN WESLEY

―――

Beware of wealth which costs too much, for
"What doth it profit a man if he gain the
whole world and lose his own soul?"

―――

There are as many troubles on
the other side of riches
as on this. —IZAAK WALTON

―――

If six hundred pounds a year would procure a man more
consequence, and of course more happiness than six pounds
a year, the same proportion will hold to six thousand, and
so on as far as opulence can be carried.
—SAMUEL JOHNSON

―――

Nobody should be rich but those who understand it.
—GOETHE

Wealth is not acquired, as many persons suppose, by fortunate speculations and splendid enterprises, but by daily practice of industry, frugality, and economy. He who relies upon these means will rarely be found destitute, and he who relies upon any other will generally become bankrupt.
—WAYLAND

Life is an arrow—therefore you must know
What mark to aim at, how to use the bow—
Then draw it to the head and let it go.
—HENRY VAN DYKE

The important thing in life is to have a great aim, and to possess the aptitude and perseverance to attain it.
—GOETHE

Concentration alone conquers. —C. BUXTON.

"He who follows two hares is sure to catch neither."

"A double-minded man is unstable in all his ways."

Let every one ascertain his special business
and calling, and then stick to it if
he would be successful.
—FRANKLIN.

"Digression is as dangerous as stagnation
in the career of a young man in business."

Every man who observes vigilantly and resolves steadfastly grows unconsciously into genius. —BULWER

Genius is intensity. —BALZAC

Be sure, my son, and remember that the best men always make themselves. —PATRICK HENRY

God gives every bird its food, but he does not throw it into the nest. —J. G. HOLLAND

Our remedies oft in ourselves do lie, which we ascribe to Heaven. —SHAKESPEARE

The best education in the world is that got by struggling to obtain a living. —WENDELL PHILLIPS

Every person has two educations, one which he receives from others, and one, more important, which he gives himself. —GIBBON

What the superior man seeks is in himself: what the small man seeks is in others. —CONFUCIUS

Who waits to have his task marked out,
Shall die and leave his errand unfulfilled.
—LOWELL

Nature, when she adds difficulties, adds brains.
—EMERSON.

Many men owe the grandeur of their lives to their tremendous difficulties. —SPURGEON.

The good are better made by ill,
As odors crushed are sweeter still. —ROGERS

Aromatic plants bestow
No spicy fragrance while they grow;
But crushed or trodden to the ground,
Diffuse their balmy sweets around.
—GOLDSMITH.

As night to stars, woe lustre gives to man. —YOUNG.

There is no possible success without some opposition as a fulcrum: force is always aggressive and crowds something.
—HOLMES.

The more difficulties one has to encounter, within and without, the more significant and the higher in inspiration his life will be. —HORACE BUSHNELL.

Adversity has the effect of eliciting talents which in prosperous circumstances would have lain dormant.
—HORACE

Possession pampers the mind; privation trains and strengthens it. —HAZLITT.

"Adversity is the prosperity of the great."

No man ever worked his way in a dead calm.
—JOHN NEAL

Victories that are easy are cheap. Those only are worth having which come as the result of hard fighting.
—BEECHER

Man owes his growth chiefly to that active striving of the will, that encounter with difficulty, which we call effort; and it is astonishing to find how often results that seemed impracticable are thus made possible.
—EPES SARGENT

Yes, to this thought I hold with firm persistence;
The last result of wisdom stamps it true;
He only earns his freedom and existence
Who daily conquers them anew.
—GOETHE

Little minds are tamed and subdued by misfortunes; but great minds rise above them.
—WASHINGTON IRVING

A penny saved is a penny earned.
—ENGLISH SAYING

All fortunes have their foundation laid in economy.
—J. G. HOLLAND

APPENDIX B

"If a man thinks sickness, poverty, and misfortune, he will meet them and claim them all eventually as his own. But he will not acknowledge the close relationship—he will deny his own children and declare they were sent to him by an evil fate."

Poverty is the open-mouthed hell which yawns beneath civilization. —HENRY GEORGE.

Wealth is created mentally first.

The stream of plenty will not flow toward the stingy, parsimonious, doubting thought.

Holding the poverty thought keeps one in touch with poverty-producing conditions.

'Tis the mind that makes the body rich.
—SHAKESPEARE

The positive man keys his life to the "I can" note, the negative man to the "I can't." Say to yourself "Health, luck, usefulness, success are mine, I claim them." Keep thinking that thought, no matter what happens.
—ELLA WHEELER WILCOX

The secret of success in life is for a man *to be ready for his opportunity* when it comes.
—DISRAELI

Our grand business is, not to see what lies dimly at a distance, but to do what lies clearly at hand. —CARLYLE

"We will remain rag pickers as long as
we have only a rag picker's vision"

Only by thinking prosperity and abundance
can you realize the abundant, prosperous life.

Fixing limitation upon ourselves is one of the
cardinal sins of mankind.

Prosperity flows only through channels
that are wide open to receive it. Doubt, fear and
lack of confidence close these channels.

A pinched mind means a pinched, limited supply.

Everything we get in life comes through the
gateway of our thought. If that is pinched, stingy,
mean, what flows to us will correspond.

By the law of affinity you may know that your own is
always seeking you if you are seeking it with all your might
and are not driving it away with your doubts.

I rave no more 'gainst Time or Fate,
For lo, my own shall come to me.
Asleep, awake, by night or day,
The friends I seek are seeking me.

> What matter if I stand alone?
> I wait with joy the coming years;
> My heart shall reap where it hath sown,
> What is mine shall know my face.
> "Nor time, nor space, nor deep, nor high
> Can keep my own away from me.
> —JOHN BURROUGHS

The person who sows failure thoughts, poverty thoughts, can no more reap success, prosperity harvests, than the farmer can get a wheat crop from sowing thistles.

No matter how hard you may work, if you keep your mind saturated with poverty thoughts, poverty pictures, you are driving away the very thing you are pursuing.

Stop thinking trouble if you want to attract its opposite; stop thinking poverty if you wish to attract plenty. Refuse to have anything to do with the things you fear, the things you do not want.

The beginning of every achievement must be in your consciousness.

We have unlimited power, boundless resources, in the great within of us, but until we awaken to a consciousness of this hidden power, those invisible resources, we cannot use them.

The consciousness of power creates power. What we are conscious of, we already possess.

Whatever we visualize intensely and persistently
and back by intelligent effort we tend to create,
vitalize into form, and build into our lives.

Limitless wealth, inexhaustible supply to meet our needs,
and undreamed of possibilities are in the great cosmic
intelligence waiting the contact of our thought to bring
them into visible form.

You have no more right to go about among others
with a vinegar expression on your face, radiating
mental poison, spreading the germs of doubt,
fear, discouragement and despondency
among them, than you have to inflict bodily
injuries on them. Indeed, to do the former
is to do the latter.

To be a conqueror in appearance, in one's bearing,
is the first step toward success.

Walk, talk, and act as though you were a somebody, and
you are much more likely to become such.

Let victory speak from your face and express itself
in your manner, your conversation, your bearing.

Never show the world a gloomy, pessimistic face,
which is an admission that life has been a
disappointment to you instead of a glorious triumph.

The moment you resolve to make your life dream come true, you have taken the first step towards its realization, but you will stop there if your efforts cease.

Keeping right after your ideals, nursing your visions, cultivating your dreams, visualizing the thing you long for vividly, intensely, and striving with all your might to match it with reality—this is what makes life count.

Our dreaming capacity gives us a peep into the glorious realities that await us further on.

Discouragement has done more to dwarf the efforts of the race, has thwarted more careers, stunted and starved more lives, than any other one agent.

Never make a decision when downhearted.
Never let the weak side of your nature take control.

Have you the grit and pluck to stand all sorts of discouragement and to struggle on after failure without losing heart; to get up again every time you fall? Can you stand criticism, misunderstanding, abuse, without flinching or weakening? Have you the perseverance to go on when others turn back, to continue the fight when everybody around you is giving up? If you can do this you are a winner. Noting can hold you back from your goal.

"You can't do it!" keeps more people with splendid ability in mediocrity than almost any other thing. "You can't do it!" meets you everywhere in life. At every turn you propose to take, you will find someone to warn you away, to tell you not to take that road, that it will lead to disaster. Unless you have unusual pluck, an iron will and a determination which never wavers, you are likely to become discouraged, and when you are once discouraged your initiative is deadened and your power paralyzed.

When all people know how to make the subconscious work for them there will be no poor people, none in distress or suffering, in pain or ill health. No one will be unhappy; no one will be a victim of thwarted ambitions.

If you impress vividly, intensely, and persistently your determination to be what you long to be upon the creative mind in the great within of you, if you register your vow to succeed in doing what you long to do and do your level best to actualize your longings, nothing in the world can stand in the way of your success.

The "lucky" person never waits for something to turn up. "Luck is the ability to recognize an opportunity and take advantage of it."

To make yourself lucky, choose the vocation nature fitted you for and then fling your life into it. Be all there.

No matter what your need is, put it into the hands of faith. Do not ask how, or why, or when. Just do your level best, and have faith, which is the great miracle worker of the ages.

Faith opens the door, sees the way. It is a soul sense, a spiritual foresight which peers far beyond the vision of the physical eyes and sees the reality long before it takes material form.

Faith increases confidence, carries conviction, multiplies ability. It doesn't think or guess. It is not discouraged or blinded by mountains of difficulties, because it sees through them— sees the goal beyond.

There is a tremendous creative power in the conviction that we can do a thing.

You may succeed when others do not believe in you, when everybody else denounces you even, but never when you do not believe in yourself.

A day of worry is more exhausting than a week of work.

The fear of tomorrow, anticipation of the trials and troubles just ahead, robs multitudes of the strength and enthusiasm that would enable them to make today a glorious success.

If you have had an unfortunate experience;
if you have made a failure in your undertaking;
if you have been placed in an embarrassing position;
if you have fallen and hurt yourself by a false step;
if you have been slandered and abused—forget it.
There is not a single redeeming feature in these memories,
and their ghosts will rob you of many a happy hour.

Few of us realize the connection between the day,
the hour, in which we are living, and our success,
our happiness, our destiny.

It is so much easier to dream of a great big success
tomorrow than to try to make today a big success.

Our todays are the blocks with which we build
our future. If these are defective, the whole structure
of our life will correspond. That marvelous future
which you have dreamed of so long will be exactly
what you put into your todays.

The world grants opportunities to those
who can use them. Power and fortune are
hidden away in the hours and moments as
they pass, awaiting the eye that can see,
the ear that can hear, the hand that can do.

The negative mind never gets anywhere;
it can only destroy, tear down.

It is very easy to develop a negative state of mind, and it is very fatal to success. We must get rid of it before we can attract prosperity or develop efficiency.

Even if sometimes wrong, it is better to decide positively and carry out your decision with energy than to be forever hanging in the balance, contemplating, and procrastinating.

Every important decision involves the letting go of something, and the more one tries to get away from the difficulty, the more one thinks over the thing to be decided, the more one typically entangles the whole situation.

It is not only necessary to keep your mind positive, but to be immune from all the enemies of prosperity and happiness, it must be vigorously positive.

If you would be sure that you are beginning right, begin to save. The habit of saving money, while it stiffens the will, also brightens the energies.
—THEODORE ROOSEVELT.

Enter into a compact with yourself to save a certain amount every week out of your salary.

The little difference between what we earn and what we spend is capital.

Nothing makes one so absolutely independent as ready cash.

We never can get more out of ourselves than we expect.
If we expect large things, if we hold the large
mental attitude toward our work, toward our life,
we shall get much greater results than if we
depreciate ourselves, and only look for little things.

The habit of expecting great things of
ourselves calls out the best that is in us.

No one can become prosperous who will all the while
expects, or half expects, to remain poor. We tend to get
what we expect, and to expect little is to get little.

We ask for little things, we expect little things,
and thus we limit our supply.

Judge yourself by what you feel capable of doing,
not by what you have done. Nothing else will
so nerve you to accomplish greatly, as a belief
in your own inherent greatness.

There is a potency inside of you which, if you would
unlock it, would make of you everything you
ever dreamed or imagined you could become.

Don't be afraid to think too highly of yourself.
If the creator made you and is not ashamed of the job,
certainly you should not be. He pronounced
His work good, and you should respect it.

Persistently hold the thought that you are eternally progressing towards something higher in every atom of your being. This will make you grow, will enrich your life.

The constant aspiration to measure up to a high ideal is the only force in heaven or on earth that can make a life great.

That vision which grips your heart, that longing of your soul to do something significant, that dream of high achievement which haunts your imagination, is not a mere fantasy, a whimsical unreality, it is a prophecy of the big things you will do if you get your higher self to work for you.

Blessed is he who has found his work—
let him ask no other blessing.
—CARLYLE

Whatever you are by nature, keep to it; never desert your line of talent. Be what nature intended you for, and you will succeed; be anything else, and you will be ten thousand times worse than nothing.
—SYDNEY SMITH

Abundance consists not alone in material possession, but in an uncovetous spirit.
—SELDEN

Less coin, less care; to know how to dispense with wealth is to possess it.
—REYNOLDS

Money never made a man happy yet; there is nothing in its nature to produce happiness. The more a man has, the more he wants. Instead of filling a vacuum, it makes one.
—FRANKLIN

Appendix C

PROSPERITY AFFIRMATIONS

It is okay for me to have everything that I want.

I am doing the work I love, and I am being richly rewarded spiritually, creatively, and financially.

Abundance is the nature of the universe I live in; I accept abundance now for myself.

It is okay for me to have all that I desire.

Money is now circulating in my life, and I use it for my good and the good of others.

Everyday in every way I become more and more prosperous.

Abundance is my true state of being, and I now live in accordance with my true being.

I easily create wealth and use it charitably and generously.

Riches flow into my life.

My thoughts and actions are a magnet for prosperity.

I am living in abundance, for there are businesses that are providing me services—electricity, gas, telephone, water—in advance of my having to pay for.

I am surrounded with the abundance of the universe—the rain and sun that nurture the soil and provide my food, the flowers that bloom and give my life fragrance; the friends and colleagues who enrich my life—and I am grateful.

www.ingramcontent.com/pod-product-compliance
Lightning Source LLC
Chambersburg PA
CBHW071215080526
44587CB00013BA/1386